# CONSULTING
## INTO THE FUTURE

THE KEY SKILLS

EDITED BY KAREN LEE

Hodder & Stoughton
A MEMBER OF THE HODDER HEADLINE GROUP

Orders: please contact Bookpoint Ltd, 130 Milton Park, Abingdon, Oxon OX14 4SB.
Telephone: (44) 01235 827720. Fax: (44) 01235 400454. Lines are open from 9.00–6.00, Monday to Saturday,
with a 24-hour message answering service. E-mail address: orders@bookpoint.co.uk

*British Library Cataloguing in Publication Data*
A catalogue record for this title is available from the British Library.

ISBN 0 340 850515

First published 2002
Impression number    10  9  8  7  6  5  4  3  2  1
Year                              2007  2006  2005  2004  2003  2002

Typeset by Servis Filmsetting Ltd, Manchester.
Printed in Great Britain for Hodder & Stoughton Educational, a division of Hodder Headline Plc, 338 Euston
Road, London NW1 3BH by J.W. Arrowsmith Ltd, Bristol.

# M·C·A
## MANAGEMENT
## CONSULTANCIES
## ASSOCIATION

Series Editor: Fiona Czerniawska, Director of MCA Think Tank.

The MCA was formed in 1956 and represents the leading UK-based consulting firms, which currently employ over 25,000 consultants and generate £4.3bn in annual fee income. The UK consulting industry is worth around £8bn, contributing £1bn to the balance of payments.

As well as setting and maintaining standards in the industry, the MCA supports its member firms with a range of services including events, publications, interest groups and public relations. The Association also works with its members to attract the top talent into the industry. The MCA provides advice on the selection and use of management consultants and is the main source of data on the UK market.

FOR MORE INFORMATION PLEASE CONTACT:
Management Consultancies Association
49 Whitehall
London
SW1A 2BX

Tel: 020 7321 3990
Fax: 020 7321 3991

E-mail: mca@mca.org.uk
www.mca.org.uk

# DEDICATION

With loving gratitude to Donald William Skilling, taken from us far too early.
Your inspiration supports me every day. And to our children, Aaron, Jesse and Gordon.
We inspire each other.

*Karen Lee 2002*

# CONTENTS

# CONTRIBUTORS

## Karen Lee BA MA

Karen is a psychologist and an independent management consultant specializing in management development and the design and delivery of specialized programs for management. She is a Visiting Fellow at Cranfield School of Management and a personal tutor to the Certificate in the Psychology of Management Program at the Chartered Institute of Personnel and Development, London. She has taught consulting skills courses, personal/professional courses to MBA students and executives for 15 years in addition to her work in organizations. As a Canadian living in the United Kingdom, she has worked in Canada, the United States, the Middle East, Hong Kong, Singapore, Korea, Western Europe and the Czech republic. She can be contacted on tel: +(44) (0)1908 505 881 mob: +(44)(0)7958 983 499 and e-mail: LSA@ftech.co.uk

## Elaine Cole MA(Dist)

Elaine Cole is a highly experienced organizational, cultural and behavioural Change Management Consultant. She has developed 20 years' specialization in effecting successful, innovative change in major organizations across the public and private sectors.

Elaine runs Corporate Transformation Associates, an independent consultancy specializing in transformational change. Elaine has a masters degree (with distinction) in Systems in Management. She additionally lectures on organizational change and is published on strategic management development.

Elaine lives in London and is married with three teenage children. Contact her on tel: +(44) (0)7977 226 258, or at elainecole@corptrans.freeserve.co.uk

## Patrick Lavin

Patrick Lavin is educated in Economics and Behavioral Science at Manchester University and Balliol College Oxford and is a Fellow of the Chartered Institute of Personnel and Development.

He has worked for over 30 years as an HR generalist in many of the international Exxon Chemical family of companies. He has led many successful organization change projects, including Startups, Restructuring, Downsizing, Mergers and Acquisitions. He has held board level HR roles in Management and Employee Development for European, Asian, UK and US organizations. In addition, he developed extensive experience in board level internal consulting to resolve people related issues through implementing effective HR strategies. For many years he combined HR Management with internal consulting. One project 10 years ago was to develop a new career management process for use by individuals to navigate their careers in an uncertain world; this was the first prototype and forerunner of Career Voyager®, now extensively used as the anchor for consulting on people development.

Patrick has recently established Pacalin Ltd. as a specialist HR Consulting Company providing Organization Recovery and Career Management consulting services. He can be contacted directly at bplpacalin@aol.com

## Carmel McConnell M.MBA

Carmel has senior business experience in change leadership, HR strategy and management development. She founded and now runs the Magic Sandwich child poverty charity, providing food and nutrition awareness to schoolchildren in the UK. The Magic Sandwich has launched a school and community based management development program with profits returned to the schools – and welcomes enquiries on how more organizations can take part in this new area of cause related development.

She has written two books for Momentum (an imprint of the FT/Pearson Education), Change Activist, May 2001, Soultrader May 2002, which draw on her strong track record as a business consultant on fast, ethically sustainable transformation. Now working as a change activist, she describes her corporate work as 'helping business leaders find more elegant, ethical business solutions'.

For more information on CSR and change activism, please contact her at carmelmcconnell@ btinternet.com or tel: mob +(44) (0) 7710 057955.

## Mick Cope

Mick Cope is founder of WizOz Ltd – a network organization that seeks to help people and businesses optimize their potential. He has three roles in his professional life as a consultant, author and musician.

As a consultant he founded his company WizOz Ltd and has consulted with a wide range of clients. He offers a range of different products and services, all of which are based around the ideas outlined in his books. More information on WizOz can be found on his web site www.wizoz.co.uk. He can be contacted directly at Mick@wizoz.co.uk

As an author he has published a number of books, including: Leading the Organisation to Learn, Seven Cs of Consulting, Know your value? Value what you know, Lead Yourself, Float-You, Personal Networking and Seven Cs of Coaching.

As a musician he has trod the torturous route of gigging around the UK and Europe. He has produced a number of CDs with his band Crisis Days and is happy to offer a free promotional copy of his latest single.

He has a number of goals in life; the simple one is to live a life of personal freedom where he is able to think, feel and behave according to his values and not be enslaved by the wishes of others. The more challenging one is to help 1000 people achieve the same by moving from a position of corporate slave and be who they are and what they want to be.

## Jean-Marc Le Tissier

Jean-Marc helps people, teams and organizations to clarify and manage their goals, and to be even more effective, so that they achieve the meaningful and lasting results they want. He has some 18 years experience as a consultant with major firms and organizations across Europe, Scandinavia and North America. He is the author of many articles on consulting and has taught at some of the UK's leading business schools. Contact him at jean-marc@wholelife.co.uk or tel: +(44) 07801 477 055.

## Nada Korac-Kakabadse B.Sc. Grad.Dip. M.Sc. MPA Ph.D.

Nada Korac-Kakabadse is currently a Senior Research Fellow at the Cranfield School of Management and the co-editor (with Andrew Kakabadse) of the Journal of Management Development and Editor of Corporate Governance: The International Journal of Business in Society. Nada has published widely in the areas of Leadership, application of IS/IT in corporations, corporate governance, government, boardroom effectiveness, diversity management and ethics. She has published five books, including Geopolitics of Governance (2001), 32 chapters in the international volumes, three monographs and over 60 scholarly and reviewed articles. Nada has acted as consultant to numerous public and private sector organizations. She can be contacted at n.korac-kakabadse@cranfield.ac.uk or write to:

Cranfield School of Management
Cranfield, Bedford, MK43 OAL, United Kingdom
Tel: +(44 1234) 751122
Fax: +(44 1234) 751 806

## Dr Joe Jaina M.Sc Ph.D. CIPD

Dr Joe Jaina is a Lecturer in Organizational Behaviour at the Cranfield School of Management. He is a veteran of numerous organizational development campaigns principally in the area of organizational change following acquisition or restructuring in Europe, the Middle East and North America. His career has also embraced a number of human resource development roles where he has been instrumental in the generation of a performance based culture through the introduction of new coaching, leadership and team development practices. His research interests are in the area of work based relationships and their influence upon business performance.

## Sergio Pellegrinelli B.Sc. M.Sc. MBA Ph.D.

Dr Sergio Pellegrinelli is a founding partner of SP Associates, a consulting firm specializing in strategic management, organizational development and program management, and is a visiting lecturer and researcher at Cranfield School of Management.

Sergio's consulting work ranges from strategy consulting interventions to tailored programs aimed at embedding new skills and/or effecting change within organizations. He has developed and facilitated courses on consulting, business strategy, commercial management, project and program management. He has also written articles on strategy implementation, consulting relationships as well as project and program management.

Sergio holds a B.Sc. in Econometrics and an M.Sc. in Economics from the London School of Economics and an MBA from London Business School. His Doctoral research at Cranfield School of Management explored the contribution and influence of management consultants in processes of strategic change within organizations. He is a Certified Management Consultant and a Member of the Institute of Management Consultants. Sergio's mother tongue is English and he speaks fluent Italian and good French.

Sergio can be contacted directly at sergio.pellegrinelli@sp-associates.com

### Jane Clarke MBA Dip.M ACII

Jane Clarke is a Director of Nicholson McBride Ltd. She has worked with large organizations, across Europe and North America, advising them on aspects of change management and leadership. Projects range from the design and implementation of large scale programs, to mentoring individuals. In particular, her work with Lloyd's of London was featured in People Management magazine.

Jane writes regularly for management journals and national newspapers, and she has published books entitled 'Office Politics' (Industrial Society 1999) and 'Wired Working' (Spiro Press 2002).

### Margaret Page Ph.D.

Margaret Page is an organization consultant, writer and action researcher who lives in London and works internationally. She has taught management development and social responsibility at Bristol University for 8 years, and is now taking up a permanent post at Surrey University where she will teach on the well known M.Sc. in Change Agency Skills and Strategies.

Margaret co-founded Maya Consultancy in 1990 and has built up a portfolio specializing in facilitating personal and professional development alongside organizational change initiatives. Her consultancy specializes in facilitating learning from diversity between individuals and organizations, and effective working across organizational boundaries and differences of culture and identity. Recent assignments include leadership development for top managers in the UK social care sector; facilitating partnerships for promoting gender mainstreaming; promoting equality and valuing diversity in UK local authorities; management development for social care professionals, service users and activists in Slovenia; and capacity building managers to use web based resources to sustain learning networks.

Margaret has lived in Italy, Switzerland and Canada. Her publications include reports and articles on partnership work, on ICT learning communities and on women's leadership. She can be contacted at MPage@maya-consultancy.demon.co.uk or via www.maya.consultancy. demon.co.uk

## Charles Sutton B.Ed Cert.Th M.Sc.

Charles Sutton is a director of the business psychology consultancy Nicholson McBride. His extensive client portfolio includes working with a number of organizations for whom the issues of social and environmental responsibility lie at the heart of their business. He also works with international clients on cross-cultural, cultural and value issues. In addition to this work Charles is a part-time Teaching Fellow in Organizational Psychology at Birkbeck College, London University, and an Anglican priest. Charles may be contacted at Nicholson McBride (London) on +44 (0)20 7724 0232 or charles.sutton@nicholson-mcbride.com

## Benjamin Hoffman Ph.D.

Benjamin C. Hoffman, Ph.D., joined The Carter Centre March 1, 2000, as director of its Conflict Resolution Program. Formerly, he was president and CEO of the Canadian International Institute of Applied Negotiation. Dr Hoffman has extensive experience as a hands-on mediator in protracted social conflict situations and civil wars and has led peacebuilding projects in Haiti, Lebanon, Lithuania, Crimea, and Romania. He is widely recognized for his work on reconciliation and the design of dispute resolution systems to support rule of law.

From 1981–1988, Dr Hoffman was executive director of the National Associations Active in Criminal Justice, a 23-member coalition of Canadian national non-governmental organizations dedicated to reform of criminal law and active in international issues of human rights and justice. Dr Hoffman earned his doctorate in 1998 at York University, UK, where he studied in the Post-War Reconstruction and Development Unit of the Institute of Advanced Architectural Studies. He was awarded a master's degree in international relations from Tufts University, and a master's degree in community psychology and a bachelor's degree in psychology and philosophy from Wilfrid Laurier University in Ontario. He also earned a specialization in dispute resolution from the Program on Negotiation at Harvard University.

## Fr. Dermot Tredget OSB

Fr. Dermot Tredget OSB is a Benedictine monk based at Douai Abbey, near Reading in Berkshire, England. Before becoming a monk he held management positions at the Hotel and Catering Industry and Higher Education.

Fr. Dermot has an MBA from the University of Bath and an MA in Applied Theology from the Graduate Theological Union, Berkeley, California. He is currently engaged in researching the Theology of Work and Business Ethics at the University of Oxford.

Fr. Dermot runs a program of retreat workshops focused on the spiritual dimension in the workplace. These have been featured in the *Financial Times* and other business publications. Using the Rule of St Benedict, contemporary management thinking and drawing on his work and management experience, these workshops are designed to help busy people face many of the challenges in their work lives including issues around leadership, organizational structures, business ethics and relationships.

In addition to conducting retreat workshops, seminars and writing, Fr. Dermot is visiting professor in Business Ethics at the Catholic University of Piacenza, Italy and an associate tutor on the Management Development Programme at Cranfield University's School of Management.

He can be contacted at dermot@douaiabbey.org.uk or tel: +(44) 118 971 5325. Or write to: Douai Abbey, Upper Woolhampton, Reading, Berkshire, England, RG7 5TQ.

## Roger Wass

Roger Wass is managing director of PALS – Peer Assisted Learning Systems Ltd and is passionate about giving people the opportunity to reach their full potential.

PALS develops software for Communities of Practice and incorporates the Training Intelligence Group for training and HR personnel (www.pals.co.uk) Zenith for CEOs and MDs (www.palsZenith.com) and Boardroom Briefings for CEOs and MDs (www.palsZenith.com).

He believes that the new technologies offer a way forward to harness people's creativity, release their energy and provide a platform for lifelong learning. At the same time they also give us all the opportunity to have a flexible approach to work which can lead to a more enriching lifestyle. Roger can be contacted directly on +44 (0)870 240 7589 or email at info@pals.co.uk

## Dr Richard Hale

Dr Richard Hale is Director of Action Learning Forums with the global association for action learning International Management Centres Association (www.i-m-c.org ) and is co-founder of Value Projects Ltd. (www.viprojects.com ) an organization which has developed processes using action learning to tackle work based problems. His doctoral research was into the dynamics of mentoring relationships and the impact on learning at the individual and organizational levels. He is author of several books in the field of management and has had a career in industry responsible for management and leadership development. He can be contacted at hale@imc.org.uk or rhale@blueyonder.co.uk

# INTRODUCTION

There are many books on the market that aim to describe the skills needed to do a credible, high quality consulting project. This book brings together a group of people who can not only speak knowledgeably about the skills required for consulting, but are also involved often in work that has the ability to inspire, educate and broaden horizons for the reader. That has been my goal – a skills book with a difference.

You will find a very broad range of topics of interest to anyone consulting today or to those employing consultants. However, this book will be of particular interest to those new to consulting or those who have been consulting for some time who wish to broaden their outlook and interests.

I am passionate about the responsibility and power that we, as consultants, have at work – literally the ability to shape and change our world. I have therefore encouraged the individual contributors to this book to write about the things that really matter to them in their consulting work – and it is not just the corporate world. The key skills of consulting are addressed in chapters that are practical and down to earth, and yet in some ways out of the ordinary:

☐ Where and how those skills are used. For example, consulting with not-for-profit organizations, which slowly alter our values and perceptions and consulting with organizations that have decided to 'own' their corporate social responsibility.

☐ Looking beneath the surface of what consultants do in organizations. For instance, issues of spirituality in leadership, psychological issues in consulting, corporate politics.

☐ Change – at both the corporate and personal levels.

What are the future concerns and trends that will directly or indirectly influence management consulting, organizations and people who work within them? What skills will consultants need to serve their clients well?

This book revisits the consulting process in the light of changing ideas about what our values are, what consulting is, and how the future will challenge us – economically, politically, socially and psychologically. It looks at new approaches and concerns, methodologies, and skills such as new interventions. It also returns to concerns that may have been underemphasized in the last few years, such as coaching, process consulting, the development of the consultant, management development, and relationship building with clients.

At this point in history the baby boomer generation is in mid-life – the time when Jung[1] said that psychologically we are looking for meaning beyond establishing family, career, and our place in this world. We are looking for 'wholeness', completion and fulfilment on a wide scale,

---

[1] Jung, C. Two essays on Analytical Psychology in *The Collected Works* Vol 7. Bollingen Series XX: Princeton University Press.

in a manner never before thought possible, global within the context of communication and travel, against a backdrop of widespread psychological awareness. In addition to individuals, organizations are called upon to address issues of 'wholeness'.

It is no longer simply the job of organizations to produce goods, jobs and profits. They are being pushed to become psychologically more healthy places to work, and to be socially and environmentally responsible. Thus individuals, organizations and consulting itself are in transition. This is reflected in Chapter 1 on the development of transactional experts through to people who are consultative in their approach. Chapters on psychology in the workplace (5), spirituality and leadership (14), cross-boundary consulting (11) and corporate social responsibility (4) also pick up on these themes.

There was a time when consultants were all-powerful. They knew best about what was happening in any particular organization; they believed this and so did their clients. The downside to this belief was that much money was spent bringing consultants into organizations to 'diagnose' what was going wrong and to recommend solutions to problems. Then the organization was left to carry out the changes. Sometimes, the companies were able to do this and sometimes not, yet any problems or mistakes were attributed often to the organization. As Fiona Czerniawska[2] pointed out in her book, *Management Consultancy in the 21st Century*, this contributed to huge gaps in the intellectual capital of organizations, making them dependent on consultancies. Also, as Charles O'Shea and Thomas Madigan[3] highlighted in *Dangerous Company*, blind reliance on consultancy companies has led to major mistakes being made, enormous amounts of money being spent and, in some cases, huge business losses.

Clients are now taking more responsibility and owning the process that they 'know best'. They diagnose their own organization's problems and needs, and often call in the 'expert consultant' that they feel they need – one with expertise in a particular area, such as software systems that will revolutionize internal communications, financial systems and so on. However, what if clients are too close to the issues to adequately diagnose the problems or to have an accurate view of the context? What if they are not experts in change management? The expert consultant may be called in to solve a problem that may not be the underlying one in the organization or be asked to supply a 'solution' that will never work given the organization's characteristics.

Enormous amounts of money have been spent installing systems that were never going to do what the client thought, wanted or needed. In the case of one organization that wanted to automate its warehouse inventory system, neither the IT consultancy, nor the organization itself considered the potential people management issues – delaying the 'go live' date by months. Other organizations have had to use their internal functions to correct mistakes made by external consultants because the basics of problem identification were neglected.

Where does that leave us? Are we looking at a future where there can be a balance of power between the client and the consultant – a cooperative working partnership in which the attributes of each are recognized and respected? A future in which the consultant's approach is one of 'I have a way of helping you to become more clear, to help you think more broadly and to put things into context', and where the clients say 'Work in conjunction with the expertise we have in this organization to do an accurate assessment of our needs and context and help us to an appropriate solution'. Could these be the mind-sets of the future?

What will happen to the three types of consultant described by Ed Schein[4] in his seminal *Process Consultation* – the expert consultant, the 'doctor-patient' consultant, and the process

[2] Czerniawska, F. *Management Consultancy in the 21st Century*. Macmillan Business. 1999.
[3] O'Shea, J. & Madigan, C. *Dangerous Company*. Nicholas Brealey Pub. London. 1997.
[4] Schein, E. *Process Consultation*. Addison-Wesley OD series. 1987.

consultant? Should old approaches in consulting be brought back? Process consulting and the doctor-patient approach have often been set aside in favour of expert consulting, but do the 'experts' know enough about the skills of the consulting approach?

What is a 'consultative approach' and why is it so important? It can be an approach that helps people to explore and to get in touch with the issues, needs and problems that have not occurred to them. It should help the client to identify and solve their problems and concerns, and so, by definition, it should show real respect for the client. Such an approach can uncover contexts and attitudes that may be detrimental to a project ahead of time, allowing contingency plans to be developed that can help to save the client expense and time.

Ultimately consultants are brought into organizations in order to change something. Therefore, it is essential that they understand how people in those organizations go through change and how to bring about effective change. Theories about people and change have been with us for many years – firstly in psychology[5] (Kubler-Ross, 1970) and now firmly in management literature[6,7] (from Adams, Hayes & Hopson, 1976 to Bridges, 1980). However, organizations still place most emphasis on the 'harder' technological, more tangible side of change and often fail to achieve all of the changes they hope to bring about. If consultants are as blind about this phenomenon as the organizations they consult to, how can this ever change? We shall revisit the 'people factor in change projects' in Chapters 2, 3 and 7 which are about change in organizations, to give new perspectives on this frequently studied topic.

What are the political and economic realities of this century and what is the interface of consulting with those realities? Chapter 13 highlights a different area in which consultants can make their mark if they have the key skill of negotiation. Borrowing negotiation skills from a peace-builder such as Ben Hoffman of the Jimmy Carter Peace Centre, means that a consultant has another key ability in his or her repertoire. This particular skill can help clients and consultants broaden their outlook from a 'win-lose' mind-set to one that honours the views and desires of the various parties concerned in the work. The chapter on ethics reflects a time-honoured value but one that seems difficult to balance with harder, bottom-line concerns in business today.

The following is some advice about attitude that a very young consultancy partnership, Strut Inc. (25 and 29 years old), with over six years of consulting experience, recommends that new, young consultants have. I would suggest that these fit consultants of any age (Salus & Selinger, 2002):

- ☐ Demonstrate passion.
- ☐ Pick your fights carefully.
- ☐ Seek out a mentor.
- ☐ Demonstrate that you are always acting in the client's best interest.
- ☐ Rationalize every decision – cite relevant references (do your research).
- ☐ Document your successes.
- ☐ Get references.
- ☐ Find ways to demonstrate wisdom/ability beyond your seniority.
- ☐ Work harder – perform beyond the call of duty.

3

[5] Kubler-Ross, E. *On Death and Dying*. Macmillan. 1970.
[6] Adams, J. Hayes, J. & Hopson, B. *Transition*. Martin Robertson. 1976.
[7] Bridges, W. *Transitions*. Consulting Psychologists' Press, CA. 1980.

☐ Perform reliably.

☐ Be clear and concise.

☐ ABD – Always Be Demonstrating.

‘We let our passion for the client's goals sell us. The fact that we were so energized, so pumped up helped a lot, but it wasn't just the passion of being new to the business, it was that the client understood that we were absolutely not willing to allow their project to fail. As new consultants, their project meant too much to us to take it lightly, and our client understood that.’

Kenneth Christopherson, *E = mc² Event Management Inc.*

This book is about the important 'stuff' in people's lives: work, passion, courage, ethical values, spirituality and psychological growth – and how to develop the skill to address these issues in our own consulting careers.

# PART 1

# THE CHANGING ROLE OF THE CONSULTANT

# C H A P T E R 1

# THE EXPERT 'CONSULTANT' – FROM TRANSACTIONAL TO CONSULTATIVE IN APPROACH?

## INTRODUCTION

There seems to be a misunderstanding about the generic role of consulting and the skills needed. This is coupled with a rising popularity and, indeed, need for organizations to increase their reliance on technology. This has lead to some interesting phenomena in the last few years:

☐ Some organizations realize that they have a wealth of expertise (internal technical experts that they have trained and invested in over the years), which they would like to 'cash in' on. They hire out their specialist experts to other organizations as external 'consultants'. Thus, regardless of their original business focus, they are partially becoming consulting firms.

☐ Different organizational departments, for example, Human Resources (HR), realize that many of the transactions traditionally done by HR personnel, can now be handled by a combination of interactive software and call centres. Therefore, these same HR experts could potentially be free to act as internal consultants to the business functions. They would offer consulting on people issues, such as people management, change management, resource planning, as well as coaching or group facilitation.

However, in both cases, if a person has one type of expertise, does that automatically mean the person is able to consult?

Is consulting a profession, a generic set of skills, an attitude towards a client or set of problems, or has the term consultant come to signify someone who is not on the payroll of an organization or a department – the outside resource, expert or extra pair of hands to help with a project that cannot be resourced internally? There is confusion about whether consulting is a way of looking at things or a set of skills that can be taught: a 'soft skill' that can be attached to any expertise or content knowledge. Is it something that you have a natural aptitude for, or is it something anyone can do? While there may be some confusion regarding what consulting really is, there is also a growing realization on the part of organizations that there is real value in a consulting approach, and in what it can accomplish.

# WHAT IS CONSULTING?

Consulting is traditionally thought of as a helping process: a personal relationship established between one or more persons trying to solve a problem or develop a plan (the client) and one or more persons trying to help in these efforts (the consultant). Schein[1] cited three models or ways of consulting with organizations (Table 1.1).

### THE DOCTOR-PATIENT MODEL

The doctor-patient style consultants are experts on organizations, their structure and the behaviour of the individuals within them. They are brought in to diagnose problems within an organization and to give recommendations for solving the problems. Issues that the consultant is called in for are often seen as 'symptoms' of an underlying problem, or situations that the consultant has to investigate. This method relies heavily on the consultant's interpersonal skills – the ability to win the trust of the client, carry out conversations in which the troubled person or group will reveal the information necessary to make an accurate diagnosis, as well as the ability to interpret the data meaningfully.

This method or style also relies on the client's willingness and ability to implement the recommended prescription. In this model, the consultant clearly has the power – initially taking the responsibility for unearthing the problems and suggesting solutions, and then handing over responsibility for carrying out the suggestions to the client. One of the most crucial issues, therefore, is the relationship of trust between the client and the consultant.

### PROCESS CONSULTING

The process model of consulting is founded on the premise that the client owns the problem and continues to own it throughout the consulting process. A process consultant enters into a relationship in order to facilitate the client's ability to think through and deal with the problems. This method or style of consulting requires similar skills to the doctor-patient style of consultant – building trust, facilitating discussions about difficult and, at times, personally sensitive issues. However, it reflects a completely different attitude towards the task and the client. The process consultant leaves the client as the owner of both the success and possible failure of the intervention. The consultant and the client share both power and responsibility.

### EXPERT CONSULTING

In the expert consulting model, clients purchase information or expertise. In this model, according to Margulies[2], 'the consultant is primarily concerned with bringing expertise to bear on a problem experienced by the client and, in this regard, . . . provides a service which the client does not have available'. The success of this model depends on whether the client has accurately diagnosed and communicated the problem and assessed the consultant's ability to successfully provide the expertise. In this sense, the client has the power. More recently, this type of consultancy has come to mean the supply of a 'product' to an organization, e.g. someone sells and installs a particular software programme.

TABLE 1.1: Schein's three models of consulting

With the technology developments of the 1980s and 1990s, process consulting fell somewhat out of favour. The expert or technical consultant became king. While the role of process consultant has been distinguished by the close 'empathetic and symbiotic relationship with the client', the relationship between the expert consultant and client has been almost 'viewed as incidental'.[2] Therefore, the expert consultant is often seen to need nothing except specialized technical knowledge.

[1] Schein, Edgar H, *Process Consultation Vol. II*. Reading, Massachusetts: Addison-Wesley Publishing Company, 1987.
[2] Margulies, Newton, Notes on the Marginality of the Consultant's Role. In R J Lee and A M Freedman (Eds.) *Consultation skills reading*. Arlington, Virginia: NTL Institute, 1977.

Margulies, nevertheless, suggests that these two main types or styles of consulting are not as polarized as suggested in the past. In fact, he states that in general, 'the role of the consultant is much more marginal and peripheral than is suggested by the process model and not as distant, uninvolved and task-oriented as suggested by the technical model'. This suggests that having technical expertise or knowledge is not enough if a person is to become a successful expert consultant – other skills are needed.

One of the biggest issues in technical, expert consulting is failing to identify the correct problem. Clients report that hundreds of thousands of dollars are spent on IT (Information Technology) systems that do not do what they want them to. In other cases, problems are solved by having IT solutions thrown at them when the original problem was not IT-related, for example, low morale in a finance department. Clients have diagnosed their own problems, but were incorrect in their diagnosis, so the solution is wrong because the consultant solved the wrong problem. Furthermore, neither the expert consultants nor the clients were experienced in people change management. Expert consultants may be knowledgeable about their area of expertise but may not realize, for example, that the systems they install will bring about massive culture change in an organization, which may be resisted by the employees.

The following situation is not uncommon. An old warehousing system staffed by unionized, long-term employees, who had their own customized system of inventory control, was to be replaced by a computerized inventory system that would require fewer personnel. Most of the time and effort in this project was spent supervising the building of the new warehouse and installing the new computerized inventory control system. No time was spent talking with the warehouse personnel at all. The organization found it very difficult to manage the transition because the warehouse staff that remained resisted retraining and operating the new system. For them, it meant losing both their long-time friends in the warehouse and a customized system that they had developed and used over many years. In other words, this was a complete culture change for the very people upon whom the organization relied to staff the new system. They were never consulted.

## WHAT IS THE PROBLEM?

Why is it not enough to know your area or field of expertise when dealing with a client or customer? What is a consultative approach and is it important? At its best, the approach allows people to explore and get in touch with the real issues, needs and problems they may not have thought of, or at least not thought of in a particular way. It is ultimately designed to help the client address or identify and solve their true problems and concerns. A consultative approach should unearth contexts and attitudes in advance that, left unexplored, could adversely affect a project. Identifying the various aspects of the context allows the client to develop contingency plans that can save both time and money.

Thus, truly solving a problem involves more than supplying the answer to a problem as defined by the client. The correct problem needs to be identified and solved.

There are many issues to consider, including:

☐ Is learning a new skill enough to turn a content expert into a consultant?

☐ Should you take a technical resource person and train them in consulting skills and personal interaction skills? A technical person may be brilliant technically, but unsuited to another career like consulting.

☐ Technically gifted people represent a big investment – the individual has invested time and effort to gain expertise and usually the organization has invested heavily in their development.

☐ The time a technical expert spends learning consulting skills takes away from time perhaps better spent updating their technical skills. Knowledge can become out of date very quickly, especially in certain industries such as pharmaceuticals.

☐ Are people attracted to working with detailed transactions or technical skills going to have the same personality characteristics as those attracted to consulting? For example, in Jungian personality types, often measured by the Myers-Briggs Type Indicator,[3] a sensing type person is often attracted to a technical career, whereas an intuitive type may be more attracted to consulting. They are, therefore, using their natural tendencies or talents. Sensing types can consult and intuitive types can do transactional tasks, but perhaps they will not do them as naturally or as well as their counterparts who play to their strengths.

☐ When a technical professional moves from a role that is largely transactional in nature to one that is consultative, one of the major shifts is motivation, i.e. what gives a feeling of accomplishment or reward? A technical person may get a feeling of accomplishment from having technical expertise or knowledge and by giving or using that knowledge or by providing a product that reflects that knowledge to someone else. The consultant role is more of a helper role and the sense of reward or accomplishment may come through helping the other party to accomplish something, by facilitating their accomplishment.

There may be a continuum of transactional people in organizations, which for simplicity we can divide into three groups:

1 There are the 'pure techies' – the 'behind the scenes' people. These people have often developed their technical expertise to a very high degree out of great personal interest. They are frequently brilliant individual performers. They prefer to handle technical design, solve technical problems or do a technical job independently – many exploration geologists and geophysicists, research scientists and IT personnel fall into this category. In the past, promotion tracks have been mainly up the management ladder. However, in order to recognize and reward their contribution to the success of the organization, technically skilled individuals can now rise through a technical route rather than the managerial route. These individuals' strongest talents may not lie in people management or people interaction.

2 There are people who are technically expert but do have a talent or interest in a helping or managerial role.

3 There are people with some technical knowledge but their strength lies in their people skills.

Any of the above categories of people may be in HR, IT, geology, pharmaceuticals or pure science. However, it is likely that only those in the last two categories have the desire or the natural ability to benefit from consultancy training in their field of expertise even though all would benefit from these skills. The expertise of the first category of employees may be better used to advise those acting in a consultative role but this is largely an individual choice or the choice of the organization.

[3] Myers, I B & McCaulley, M H, *Manual: A guide to the development and use of the Myers-Briggs Type Indicator*. Palo Alto, California: Consulting Psychologists Press, 1985.

If organizations decide they want their technical people to consult, is the issue of transactional people becoming consultants dealt with too simplistically? In addition to the previously mentioned issues, the organization that decides to go ahead and train their technical experts needs to consider:

☐ How can you evaluate who will most benefit from training?

☐ Is the organization willing to develop its personnel over the time period that is necessary?

☐ Is it able and willing to provide ongoing supportive structures for the change (courses, opportunities to practise the new skills, coaching in the new skills)?

How does an organization decide who to keep in the purely advisory or technical design role and who to train as consultants? Observation will be the key method of evaluation. Observers can be used in a development centre setting to assess prospective candidates while they participate in a number of scenarios. They can also participate in one-to-one interviews, which explore the candidate's own personal career aspirations.

## SUMMARY

1   There are many organizations which want to benefit from the technical expertise of their personnel. They want them to consult internally and, sometimes, externally. They want them to be able to work with clients in a manner that helps to identify the real issues in the client situation, takes a more systemic or contextual view of problems and helps the client to achieve a real and lasting solution – not to impose a solution or sell a product that does not meet expectations.

2   These personnel can only do this if they have consulting skills – the ability to work with a client, form a relationship, have meaningful discussions about problems and know what change in organizations entails. These are a set of skills that are as essential as the content expertise that the technical expert has.

# CHAPTER 2

# CHANGE MANAGEMENT

## INTRODUCTION

Change management is the process that catalyzes an organization to become different. The key is to enable people to *think differently* about their situation in order to open up possibilities to *do things differently*. This chapter explores how this can happen and how the consultant can help a client to manage both the process and the outcomes to explore and embed desirable differences. We will explore the current status of change management, both as a theory and in reality, and how it is likely to develop in the future. This chapter also provides practical tools to help consultants to develop their own and their clients' understanding, to bring about effective change in their organizations. However, the intention is not to provide an all-embracing analysis across every approach and philosophy: other practitioners will have had other experiences. Frankly, whatever works is valid.

## THE MANY FACES OF CHANGE

All the many variations of what change means for specific organizations – business context, drivers, goals, approach, issues, management philosophies, politics, commodities of power, structure, culture – contribute to change management's inherent complexity. Hence, 'Change Management' is a phrase that has many possible interpretations, and any practitioner needs to keep in mind constantly the fact that other people may have a completely different set of views and assumptions. Nevertheless, in practice, all change projects sit somewhere on a spectrum between two extremes. The extremes take necessarily simplistic views – change is always more complex than it is given credit for beforehand. Large-scale projects and those incorporating IT implementation, will contain elements that sit in more than one position on the spectrum and will, therefore, require different approaches within the overall project or programme scheme.

At one end of the spectrum there are projects where the change is the process of enabling people, processes and technology to transition to a known, foreseeable and plannable future. An example is rolling out 1000 new replacement desktops into an otherwise unchanging

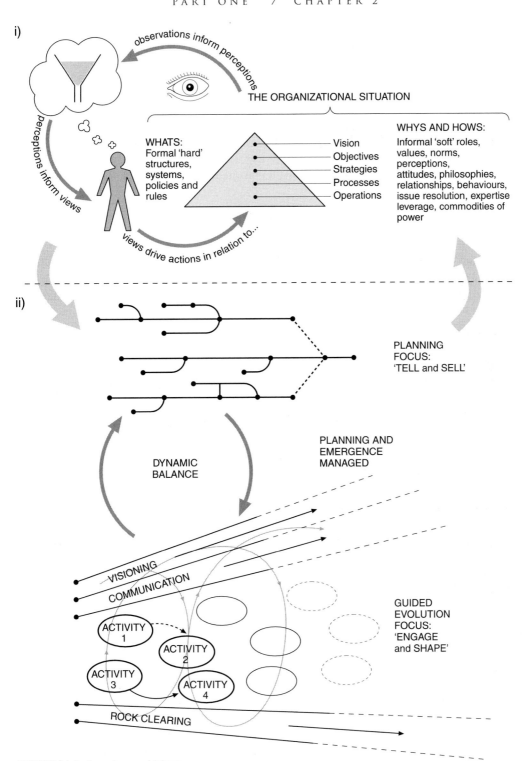

FIGURE 2.1: Key themes for successful change
i) understanding the relationship between views/perceptions of the client situation and driving actions within it.
ii) creating a dynamic balance between planning and emergence in the development of organizational change.

organizational situation. This is an extreme example of 'reactive' change – the future is known, the change is reactive to it and, therefore, plannable. At the other end, are projects where the change involved is the process of discovering an unknown future via an iterative cycle of envisioning, taking action, reflecting on the outcome, envisioning and so on. At the same time, shaping the developing direction and managing the surrounding uncertainty on an ongoing basis. An example is where the culture and business functioning of an organization are felt not to be working but the future can not be described, except as 'not like this'. This is an extreme example of 'proactive' change. The future is unknown, the change framework can be outlined, at least in the short term, but the timing and content cannot be predicted overall and can only be planned for in terms of the immediately foreseeable future. Ultimately the framework itself may adapt.

## UNDERSTANDING HUMANS AND CHANGE

Humans are 'sense-making' creatures (see section (i) of 2.1 above). As individuals, we continuously interpret the world around us and interact with it, guided by a complex set of influences that comprise a 'logic filter' in our minds. This logic filter is informed by genetic predisposition, upbringing, experiences (either direct, reported or surrogate), emotions and whether we argued with a loved one, missed the bus or won the lottery etc on that particular day. We refer to it collectively by nouns such as mind-set (or the broader German term *weltangschauung*, loosely meaning worldview). Our actions are driven by our intentions (at some level, not always conscious) and we tend to see them as logical. Note that 'logic' sounds solidly and comfortably objective. We tend to forget that it is conditional, subjective and very personal. One person's 'freedom fighter' is another's 'urban guerilla'. The filter is also largely hidden, even from our conscious selves. We do not notice what we do not notice. We do not see what is going on in others' minds – the 'drivers'. We only see the outputs expressed in their decisions and actions. We then pass those through our own filter in our interpretation of, and assumptions about, them. This is a continuous and, generally, unchallenged process. So, what of it?

When we come together to make things happen, as we do in organizations – particularly when we try to change the status quo in any way – we have to address this nexus. Those around us have a multitude of conscious and unconscious drivers, which influence their actions and reactions over time and, corporately, will have a significant impact on our work and how we go about it.

This reflects the reality that organizations are inherently very complex, and bringing about attitudinal and behavioural change is especially so. Managing this overall complexity is, therefore, a key component skill in managing change.

A later section describes helpful approaches for getting 'under the skin' of these complexities to tackle the underlying issues, rather than simply the symptoms.

## THE DEVELOPMENT OF THEORIES AND PRACTICE

Reductionist, mechanistic views of organizations and management theory had, until the 1980s, held sway for many years. Analogies with machines included a general assumption that most organizations were run along some form of command and control lines. Making changes was theoretically easy – tip the change in at the top and the organizational mechanisms and feedback loops would do the trick of disseminating it. The basis of action was 'decide, plan, do'. The 1980s, however, brought two spectacular changes that turned previous notions on their head.

Firstly, the more developed world was starting to realize the impact of computers, whose development was moving towards desktop machines and network capabilities. This brought unprecedented opportunities for increased speed and flexibility and challenged the traditional hierarchical organization structures in terms of resource locations, communication and who could make decisions, based on what information. Secondly, specific industries faced unprecedented upheaval. In financial services, the changing operation and regulation of the stock markets exposed organizations of all kinds to the impact that their culture had on their management and fortunes, which was similarly remarkable. Prior to this, culture was the spectre at the feast in organizations: it was barely acknowledged. Big Bangs, like that in London in 1987, opened stock markets to outsiders and enabled some corporate marriages that forced businesses to reassess explicitly what made them 'tick'. By the 1990s, the concepts of managing organizational and cultural change moved on to the management agenda, as business leaders started to recognize their fundamental importance in the new business context.

## UNDERSTANDING AND USING THE LEGACIES – TREASURE AND TRASH

As demand for change management advice and assistance grew among client organizations, so consultancies and gurus filled the gap by developing new thinking and methodologies to tackle the issues. Many successive themes emerged, promising global, holistic, systemic all-embracing answers to the complex change conundrum. Most theories got sucked into particular issues and associations and had their 'currency' devalued. Total Quality Management (TQM) and Business Process Re-engineering (BPR) both fell into this camp: many good things came out of both, but neither one delivered on the original promise of broad change. TQM implementation was devalued by a rush to codify what existed rather than to challenge it; BPR suffered a similar fate by questioning 'Which process shall we re-engineer?', rather than 'What are the strategic purposes that this business intends to serve and what core processes are, therefore, required to support those purposes?'

In terms of general approaches to change and consultancies' market offerings, the 1990s saw the outbreak of 'methodology wars', with consultancies vying for change management business on the strength of the logic of their approach. The logic stream underpinning these approaches was: define the change, develop change vision, design new organization/structure/processes/other 'change' solutions, assess current resources, perform gap analyses, design change implementation and communication interventions, implement. Most of the diagrams depicting these approaches had a plethora of action arrows flowing forwards. There was little indication or recognition that reflection and review would be a necessary part of the process. This period effectively represented a massive experiment in how to manage organizational and cultural change: some good developments in thinking and practice emerged as a result, and these are explored later in this chapter.

However, research undertaken in this period shows that 80 per cent of major change initiatives were perceived to have failed. This shocking indictment caused the client and consulting world to take serious stock of why so many, apparently logical and well-planned, programmes were not achieving their targets. Many individuals and organizations, in the light of their experience of perceived failure (or less than optimal success), assumed they had not planned well enough. This was usually because so many unexpected things had come out of the corporate woodwork during the programme and caused other developments to happen, i.e. the plans had gone off course. They decided they needed to plan more and to plan better. In fact, what they needed to do was to plan less and become more adaptive and flexible.

## CHANGE PROGRAMMES AND TRADITIONAL PROJECT MANAGEMENT APPROACHES

An unfortunate attitude to change management, still prevailing in some corporate quarters, is that it is much the same as any other project and you can, therefore, apply project management principles to it for management purposes. This attitude relates back to thinking differently. The attitude results, in reality, in trying to do new things by applying old mind-sets. The principles of traditional project management approaches are rooted in the mind-set of 'decide, plan, do', i.e. decide the change, plan how to do it and do it.

Notice the similarity to the change logic stream outlined above: define the change, develop change vision, design new organization/structure/processes/other 'change' solutions, assess current resources, perform gap analyses, design change implementation and communication interventions, implement. The unchallenged assumption here is that the change is 'done to' the organization. Several further assumptions follow from this:

- ☐ Change is decided by few and imposed on many.

- ☐ Change will mean loss of control for the individual and they will, therefore, resist it.

- ☐ People must be convinced of the need to change, otherwise they will not, hence an emphasis on extensive communications programmes.

- ☐ Change must be delivered in measured doses, otherwise people's resilience will be overloaded.

The above factors are reflected in many of the formal change methodologies that have had currency in the past few years. These approaches, in combination with the project management vehicles that carry them, have contributed to the perceived failure of complex change initiatives.

This is not to say that traditional project management approaches cannot be helpful. For example, the standard project management disciplines of looking ahead and questioning how much is known, who is involved (or needs to be), what is the timeline of significant events that could relate to the envisaged change, what events and activities already exist in the corporate diary that could be useful to the change process and so on, are all useful. However, experience shows that much of what needs to be achieved, especially in the very early stages, lies in identifying and gaining the involvement and commitment of key individuals in the organization in order to set other activities in train. In this respect, some of the planning emphases and assumptions inherent in a project management approach are not helpful. For example, you cannot predict with certainty that person A will commit to the project on day 147. Time needed for 'sponsorship commitment' requirements (and the consequences of not doing them) tend to be underestimated. Communications alone will not suffice.

This brings us to the caveats about traditional project management and its use as a vehicle for managing change. These are that it:

- ☐ Views the future using the context and mind-set of the past (which may be limiting).

- ☐ Assumes that the goals are agreed and a shared understanding of their implications exists among the interested parties.

☐ Assumes that a desired future 'ideal situation' can be seen and articulated in sufficient detail, in advance, to formulate timelined project plans (this may be beguiling but ultimately misleading).

☐ Assumes that timed milestones can be articulated and agreed – so that 'ahead' and 'behind' judgements can be attributable to 'progress'.

☐ Assumes that the issues perceived which drive this response will be addressed by it over the elapsed time to implement, without significant change (i.e. that the 'goalposts' will not move).

☐ Adopts, unchallenged, the 'decide, plan, do' project management approach. This further implies a 'tell and sell' approach for the outcome plan, with the risk of resistance in the organization.

☐ Restricts creativity, i.e. once the plan is blueprinted then 'creativity' is only welcome if it fits. This can disenfranchise the very people who could contribute most – those who know the organization best.

These caveats create real issues for the change process:

☐ If you bring about fundamental changes, the above assumptions are not viable because the information to fulfil the project planning cannot be foreseen, or seen in sufficient detail.

☐ Formal project management is inherently reductionist and seeks to break project components down into manageable chunks. However, the reality of genuine organizational and cultural change is in the complex interplay of component elements and influences. Therefore, a holistic approach, that manages in the context of the complex whole, is required.

☐ If you plan to engage (rather than simply consult) the client organization's people and encourage them to be creative to introduce some new thinking on old issues, then you cannot predict what form or outcomes will emerge.

☐ With regard to the implied assumption that the goalposts will stay still: the corporate issues driving the change initiative will usually change. Often they would have done so anyway (e.g. market conditions may change over time), or the change initiative itself will encourage new perceptions that cause different views of the organization. Fundamental change means that the way the business conceptualizes itself, and performs and measures its performance on that basis, will probably change too. Therefore 'reflection' and 'adaptation' need to be built into the approach. Heavily predictive planning processes find this difficult to accommodate.

In the above (project management based) approach, expert consulting skill is deployed to design the proposed change outcomes, and process skills are deployed to tell and sell and convince the organisation of the approach's appropriateness and how to fit with it. The alternative approach (described below), deploys expert skill continuously through a process approach that engages the organization in the development and shaping of the change itself, right through to implementation. The discussion is not about which approach is best – both may be applicable, depending on the circumstances. It is about the opportunities that each approach makes available and about challenging the above with a different approach. In practice, I would recommend that most projects would benefit from managing a dynamic balance between the two approaches (see Figure 2.1). Further sections give tools that can assist in achieving this dynamic balance.

What is the alternative approach?

☐ An approach that works on developing visioning skills in the organization, rather than a single vision 'upfront'. This is not to say that a guiding vision is not developed, rather that the process does not stop there.

☐ Recognition that significant organizational change, of whatever kind, requires a process akin, metaphorically, to hill-walking. Having envisioned the end goals (in high level terms to start with), planning is only done in detail for the 'hill you can see', and then on a high involvement 'engagement' basis with the client organization.

☐ The consultant acts in a 'sherpa/guide' role, i.e. they know all the various contextual components – terrain, weather conditions, tools required, difficulty of climb, experience level of the climbers – but recognize that the climb belongs to the climbers. Once the first hill is attained, the terrain for the next part of the journey can be seen in detail and the climbers' increased experience level incorporated to develop the detailed plan for that stage, as well as firming up outline views of the further stages.

☐ Detailed planning is, therefore, conducted on a rolling development basis, incorporating reflections on experience to date at each stage. As needs emerge or are identified through the expert/process input from the consultants, appropriate groups are set up to tackle them. These are networked into the existing groups to maintain a shared overview across the work.

☐ Progress/developments across different groups working in parallel, on different aspects, is monitored and knowledge is shared and communicated through a variety of interactive mechanisms. A rich, shared understanding of the contextual overview is maintained, fed by reflections on experience and used in turn to guide shaping of future action/ commitment developments.

☐ Viral communication is supported, while maintaining formal core communication mechanisms.

A range of creativity, systemic thinking, varying analyses and approaches, problem-solving and facilitation tools and skills are drawn upon to engage and support the participants. These are from all levels, as appropriate to the situation. Strategic intentions and tactical realities are examined to surface issues relevant to developing and shaping the change, whether re-structuring, new processes, new ways of working, capability requirements or appropriate skills assessments. This approach actively combines planning with emergence.

However, it is also important to recognize that this alternative approach adopts a quite different mind-set. The arguments against it need to be recognized and addressed:

☐ Many organizations, used to doing things on the basis of project plans, may find it difficult to manage without their usual 'comfort blanket'. Without a detailed plan upfront, clients may lack reassurance that the process will deliver something that works. They will have a plan for the kick-off and outlines of how the initial stages will be undertaken, i.e. a plan for the process is prepared in advance. Further plans and refinements of goals are produced in the light of developments over time. Perceiving uncertainty as a space for creativity and opportunity, rather than a scary indication that management does not know what it is doing (an old 'management as planners and controllers – rather than leaders' mind-set), may be part of the required change. In practice, these 'engage and shape' change projects are not unplanned. It is important to recognize that the nature of the planning is different from the project management approach. The crucial difference lies in the need to manage a dynamic balance between 'planning' and 'emergence'. Clients need to be reassured that the process itself is robust and that the combination of internal knowledge with support expertise will ensure that effective delivery outputs are gained.

☐ This alternative approach has the appearance of being more involvement-intensive, than the project management approach. Client leaders may think they want to be 'done to' because it seems in prospect to be quicker and more painless. However, experience says that in reality, given the (usually hidden) effort that the project management approach requires to counter resistance (because inevitably it is negatively perceived as 'done to' within the client organization), both approaches come out the same in terms of required involvement. The key point in selling this alternative approach is that the levels of engagement rather than simple consultation involved, mean that ownership of outcomes is high and resistance levels are low. Involvement is positively invited and proactive, rather than negatively imposed and reactive.

☐ The alternative 'engage and shape' approach may appear chaotic. Many organizational change, design and development approaches talk about engagement when they mean consultation. They pay lip-service to creativity. Remember, if you intend to engage the organization and to release and utilize its creative capabilities, you cannot predict the outcome. This is not usually tidy, but it is productive. The 'encasing' approach needs to be flexible and adaptable, with capacity to incorporate creative output and shape it in helpful directions.

☐ The alternative approach appears to assume a democracy that may be seen as idealistic. This approach is not democratic. It starts, as all change must, with the senior organizational sponsors who have the power to initiate and support action to address their strategic issues. It allows a high degree of self-selection of participants. No false promises are made that all ideas and suggestions will be incorporated. Nevertheless, it does promise that all ideas and suggestions will be welcomed and considered. Since the participants are engaging in the design of the changes, rather than being asked to produce ideas against a perceived, externally imposed design, there is more capacity to engage in genuine creative problem solving. Motivation levels tend to be high.

☐ The aternative approach may appear to incorporate an assumption that everyone will have the organization's best interests at heart and will want to participate, even if they personally may not eventually benefit from it. Most organizations would view this as a naive stance. In practice, this approach brings the organizational issues that need to be resolved to the surface; it tackles them in the context of the strategic requirements. The resulting high levels of creativity, engagement and ownership counter one of the more significant risks of other approaches – that in the atmosphere of secrecy and/or imposed change, good people (whom the organization would most like to keep) leave prematurely, out of fear that they will be victims. Further, because there is more scope for new ideas and developments to emerge from this process, new organizational opportunities can arise, giving more potential scope for development and deployment of staff. Enlightened self-interest is as good a reason as any to start to be involved.

## MANAGING EXPECTATIONS

Most change projects have some kind of time constraint: few have the luxury of a brief that says at the beginning, 'Make this change, whatever it takes'. Contrarily, few clients would voluntarily close down a project that was seen to be working successfully, even if the original dates envisaged have gone by. It is, therefore, important to be as clear as possible with your client about what kind of progress may be expected within each different, foreseeable component element, within the overall time allowed or predicted. You need to be explicit also about the areas of the project that cannot be assessed for progress and pace (or even for some elements of content), until some initiatives are actually in place. In this context, the organization is required to address itself to teasing out what is desirable overall and what is minimally acceptable within any constraining time framework. It can then address how to handle the differences.

Most complex change projects, whether proactive, reactive or a mixture, have experienced changes to their time-scales. Many reasons account for this. Lack of real senior level sign-off, lack of real sponsor commitment or technology development delays can cause project time-scales to stretch. Similarly, where engagement has 'taken off', extraordinary progress can be achieved in a short space of time (e.g. by different groups parallel processing different issues).

A key service the consultant can offer the client is to tease out and represent in graphical form (to clarify), the many hopes and expectations that are discovered, from their research, to impinge on perceptions of success. For example, in one major public sector (remedial) change programme, five key senior sponsors all described their organization's desired change as seeking to achieve different aims. These were cross-referenced with the ten action teams that had already been set up. It was found that some aims were not sufficiently supported by the action plans. Similarly, some teams' goals would not achieve any of the overall aims. Perspectives had changed across the piece since the project's initial inception. Work was immediately put in place to:

☐ Take a fresh perspective on desired aims in the light of the experiences to date.

☐ Bring the accumulated achievements together.

☐ Reconfigure the effort so that each team could relate their future work to the new assessment.

☐ Initiate a rolling review programme so that real achievement could be attained and recognized, with newly emerging needs identified and addressed.

One helpful approach is called Goal Directed Project Management. This operates on the principle of identifying and prioritizing desired outcomes, and what needs to be in place to know that they have been achieved, rather than timed milestones. In cases where the change management task is associated with implementation of a technology, particularly information technology (IT), the change management expectations need to be very carefully analysed. It is necessary to examine which elements of the overall desired results are related to the transition to the new technology (where some change activities will necessarily be tied to technology implementation goals) and which elements relate to a more fundamental reassessment of organization and activities, goals and 'driving mind-set' requirements. Different expectations need to be teased out and managed accordingly.

Many projects have suffered and been perceived as failures because these analyses were not done and change management was seen simply as a soft, cuddly add-on to the technology implementation, rather than technology being seen as the enabler of organizational change. Similarly, projects have failed because insufficient recognition was given to the different demands of the changes involved.

Managing expectations is vested in managing client relationships. Achieving both individually and across the consulting team, as broad a network of successful, informative relationships with client people as possible, is the best defence against misconceptions and false expectations.

# HELPFUL TOOLS AND APPROACHES

The focus in this section is on tools that help the development of proactive 'engage and shape' change. These are a key tools that will help to manage the uncertainties involved and reassure the client that the process is a productive one, in which the organization's capacity for creativity and for learning will be utilized beneficially to develop effective, sustainable change.

In a well-run organization, (see Figure 2.1, section (i)) individuals at any level should be able to understand the corporate vision, how the structure and processes of the organization work and how the tactical actions delivered through those add up to deliver strategic intent. They should be able to see how their own role fits into the scheme of things and how their efforts contribute. Further, individuals should have a reasonable idea about the fit and contribution of other roles. The organizational attitudes and management philosophies, commodities of power, behavioural norms, value systems and culture should all support the overall strategic intentions and tactical needs of the organization.

Consultants entering a new client situation need to assimilate quickly the factors outlined above, particularly the way they relate to the area of the organization in which change has been identified as needed.

## Rich picture building

Figure 2.1 gives an example of the general style of a rich picture. Constructing a graphical drawing can be immensely helpful – both to the consultant and the client. Its purpose is to plot an overview snapshot of the situation in which you find yourself. This is a key tool for mapping complexity and monitoring developments. Clearly, as an observer, it is helpful to be aware of your own perspectives and their influence on what you will 'notice', or not, in any given situation. Try not to focus on the 'problem' (the diagnosis may not be correct or may simply be a symptom), but on the situation in which problems are perceived to exist and the identities and interrelationships of those who perceive the problems to exist and why.

Situational rich pictures usually contain representations of key people; significant views expressed; key influencing elements in the situation; indications of structure or different organizational entities and the relationships between them; and key values factors in different parts of the organization and so on. In summary, they should show the interconnections of all the headline elements that look meaningful in terms of understanding the situation as you find it. There are numerous software packages that can help with this process, but hand-drawn pictures are still often richest (and quickest) for conveying the dynamics of a situation. However, they have the drawback of needing a scanner to enable electronic sharing, and they cannot be manipulated further easily.

Resist the temptation to over-analyse and classify the information you receive in the early stages of your interaction with the client, particularly if the project is just starting. Try instead to plot a picture that gives an overall context of the situation. This will help you to map the complexities of the situation with the key personalities who will shape its development. It will also help you to identify where key issues may be sourced (e.g. differing views from key sponsors, conflicting values systems in parts of the organization that work together).

Practitioners understand that there is never just one 'problem' that change needs to solve. Your client may, however, be conceptualizing matters in this way. All situations evolve in response to events and activities. Change management is the process of guiding that evolution in helpful ways. Part of the role of the change management practitioner is constantly to help open their clients' eyes (and keep them open) to the broader picture. Rich pictures are a very effective way of helping to articulate and share a number of key views held and their impact on the situation and each other.

Pictures can be used for:

☐ Capturing the complex interrelationships within a situation in which change is envisaged – people, structures, processes, events, ideas, perspectives, etc.

☐ Helping to make key impact factors (views held, key issues) explicit and shareable.

☐ Visioning and scenario exploration.

☐ Clearly articulating the overall conceptual framework and route of the change process – as it develops – and the kinds of activities required at each stage and who is likely to be involved, as these factors are firmed up during the rolling development planning.

☐ Plotting key progression points over time (situation snapshots), as the change process develops. For example, impact on the whole situation of recognizable changes of perspective in key parts of the organization.

☐ Developing a detailed understanding of a particular element of the situation and the factors that impact on it.

Any of these applications can be made into useful exercises in workshop-type settings, where your clients draw the picture. They are particularly useful in helping client people to gain a shared understanding across different organizational settings. Alternatively, you may draw pictures yourself to develop your own analyses, or to facilitate discussions with the client.

## Change role identification and analysis

Organizational change may be an exhilarating or a threatening prospect to individuals within the client organization. Naturally, one of the things consultants will be interested in, especially during the initial researches into the situation, is who the key people are and what views they hold about the situation and about any change foci that have been discussed. When you try and analyse how individuals and groups respond (or might do) to change processes or goals, you need to acknowledge that the picture you get may be of symptoms, rather than underlying truths and, in any case, will only be a snapshot in time. Very resistant individuals have turned into champions overnight and vice versa. Resist the temptation to put people and situations into category boxes. And where you do, for the purposes of analysis, ensure you do not assume they will stay there.

Change role analysis helps us to analyse and also challenge our analyses about, who in the situation is driving or is instrumental in, the change initiative and the impact that they can have. Therefore, it is important to effect change role identification with reference to the change brief given (or to discussions that will lead to the development of a brief) and in relation to where those key people sit in the organizational hierarchy. It will help you to assess whether your client for the change management is appropriately placed to instigate and authorize action and, in particular, to take a tough leadership stance when the going gets tough (as it will).

Numerous role structures have been developed in different change approaches:

☐ **Initiating sponsor** – Who has the authority and political power to initiate, shape and drive through the change programme.

☐ **Sustaining sponsor** – Who has the authority and political power to support, shape and drive through the change programme.

☐ **Advocate** – Someone without sponsor level authority but who nevertheless has political or organizational authority or influence and can encourage support of the change programme.

☐ **Agent/champion** – Focal centres of change activity with the motivation and position or authority to act in driving, shaping and support of the change programme.

☐ **Actor/respondent** – Individuals who will participate in and help shape the change. It is an interesting reflection on early methodologies that this role was originally termed 'target', with no questioning of the implied assumption that change was 'applied to' those individuals rather than that it could be participated in and shaped by them.

☐ **Assassin** – Not usually mentioned but essential to recognize, at least as a potential threat. These individuals could be at any level.

Much has been written elsewhere about these role analyses and their uses. The priority when researching this subject is deciding whether the author is in a reactive change 'tell and sell' mind-set, in which case they are likely to talk about identifying people to occupy these roles ('Who shall we choose to champion 'x' activity that we're planning?'). Or whether, the author is in a proactive change 'engage and shape' mind-set, and may talk more about people self-selecting for these roles, for instance, increasing numbers of champions self-selecting over time as the organization engages in and takes ownership of the change process.

## Systemic analysis and 'purposeful activity' modelling

The concept of systems thinking as an aid to management problem solving and, more particularly, change management practice, has entered management dialogue in recent years. In fact it has been around for much longer than most practitioners realize (50 years or more).

Much of systemic analysis' current prominence is owed to the popularity of Peter Senge's ideas in his *Fifth Discipline* series (Nicholas Brealey, 1994). His ideas form a useful introduction to holistic thinking. However, anyone wanting to use systems thinking and practice to get under the skin of client organizations should read *Soft Systems Methodology in Action* by Peter Checkland and Jim Scholes (Wiley). This offers a powerful understanding of, and methodology for, using systems concepts to understand and shape organizational change. The systemic modelling outlined in this chapter is part of the approach detailed in this book.

*Soft Systems Methodology* uses an intellectually rigorous approach to grapple with the soft complexities of human actions and intentions in organizations. Its premise is the use of systems concepts to help structure the process of enquiry into a situation that is perceived to be problematic, leading to beneficial action to improve it.

Most of us know what we mean when we refer to the 'system' in any context. We do not usually dig to see if the 'system' the other person has in their mind in relation to the reference is the same as that in our own. One person might talk about the 'education system' and have in mind formal education for 4–21 year olds, but another might talk about the education system and have in mind whole life learning in every context. Similarly, when we refer to the organization, we may be discussing apples and pears. The drawback of talking about systems as if they exist in the real world, is that the boundaries of the concept referred to may not be clear or shared, and may not map onto what we are discussing – causing confusion. The more sophisticated approach is to use systems concepts as constructs to support our intellectual process of enquiry *about* the real world. When we are talking about potentially useful ideas – concepts – we can specify exactly where the boundaries are. To clarify, someone once remarked that the world and the universe are not innately divided into chemistry, physics and biology etc. These concepts are constructs we place on the natural world to help us relate to and make sense of it.

Systemic activity models are powerful 'construct development' tools, which can help to underpin proactive organizational change. You can take any ideas that feel useful for taking the organization forward, and any mind-sets that makes sense of them, and quickly create activity models that explore those combinations. Each is a conceptual model (i.e. it does not necessarily map what actually happens in the real world). It can be used to help you to challenge what is happening in the real world of the organization, or it can help to explore scenarios for the future.

This sounds quite academic and theoretical, so let us look at a practical example. A client took TV and radio programmes and turned them into video, audio and merchandise products. Financially, it was a very successful company, but two key parts of the organization were not working effectively together. The managing director took a strong position on addressing this because he felt that greater success would come from better integration. His brief was 'I don't want to see a report – if I don't see change happening, you've failed.'

This was proactive change – the future was unknown. Some initial research was undertaken that produced a complex picture of interwoven strands in the situation. A project 'plan' was produced in the form of a 'rich picture'. This consisted of a process framework with some rough time-scales, based on practical organization logistics. The rich picture contained a series of workshops. Only the first two workshops had a pre-specified focus (strategic and related to the two key organization groups) and promised that some useful output would be achieved that would feed the rest of the process. A steering process was also shown. In these two first workshops, brainstorming, SWOT (Strengths, Weaknesses, Opportunities and Threats) analyses and creativity exercises were used to identify and understand the issues. Participants (the most senior three management levels across the two groups) were divided into mixed syndicate groups and shown how to do the conceptual activity modelling. They then took a key issue each and explored it using the modelling process.

One of the strategic issues identified by the workshop was that the organization would have to be able to nurture talent in order to feed its future stream of work (products from talent-based programmes). It was recognized that talent nurturing must exist because the business survived on that basis. However, you could not look at the business and identify a talent nurturing system or process, so the particular syndicate group decided to model one to see what it could look like. They named what they were exploring as 'a purposeful activity system to nurture talent'. Next they debated how to populate the required framework to build the model of that system. There is always a range of choice options for each category. The framework required them to decide the following:

**Customer:** Who would be the beneficiary of such a system? (In this case they chose the organization.)

**Actors:** Who would be the people who would do the activities in the system as if it existed in the real world? (In this case the choice was the organization's people.)

**Transformation:** What inputs would be transformed into what outputs by the activities in the system? (The choice was talent resources available transformed into talent resources nurtured.)

*Weltanschauungen*: What mind-set would make sense of this transformation? (They chose the rationale that it would help to make more money.)

**Owner:** Who could be the owner of such a system, i.e. who could shut it down? (They chose the managing director.)

**Environmental constraints:** What elements in the environment where such a system would notionally operate would they take as given and that the system would not address? (They chose the fact that agents who acted for talent were in contact with each other and could influence the responses to their activities from the talent individuals themselves.)

Jointly agreeing such a framework across mixed groups from two different parts of the organization – that did not work well together and who usually would not meet in this context – proved a lively process, as did constructing the models. From the choices made to populate the framework, the model building task is to debate and decide the minimum set of logically defensible activities (expressed as verbs, e.g. 'Identify talent' etc.) that, connected together could notionally operationalize the framework. In other words, the activities that would – connected together as a system – transform the inputs into the outputs as described in the transformation part of the framework, and incorporate the other framework elements. Each group produced a model to address a different issue of strategic importance, as defined by themselves. The process of arguing about which words appropriately described each activity in the models (and how they should connect together in the logic of the mind-set they had chosen to model), really helped unpack the meanings and assumptions that these key individuals attached to them, in turn enlightening their colleagues in relation to their beliefs about the business.

None of the models were of 'systems' that you could point at in the real world of the organization. Therefore, the next stage of the process where each activity (and connections) in the model is used to challenge the real world was interesting. In the case above, the comparison of logic and reality resulted in the realization that many things that appeared in the model did happen in practice but were unconnected and carried out by different individuals who perhaps did not have contact with each other in that context. The model gave a framework that could help them shape what such a system might look like in the real situation. Models are not 'ideals'. They are a framework for notionally operationalizing a purposeful idea, driven by a mind-set, in a way that helps challenge and understand the real situation.

While these models are very useful for achieving the multi-level development and sharing of ideas that a workshop can enable, they are also useful as a tool for the consultant. They can help to:

☐ Clarify thinking about an issue.

☐ Explore different viewpoints on a single subject.

☐ Explore different views within the situation in general.

☐ Prepare ideas for discussion with the client.

☐ Prepare a robust challenge for situations in which people seem to believe they are doing one thing, but in practice are doing something else.

In the example client situation, the first workshop produced one group who were determined to develop their ideas back in the workplace. This went ahead as a guinea pig for the approach. Their work (a cross-functional 'first') generated some developments that fed into the second workshop, which was run on the same process. Out of that process came three new key streams of activity. The organization (having involved its entire management team across the two organizational groups) threw participation in the next phase of development open to the rest of the hierarchy. This was on the basis that anyone who thought they could contribute was welcomed to do so. Enthusiasm and ownership were startlingly high. Viral communication about progress 'took off'. The steering process ensured that the change process's pace was appropriate and that 'cross-fertilization' reflection and review informed the subsequent development activities. Individuals at all levels felt their connection to the business's strategic development. The process fast-tracked some individuals who might have otherwise been buried in the hierarchy, but whose ideas were important. It also, over time, identified some managers whose ideas and style were not supportive of the way the organization was developing. This was a valid issue for the business to tackle.

The successful conclusion to the consultancy input was when the client felt that the 'engine of change' had transferred successfully into the management of the organization. They saw for themselves that a whole new way of conceptualizing their business had developed and that this meant they needed to restructure to meet changing market demands – which they did successfully. This left them focused on new business growth and working successfully internally to support it. The client acknowledged that the systemic modelling had enabled them to open their thinking up in previously unimaginable ways and gave a rigorous means to follow their ideas through and explore new developments. The organization had successfully changed.

## Engagement and resistance

Increasing experience over the years has shown the need for consultants and client organizations to engage and involve staff in their change. However, disappointingly, often this has still been from the mind-set that staff are being taken along a largely predetermined path, to counter assumed (and often self-fulfilling) resistance. This is effectively 'interactive communication messaging'. While better than nothing, this approach frustrates the opportunities for real creative development and organizational learning that could blossom. Experience suggests that there is an inverse relationship between engagement and resistance: the higher the level of real engagement, the lower the level of resistance encountered. However, this is not to say that resistance does not exist. Consider this Chinese proverb:

I hear – I forget

I see – I remember

I do – I understand

Engaging the organization's people to shape their change is part of the element of 'emergence', referred to earlier in managing a dynamic balance. People are part of the creative force that shapes the process, not simply recipients of the output of others. Most people, concerned about and involved in a situation, respond better to an invitation to participate in decisions about it, than an instruction to do something differently. Similarly, no one appreciates wasting their time with spurious decision making over something that is already settled.

To translate that principle into change management practice, try to create the change project environment, structure and processes that allow a level of engagement that is as high as possible for shaping the process of change, with a clear set of explicit parameters about what is known or fixed about the situation. That then defines the space in which real creative, interactive change activity can take place. These parameters may be pushed and may move as a development of the change process, but recognizing where they are explicitly at any given time is important. Explicit discussion will illuminate any differences of perception (among colleagues and clients) about what is possible and about what the parameters themselves are.

An important blocker to recognize in this process, is fear. Sometimes it is client management fear and sometimes it is inexperienced consultant fear. Fear that choices and their outcomes will clutter or impair neat careful project plans. Fear that the unknown will be bad. Fear that too many cooks will spoil the broth and that, having encouraged people to contribute their ideas, there will be trouble if they cannot all be accommodated.

This fear does not recognize the levels of good sense existing in most individuals. Nor does it recognize that processes can be instigated to deal with these issues. Engagement vehicles can involve all or any of:

- [ ] One-to-one discussions.
- [ ] Group discussions.
- [ ] Workshops.
- [ ] Idea factories.
- [ ] Focus groups.
- [ ] Seminars.
- [ ] Surgeries.
- [ ] E-mail and discussion databases.
- [ ] Research activities – questionnaires and interviews.
- [ ] Communication – formal or viral.

## SUMMARY

1  Since the 1980s, change management has matured to a point where consultants are now in a situation to add real value to clients with more assured prospects of success.

2  It has taken many years to convince clients that change management is a serious, real issue. Helping an organization to become different involves altering the dynamic between people, processes, structure and culture – at the core of operations. Change management is not a soft cuddly add-on to the periphery of the business activity to keep the troops happy. Rather, it involves a fundamental re-thinking of the business, its rationale, how it conceptualizes itself and how it wants to operate in the markets it is (or seeks to be) active in.

3  Moreover, change management has become 'fashionable', and everyone says they can do it. In the heat of competition, every consultancy claims their methodology is 'better than the others' and all sorts of activities are inappropriately labelled 'change management' (e.g. training, communication, etc.). As a result, change management is in danger of becoming completely oversold and client expectations unrealistic – combining fairy dust and 'magic wand' to keep people happy, regardless of corporate realities.

4  Clients are now more experienced at change and sophisticated in their understanding of their needs. They are clearer about what is involved and prepared to 'cherry pick' teams of appropriately skilled individual consultants – not necessarily from the same practices – to undertake their project. Consultancy practices have become more sophisticated and are able to position their change offering more appropriately to the range of client needs.

5  Effective change will not come from a particular methodology – all of those available can only inform at the mind-set level. Effective change comes through experience and sensitivity to needs and realities, addressed by tailoring many different approaches, including creating new ideas in situ, and balancing planning with emergence to shape the process overall.

# CHAPTER 3

## CONSULTING ON SECOND-WAVE CHANGE

### INTRODUCTION

The advent of process engineering in the 1990s brought massive waves of organization change through downsizing, restructuring, mergers and acquisitions. This had a powerfully destabilizing effect on people, their development and their careers, and, in consequence, organizations are now finding cracks in their people-development processes.

The resulting people problems constitute one of the most significant challenges consultants will face in the future. This chapter explores what consultants can do to recover the situation and, where necessary, initiate another 'second wave' of change.

### DOWNSIZE AND CAPSIZE?

The academic who led the process re-engineering revolution, Michael Hammer, a professor at MIT (Massachusetts Institute of Technology) wrote with James Champy the influential *Reengineering the Corporation*.[1] He has now published research work on the radical organizational changes that characterized the 1990s, many of which, arguably, he and Champy helped to precipitate. Hammer admits that he did not get it quite right in his later book, *Beyond Reengineering*.[2] With commendable honesty, based on innumerable case studies in the US and Europe, he acknowledges that he was wrong to emphasize 'radical change' versus 'changing the processes' that actually create added value for organizations.

It might be that Hammer and Champy had a change of heart, partly influenced by the statistics from the last decade, which indicate that over 85 per cent of process re-engineering projects failed to meet their original objectives. A further study of transformation projects by John Kotter, among 100 top corporations, identified the failure rate as over 70 per cent.[3] Gary Hamel and C K Prahalad found that most re-engineering fails because of its dangerous focus on 'being better at what the company is doing currently, not on being different'.[4] The latter would give a better chance of long-term, and increasingly of short-term, survival. In

[1] Michael Hammer and James Champy, *Reengineering the Corporation*, Harper Business, 1993.
[2] Michael Hammer *Beyond Reengineering*, Harper Collins, 1998.
[3] Peter Senge et al, *The Dance of Change*, Nicholas Brearley, 1999.
[4] Gary Hamel and C K Prahalad, *Competing for the Future*, Harvard Business School Press, 1996.

addition, another alarming phenomenon is now beginning to be reported in the 15–30 per cent of organizations that initially met their objectives after a first wave of change. This is the organization turbulence in the years (approximately two to three) after implementation of the original changes. Early ripples following change implementations are not receding but turning into a succession of waves threatening, or capsizing, some of these formerly successful organizations. It is becoming apparent that skilful management is crucial in the dangerous period following radical change and that a seemingly successful project can quickly go wrong.

## CONSULTING ON SECOND-WAVE CHANGE

While consultants continue to acquire more and more expertise in facilitating and directing change, the most accepted model of change used continues to be the 'single u – loop model' (i.e. things get worse before they get better). Those who have experienced radical change at first hand, find that effects stretch far beyond the time span, scope and intent of the first original change intervention (i.e. after things should be 'getting better'). Poor handling in this period produces long-lasting implications for organizations. It is the moment when the classic symptoms of an ailing or failing organization first present themselves. Frequently people-related issues become a root cause of failure. People are often seen primarily as 'change enablers' in the first wave of change and of secondary importance to the main change objectives. Later they become the prime causes of new resistance to the continuing success of the change project, or of under-performance versus original change objectives. In any case, their reactions undermine optimization.

Unfortunately, the static single u-shaped model of change does not explain the dynamics of organization behaviour after an initial wave of change has spent its force and before the appearance of a second wave of change emerges and engulfs the organization (see Figure 3.1). If we look at the flow of energy in a wave of water, we see one wave following another. How soon the next wave will arrive and its size, direction and the energy it releases, will depend on the characteristics of its source. Many change projects simply fail to prepare organizations to anticipate the second wave of change (or subsequent waves, e.g. W2 on Figure 3.1). Change is not an isolated occurrence and the paradox is that change is a 'steady state' and an ever-present part of the life-force in any functioning organization.

In nature, wave energy is created by the gravitational pull from the sun and moon, earthquakes, volcanic eruptions under the sea, changes in atmospheric pressure and, most commonly, from the forces of the wind. A steep choppy wave is usually formed from local storm winds, while a mature steady wave with a high crest near the shore may come from winds formed at the other side of the world. For any organization, the causes of change also find their source locally or globally.

*Tsunami* (translated as 'harbour waves') is the name the Japanese give to the giant waves up to 128.5 km (80 miles) wide, up to 27.5 m (90 feet) high, which sweep across oceans at a speed of up to 800 kph (500 mph). In 1960, an earthquake and landslip in Chile killed 150 people in Japan 22 hours later, after the tsunami which it had created crossed over 16,090 km (10,000 miles) of ocean. Was 11 September 2001 an organizational tsunami? One characteristic of a tsunami is that while you may get some warning of its coming, you will still be unable to get out of its way. Was the Enron corporate collapse a smaller but no less lethal tsunami for Andersen Consulting? Did the WorldCom collapse create the wave that swamped the world's financial institutions?

Weather forecasts are predictors of changing wind force, which show where and when a storm will break and change the ocean from a calm to a brisk swell. Second-wave consultants need to scan organization and business horizons to predict change and prepare for it as best they can; a second wave may release powerful energy, but happily it rarely has the force of a tsunami.

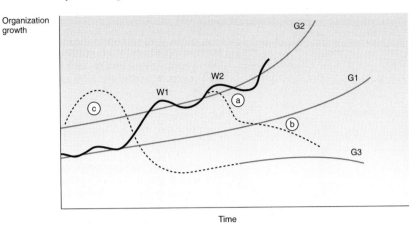

FIGURE 3.1: Consulting on second-wave change

Figure 3.1 shows an organization using a change strategy (W1 – wave one) to move itself successfully from a low growth curve (G1 – growth curve one) to a significantly higher one (G2 – growth curve two). Over time, as successive waves of change occur, the challenge for the organization is to move ahead from the first wave (W1) to the second wave (W2). Embarking on a wave-one strategy (W1) is not without danger. Not only is the effort required to move an organization to a higher growth curve (from G1 to G2) significant, but the risks of failure are high. Compare this to a 'steady-state' strategy (staying on growth curve G1) of growing through continuous improvement. A proper risk assessment before launching radical change could lead organizations to reconsider radical growth options, or prepare better to manage the long-term effects of change.

The first challenge for the second-wave change consultant is to prevent an organization from slipping (a) off the second wave back to the original growth curve (G1) or even below (b). After organizations accommodate a first wave of change, they may still need to take specific action to avoid going into free-fall. What successful organizations do (either by luck or judgement) is to weather successive waves of change and keep on moving up the growth curve (G2). Survival cannot be guaranteed necessarily by the rationale for or a repeat of the program used to address the challenges in the first wave (W1); new thinking is required for successive waves of change.

The second challenge for the second-wave consultant lies in identifying and preparing for potential threats (on the left-hand side of Figure 3.1), shown as the large shadow of a wave of change (c), which could overwhelm the organization and move it to a much lower growth projection curve (G3).

## CONSULTING BARRIERS TO ENTRY

All consultants experience barriers. However, consultants working on second-wave projects need to overcome particular challenges (Table 3.1). They need to confront the issue of their visibility and reputation, and develop effective relationships with potential clients, as well as bearing in mind their specific approach strategies.

| TYPE OF BARRIER | SECOND-WAVE ENTRY APPROACHES |
|---|---|
| LOYALTY TO OLD IDEAS | ☐ Entry only likely when client's short-term problems outweigh past loyalties. |
| | ☐ Never challenge old ideas initially. Work through problem diagnosis towards new insights and solutions, which become the nucleus of the new framework for the client and second-wave consultant to work together. |
| WHY BETTER THAN THE FIRST CONSULTANT? | ☐ Highly sensitive issue for organizations in trouble who may have developed consultant loyalty or aversion. Either way trust and confidence in a second-wave consultant becomes a major issue. |
| | ☐ Best to differentiate from conventional change consultants on basis of breadth and depth of experience, and of an individual approach and not being bound to a single methodology, 'one size fits all' approach. |
| CREDENTIALS FOR GETTING ORGANIZATIONS OUT OF TROUBLE | ☐ Staff the project with experienced consultants who have high personal credibility and breadth of expertise. |
| | ☐ Emphasize own 'internal', 'sharp end' expertise, as well as external consulting experience of radical change such as downsizing, restructuring, joint ventures/mergers and acquisitions, start ups and organization renewal (i.e. cycles of decay and renewal experienced by all industries) plus relevant client experience. Above all, a track record of successful change intervention in varied circumstances and organizations brings essential credibility. |
| LACK OF CLIENT UNDERSTANDING OF SECOND-WAVE PRIORITIES | ☐ Many clients only call for help on painful surface issues, which may be no more than irritants. Root cause problems need addressing to create lasting solutions. |
| | ☐ Expand client perspective as you progress diagnostic work on their priority issues and develop a systemic approach to their solution. |
| RECOGNIZING THAT PEOPLE ISSUES HAVE BEEN OVERLOOKED | ☐ Managements may find themselves embarrassed when they realize the imbalance of their past first-wave strategies; dangers exist in both ignoring the problem and overcompensating with uncoordinated initiatives. |
| | ☐ Need to move organization away from treatment of people as enablers of transactional processes (i.e. as things), to being treated as individuals with their own needs. |
| COMPETITION WITH INTERNAL CONSULTANTS | ☐ An issue particularly if internal consultants were part of an ailing first-wave change strategy and/or they feel that a new consultant is taking over their previous territory. |
| | ☐ Ensure consulting contract scope is clear and explored in depth with the client. Lay out boundary conditions and role of consultants (external and internal – if involved). |
| | ☐ Work alongside internal consultants, not around them. |

TABLE 3.1: Barriers to entry

# SECOND-WAVE CHANGE COMMUNICATION

In an era of warp-speed change, communicating clearly and simply why, how and when a change will occur presents organizations with a variety of headaches. It is not often identified that first-wave change communications create a lasting legacy for organizations. They also have the potential to create misunderstandings and false expectations against which both management and employee judgements of success and failure are made. The power of these employee perceptions remain highly influential for many years after the conclusion of the change project, and certainly affect second and successive waves. All radical change has its own momentum, pace, scale and churn. Each new change or recovery project must have a clear, concise, believable, relevant message, with the potential to inspire or at least engage and involve people in its delivery.

The difference between the success or failure of first and second-wave change programmes may simply rest on whether the 'words actually match the music'; in other words, whether the aspiration gap between the organization today and the organization tomorrow appears to be realistic and achievable. From a communications perspective, the three most typical forms of first-wave change each create a very different impact and challenge.

1  **Crisis change** – Typically in downsizing and restructuring, with a largely negative employee impact. At first, change communication may be seen as clear, to the point and relevant. Subsequently, disillusion may set in, particularly if the change involves redundancy and/or relocation. Then it is likely that employee communication has the potential to become negative as 'survivor syndrome' sets in and scepticism changes to hostility. David Noer in *The Organization in Crisis*[5] identifies three types of 'violation' experienced as threats. They are the violation of the psychological contract, of the corporate culture and of the self. When it comes to communication, then, for most employees 'the jury is out', for they are constantly looking for signs that change is over and normality has returned.

2  **Growth change** – Usually in startups and expansions, with a largely positive employee impact. Change communication has enormous potential to inspire people with the possibility of a more secure future, and gain their commitment in working towards it. However, this can backfire if all does not go to plan and employees begin to feel that their expectations have not been met. Even after successful growth change, for example, a start up of a new organization, it is typical that 'post start-up blues' set in a year or so after start up, when the new organization people-development systems are used and tested. Employees begin to weigh up the reality of their delivery against their original expectations. This is often where growth change goes wrong.

3  **Renewal change** – Classically in improving the performance of organizations, with a largely low employee impact. Undoubtedly the greatest communications challenge, renewal change is likely to be aspirational, broad in scope and clear. However, it is often clouded by employee scepticism and its relevance is challenged. Unfortunately, employees rarely get engaged or too excited or energized by this sort of change. The communications climate generated by first-wave renewal initiatives is generally found to be weak: it fails to create interest. It makes it tough to follow with a second wave of change.

A daunting statistic covering a typical three-month period following major change[6] reveals that employees receive on average 2.3 million words or numbers in communications at work (representing 99.42 per cent of all communications received), compared with 0.58 per cent

[5] David Noer (ed. R J Burke and C L Cooper ), 'Leading Organizations through Survivor Sickness', *The Organisation in Crisis*, Blackwell, 2000.
[6] John P Kotter, *Leading Change*, Harvard Business School Press, 1996.

concerning change itself. This change communication is equivalent to one 30-minute presentation, one 60-minute meeting, one 600-word article in the company house journal and one 2000-word memo. Perhaps this is the reason that the common denominators in employee response to all types of change communication are 'lack of credibility' and 'disillusion', either during or after the first-wave change.

The usual error in communicating change is to bypass middle managers and more particularly supervisors, relying exclusively on senior management or a change team to communicate directly to employees, above the heads of their supervisors. For most employees, middle managers and supervisors represent the organization and what it seeks to achieve. They are organization opinion leaders. They reinforce new or old behaviour. They are closest to employees and in the best position to deliver a credible message.[7] Effective change communication increases the readiness of employees to change. It enlists their willingness, capability and commitment to change.

For these reasons, getting communication right is essential to deliver effective change. It has to be well developed, simple, brief and arresting. If it is to have any chance of capturing the attention and engaging employees, the right people need to deliver it. It is not corporate video time. It must be clear, realistic and open and, most importantly, delivered by well-trained supervisors. This is the only effective base from which to rebuild a credible change communication strategy, to defeat the usual first-wave employee trust deficit.

## IMPACT OF SECOND WAVE ON PEOPLE DEVELOPMENT

The vast majority of first-wave change problems are people related. For this reason, approaches to recovery develop people themes. Although no two second-wave change strategies are exactly the same, consultants need to take into account the following issues:

☐ 'Unfinished business' remaining after first-wave initiatives (solving immediate problems).

☐ The current employee communications climate, based on previous first-wave initiatives (identifying expectations created in the first wave).

☐ The current and desired future career paradigm (type of career partnership) within which new career development processes will need to operate (aspirant organization values on careers).

☐ The current effectiveness of people-development processes after first-wave change (do they still work in the changed organization or do they need to be replaced or renewed?).

☐ The spirit of the organization and the way to rebuild it. (The observation of Harrison Owen in *The Power of the Spirit* that

❛Apparently successful organizations with strong bottom lines and good reputations will often have a nasty secret. The spirit is weak or broken and just hanging on.' They need to answer the question, 'Why do we look so good when we feel so bad?❜[8])

Before developing a recovery strategy, consultants need to prepare an assessment of both existing people processes and people problems. The scale on Table 3.2 illustrates the divergence between typical management and employee reactions to people development in the wake of various types of change. Both the strength and direction of response need to be taken into account in recovery initiatives.

[7] T J Larkin and Sandar Larkin, *Communicating Change*, McGraw Hill, 1994.
[8] Harrison Owen, *The Power of Spirit*, Berrett-Koehler, 2000.

| TYPE OF CHANGE | ACTION IN ANTICIPATION | ORGANIZATION RESPONSE | EMPLOYEE REACTION SCALE: −5 TO +5* | MANAGEMENT REACTION SCALE: −5 TO +5* | RECOVERY ORIENTATION |
|---|---|---|---|---|---|
| Downsizing | None | ☐ Retain existing systems<br>☐ Reassess 12 months after downsizing | −5 | −1 to +1 | ☐ Find ways to rebuild and regain trust<br>☐ Open employee communication<br>☐ Respond to 'survivor syndrome' |
| Restructuring | Advance planning | ☐ Reassess 6 months after restructuring<br>☐ Confirm if old systems continue to meet new needs | −4 | +2 | ☐ Re-energize people agenda<br>☐ Relaunch people processes with high level of employee involvement |
| Mergers and acquisitions | Major program | ☐ Implement within new merger and acquisition start up | −3 | +4 | ☐ Ensure new systems reflect 'best of both parent organizations' |
| Start ups and growth steps | Design to reinforce new desired culture | ☐ Implement during start up<br>☐ Reassess 12 months after start up | +5 | +5 | ☐ Assess effectiveness of new processes<br>☐ Relaunch to avoid 'post start-up 'blues'' |
| Organization renewal | Scope future business and employee needs | ☐ Make case for change<br>☐ Renew and relaunch career processes<br>☐ Reconfirm employee/organization deal or psychological contract | −2 | +1 | ☐ Recognize the symptoms<br>☐ Develop solutions with high level of employee involvement in new career processes |

* Scale from −5 to +5, where −5 and +5 reflects extreme negative and positive reaction respectively and 0, nil a minimal reaction.

TABLE 3.2: The impact of second-wave change on an organization's people development processes

☐ **Downsizing** – Usually this creates employee cynicism and a massive negative reaction to continued involvement with people-development. Sometimes, employees moving through 'survivor syndrome' feel too guilty to continue development activities after their previous co-employees have been made redundant. Rebuilding and regaining trust in the organization's people-development processes is a difficult, sensitive and long-term project, needing high levels of open communication and employee involvement. Managers have few expectations after downsizing, and tend to expect the worse. Unfortunately this can become a self-fulfilling prophesy.

☐ **Restructuring** – Typically, managers may be quite positive about restructuring, as usually they are pragmatic enough to see short-term operational gains which will be appreciated by shareholders or governing bodies. Even without actual redundancies, employees see discontinuity from restructuring very negatively, including learning new roles, reassignment and retraining.

☐ **Mergers and acquisitions** – Managers, having invested many months into developing merger and acquisition strategies, are normally optimistic and buoyant about the benefits of merging. Often they themselves could be financial beneficiaries. Employees from both organizations can be very suspicious or even hostile towards change in people-development processes, which they may associate closely with the identity and values in their old organization. Forcing implementation of a system from the dominant partner is likely to be seen as lasting evidence of 'take-over' rather than truly merging. The optimal solution is to select from the 'best of both parent organizations' in a combined and more widely-owned people-development process.

☐ **Start ups and growth steps** – The difficulty in this case is the uncritical nature of initial commitment of both employees and managers to the process developed for start up, whether it is functioning well or not. The problem with uncritical commitment is that if expectations are not met, disillusionment quickly sets in. The organization's experience of start up is likely to reinforce commitment for its continuing use. This may not be an issue if it functions well, but if the organization has moved away from its original goals, then tough decisions need to be taken.

☐ **Organizational renewal** – Here the issue is the credibility of any renewal initiatives and of making it a priority for employees, as well as managers, who both tend to see such initiatives as, at best, of marginal value. It takes senior management leadership and an exceptionally good initiative to launch renewal effectively.

Whatever the divergences in view, the consultant has to assess the context into which a second-wave programme of recovery and change needs to be launched. Organizations may have already chosen an effective approach to accommodate or facilitate change when the consultant arrives on the scene. If entirely ineffective approaches were implemented, it is much easier to move on rather than moving into rescue mode.

People development processes in any organization provide significant indicators of which values the organization seeks to reinforce. Recruitment information, induction, appraisal and coaching, promotion and reward systems, talent identification, supervisor and management training and skills training are all value laden. Changing the functionality of an organization (restructuring, growth or downsizing) or adding external influences (from mergers or acquisitions) means that organizations need to reassess whether existing processes still work. If they do, they need to be reinforced. If they do not, then new career paradigms need to be promoted.

There is another problem which many organizations experience after radical change. If people systems fail to deal with spiralling attrition, development of new talent, 'survivor syndrome' and new personal needs in a new or changed work environment, employees and supervisors will quickly show disinterest and distrust and people systems will go into virtual hibernation. The job of the consultant is to convince the client that although management and employees both have different priorities, a balance needs to be achieved to enable a recovery programme to succeed. Typically these priorities are:

☐ **Employee priorities** – Unmet change expectations, lack of open employee communication, lack of credible career options, insecurity, low morale, people systems which do not deliver.

☐ **Management priorities** – Spiralling attrition, poor productivity, underperformance versus original change goals and shareholder/stakeholder expectations, too few management replacements.

It is common to encounter real surprise from clients, and then denial, that people-problems have actually arisen, and that their cause is rooted in the original first wave of change. The consultant has to find a way to detach the organization from the recent past, while finding a pathway to recovery which builds on and is aligned to the new aspirations of the organization.

## SUMMARY

1   Although organizations are constantly evolving, radical change (such as from downsizing) sets up a first wave of change which many fail to navigate successfully. This creates significant barriers to entry for second-wave consultants. It means that they have to be broadly experienced in change as well as both able to resolve acute first-wave problems fast, with the ability to develop customized long-term recovery strategies.

2   It is also critical for consultants engaged in second-wave work to understand that all does not end with a first wave: its influence continues on subsequent initiatives. They need to avoid organization 'capsize' in its many forms, by addressing second-wave change in its own right; firstly as a recovery and secondly as a new change initiative. The challenge lies in rebuilding trust in organizations at the same time as finding and implementing effective recovery strategies.

# CHAPTER 4

## CONSULTING IN THE AREA OF CORPORATE SOCIAL RESPONSIBILITY

### INTRODUCTION

‘ I think consultancy can form a valuable part of developing corporate social responsibility strategy, particularly where companies are relatively new to the subject. Guidance on key issues of good practice, intelligence and communication can be invaluable. However, corporate social responsibility is about the values of a company: without belief, the tree withers and dies. A company must define this for themselves and it must be top to bottom. It cannot work if this is delegated outside. ’

Chris Staples, Community Affairs Director, Zurich Financial Services (April 2002).

Corporate social responsibility (CSR) is front-page news these days. Business leaders want to make their organizations better corporate citizens, not least because the low trust brand, i.e. one without sufficient investor and consumer confidence, is also a low value brand. CSR is the umbrella term given to all the activities designed to align business activity with social and environmental improvement. With the eyes of an increasingly demanding marketplace upon them, business leaders are keen to produce evidence to support their claims to goodness. And, as you would expect from a relatively new area of business activity, CSR is a hotbed of consultancy growth. For consultants wishing to create a better world, working with organizations embarking on the road to better CSR can be a challenging, but satisfying road to both principle and profits.

This chapter is not about the rights or wrongs or even history of CSR. Its starting point is that corporate social responsibility is an increasingly important part of twenty-first century business activity, and therefore merits space in the mind of the twenty-first century business consultant. This chapter will consider some of the consulting challenges raised by this new dimension of corporate activity, the range of consultancy services being bought and utilized in this area and skills needed to make an effective CSR consultancy intervention.

# A BRIEF HISTORY OF CORPORATE SOCIAL RESPONSIBILITY (CSR)

While CSR is a relatively new area of corporate activity, the concept of ethical management is as old as business itself. According to Scottish philosopher and economist Adam Smith, (1723–90), 'an invisible hand' of conscience and sympathy was needed to balance the natural greed of private corporations, and create 'orderly and beneficial social organisations'. However, 2002 witnessed a turning point. The financial downfall of those leading the Enron Corporation, a global oil producer, caused business leaders to ask a wider set of questions: are we managing our firms in a responsible way? Are we susceptible to allegations of financial impropriety? The stakes are high. Large profitable organizations increasingly feel the need to portray a decent, truthful and ethical face to the marketplace. It is not only what you do, but also what you are perceived to be doing that impacts on business survival. The old order of unfettered free market activity seems to be giving way to a new world of stakeholder engagement and social accounting. Furthermore, there is evidence that business is being rewarded for its CSR efforts. BT has become the second company, after the Co-operative Bank, to publish official figures on the link between CSR and financial performance. The telecoms giant has identified four drivers of customer satisfaction and found that over one-quarter of the overall figure for image and reputation was attributed to CSR-related activities. The study's results, compiled by independent statisticians, strongly suggest that CSR activities play a large role, via image and reputation in maintaining and building BT's market share in a competitive market. This approach contrasts with the 'sustainable cost-benefit analysis' approach taken by the Co-operative Bank last summer, which declared that 15–20 per cent of the company's pre-tax profits could be directly attributed to its ethical stance.

Some organizations have a history of social responsibility and contribution, of demonstrating a core set of beliefs that go further than the bottom line. The Body Shop, Co-operative Bank and Ben and Jerry's Ice Cream are well-known examples of companies with a highly visible set of socially responsible values. For many firms, responsible business is simply living the values of their founders, who were decent individuals and imbued their personal values into the decision-making process throughout years of growth. One example of this is Hewlett Packard (HP), where employees strive to continue a tradition of behaviours and attitudes in keeping with 'The HP Way'. In the best-selling *Built to Last*,[1] authors Collins and Porras show that a cohesive culture, societal vision and clear guidelines for individual behaviour have all been instrumental in keeping companies such as HP at the top of international business over many decades. CSR has been part of the cultural DNA of some organizations and, according to the research by those authors, there are clear rewards for those who stay on that path. For other firms, being a responsible corporation is simply the asking price for a place at the increasingly transparent top table of global business. No self-respecting blue chip will publish an annual report without mention of a stirring societal vision. We have moved from Big Hairy Audacious Goals to Big Hairy Audacious Goals Which Save the World as Well as Our Share Price.

Whatever the motivation, there is little doubt that for those organizations capable of creating and maintaining corporate social responsibility or CSR, being seen as a good and trustworthy operation is a source of competitive advantage. There are four reasons why CSR has become such an important issue:

1  **Mobility** – Customers and suppliers now enjoy greater mobility: if your company does not live up to expectations on both quality and decency, consumers will go elsewhere. Technology and improved communications mean that corporate reputation is increasingly vital to the success of all businesses, whether in the brand value of a large multinational or

[1] Collins and Porras, *Built to Last*, Random House, 1997.

the reputation of the local shop for customer service. Shakespeare was right to call reputation 'the one immortal part of man'.

2 **The war for talent** – The most sought after employees are also increasingly mobile. For employers wishing to recruit and retain their employee of choice, evidence exists to support the idea that a strong track record on CSR will be a powerful asset in a competitive job market. A recent Mori survey concluded that when people are spending more and more hours working, they want more out of it, and the growing emphasis on ethical business and social accountability seems to suggest that business feels the same way. Employees increasingly expect to be treated as individuals, and employers are trying to make the package fit the person, not the other way round.[2]

3 **Global interdependency** – The global marketplace has become a more open, dynamic environment. It may be that your firm needs to jointly bid for work with a local partner – in India, South Africa or Finland. This means a significant shift in attitudes and behaviours. Organizations need to become brokers of culture as well as products and services; success often depends on the ability to work effectively with local communities and cultures. A review of corporate citizenship in six global markets (Germany, UK, Italy, France, Hong Kong and Singapore) has revealed a growing recognition that the issue has become an 'integral part of doing business well'.[3]

4 **The anti-globalization lobby** – CSR has also grown from the efforts of consumer activists. Moreover, some firms – notably the oil companies and clothing retailers – have been more publicly taken to task. Many companies cannot afford to ignore social responsibility. Anti-globalizers can take your hard-won brand and blockade it.

Growing expectations and concerns about the increasing power of business mean that there is increasing pressure for companies – especially large ones – to behave responsibly. Your company makes a mistake in handling an environmental issue and you get a starring role in the pages of *No Logo*[4] or *Change Activist*.[5] Consumer boycotts impact investor confidence.

## WHO IS THE CSR CONSULTANT?

Given the wide ranging parameters of CSR, it is no surprise that the CSR consultant comes in many shapes and guises, and is either a niche specialist, or all-round change manager with a range of skills. In many ways, the need to find a balance between profit and good corporate behaviour has given rise to a generation of hybrid business and social consultants, able to understand both sides of the profit and principle argument. Indeed, the activists and management have become interchangeable in some organizations. Table 4.1 describes the range of roles played by CSR consultants.

Experience suggests that traditional change skills are enough to create the infrastructure and to gather new information, but not enough to define the specialist content or analysis of the data. They may be enough to define the process and procedures, but not to determine the priority areas of responsibility.

Let's take the case of a manufacturing firm, producing blue widgets. The board has decided that this family firm will become known as champions of environmentally friendly blue widget making. Imagine you are the director responsible for the initiative, sitting down to plan the necessary resources. With your career history, you feel able to set the scene for CSR, but it would probably be a step too far outside your experience to work out the performance data

---

[2] www.mori.com/digest/2001/pd01615.shtml
[3] Report published by Probus BNW for the Sprint Corporation, February 2002.
[4] Naomi Klein, *No Logo*, Flamingo, 2001.
[5] Carmel McConnell, *Change Activist*, Momentum, 2001.

| | |
|---|---|
| Providing specialist knowledge, external | The social activist with expert knowledge on environmental efficiency in one part of the world might be the best person to provide a strategic overview for the directors of a firm about to embark on a commercial venture in that region. Clearly the mutual benefits would need to stack up, or else it is unlikely that the environmental activist would want to engage in detailed discussion about the pros and cons of operations management in Ecuador. For example, can the company give assurances on consultation with indigenous groups? What would the long-term benefit be on the local economy? Will there be any damage to primary rainforest in the area?

One area of prime importance to the CSR agenda is the right level of stakeholder engagement. For this, it may be that expertise does not exist in-house, and will have to be obtained as external 'expert' consultancy.

There is an increasing amount of knowledge sharing and staff traffic between charities and NGO organizations into the CSR functions of large organizations. Getting an activist on board has, for many firms, been critical to establishing corporate social responsibility. Equally, a position of genuine influence at the top table is important to social and environmental organizations. This increasingly ambiguous boundary raises some fascinating new questions for the twenty-first century consultant. Given that many business leaders are concerned with creating a responsible image of their organization, is it likely that we will see a new breed of senior corporate activist? How far can the CSR champion go to build a 'good' company from the inside, and what kind of external support could be needed? Will the business leader require external consultancy at all, if the internal skills are increased, such that CSR is something that everyone is trained to understand? |
| Providing specialist knowledge, internal | One European sportswear firm recruited the ex-head of a Non-Governmental Organization (NGO) with experience in South East Asia, to increase in-house understanding of that region, prior to an expansion in manufacturing activity. That local knowledge and cultural expertise was vital in creating better labour and supplier relations over time – even though the firm had, in the past, been accused of labour malpractice. The activist became an internal change agent, convincing the Board of Directors that increased investment in local management, housing and childcare facilities would result in a more efficient and humane outsourced value chain operation. It also meant that the firm was happy to be filmed in South East Asia, allowed employees to speak to media cameras, at a time when other clothing manufacturers were suffering from detailed scrutiny under the same public spotlight. The activist turned internal consultant had, undoubtedly, made a valuable intervention. |
| CSR Consultant Internal Change Agent | Is it possible to be an internal CSR consultant, if you have no direct experience of working on social or environmental issues? Let us consider this from the point of view of one experienced change manager, in a large manufacturing organization.

You have a good reputation for delivering large change programs to time and budget. The next call from your boss is surprising. 'We're going to set up a Head of Corporate Social Responsibility, working within the chairperson's staff office. Next year we'll start reporting against a range of environmental and social measures helped by a team of investor relations guys in the PR department. Are you up for it?'

'Sorry?'

'They've recommended you establish the CSR program, set up the mechanisms and procedures, get the whole thing moving. Oh, and you've got six months. The chairperson has announced our reporting schedule already, apparently.'

'Sounds interesting – you know I have never worked on CSR before – maybe I should set up some time to see the chairperson.'

'Fine, just don't go in there talking barriers. You know what she's like when she wants something done.'

How would you feel in that situation? Being able to contribute to a high profile initiative is great, but how would your traditional change leadership skills translate into this environment? You have senior buy in, time-scales, budget (presumably) – perhaps that is enough to create a credible CSR program? |

TABLE 4.1: CSR consultancy roles

on pollution, or the educational programme to support future blue widget makers from all sections of the community. Unless your organization has given you the chance to develop your organizational and societal vision in a very real sense, it would be advisable to create a 'founders and advisers' guiding coalition to ensure the right areas are monitored. You would probably invite some level of external CSR consultancy support to guide the board on CSR trends and benchmarks. That way, both the mechanism and right content data could be collated in time for the chairperson's address. And you, as the internal change agent, would be rightly acclaimed as the enabler for the historic move made by Blue Widgets PLC toward environmental and social responsibility.

## WHAT DO CSR CONSULTANTS DO?

Leaving aside the wider trends within CSR consulting, if you were keen to start your own CSR consulting firm, what might you wish to have in your client portfolio? The CSR consultant could be asked to provide support in any of the following areas:

☐ **Developing a CSR strategy** – This could include design, development and implementation of a company's overall CSR objectives and strategy.

☐ **Management and staff development** – This is likely to be a bespoke programme to ensure that all management, employees and suppliers are sufficiently aware and skilled in CSR issues, trends and specific company requirements. Some organizations benefit from having a board level CSR 'coach' who understands the individual market issues facing the firm, and is able to advise the senior team in a way that allows for genuine learning in a supportive environment.

☐ **Assessing CSR policy and practice** – For example, an audit of the company's activities and commitments relating to CSR. It might include interviews with employees and external stakeholder surveys.

☐ **Stakeholder management** – Consultants with particular expertise in this field would seek out the kinds of stakeholders likely to be impacted by products and services produced by the organization, and seek to promote productive dialogue. This could include selection of third-party suppliers and a range of stakeholder meetings.

☐ **PR and reporting guidance** – This would entail specialist advice on the structure and content of reporting efforts to internal and external audiences, particularly in the area of environmental and social performance.

☐ **Benchmarking** – Surveys on CSR best practices against key standards, within industries or geographies, or among leadership companies.

☐ **Analysis and reporting** – The CSR consultant would provide an analysis of current trends and recommendations on corporate strategy for topics ranging from the impact of local consumer campaigns to sustainable development.

☐ **CSR standards analysis** – The consultant would consider the value of accreditation and adoption requirements of international CSR standards. In the same way as a quality assurance consultant might undertake a Total Quality Management or Six Sigma business process improvement consultancy assignment, the CSR consultant would set up procedures and processes for measurement and reporting of national, international and industry-specific CSR standards.

Can the CSR consultant create ethical advantage? The simple answer is yes, if the organization is prepared to act.

☐ Reports from Nigeria, focusing on the activity of a sister company of leading oil producer Shell during the 1980s and early 1990s, sparked a significant consumer boycott. Robin Aram, ex head of external relations at Shell International[6] had this to say: 'We have got this message from society, which is: if you don't meet our expectations we will punish you. As a company today you can't run and you can't hide. Social investment or social altruism has its part to play of course, and we are spending $50m in Nigeria alone. But the most important contribution we can make is to do our day to day business in a responsible way.'

In the days before CSR, many companies believed that they had a mandate to do whatever it took to keep the shareholder dividend high. Stakeholders, by implication, were given data on a need to know basis, usually restricted to where it would impact investor confidence in the area of financial performance. By contrast, consumers now believe they have a right to know about the behind the scenes machinations of their favourite brands. This is a significant shift. The concept of marketplace transparency as an ingredient of competitive advantage is itself a driver for cultural and behavioural change. This is outside the range of expertise and skills within most organizations. The CSR consultant can help by bringing a range of traditional consultancy skills – persuasion, negotiation, change management – and supplementing those with experience of social and environmental issues. The CSR consultant is an essential guide in this largely uncharted area of business management territory.

## SUMMARY

CSR consultant aids and advises, whereas company behaviour is largely based on values. Johnson and Johnson gained respect in the US when they quickly withdrew all supplies of Tylenol during a crisis in the late 1980s. They were able to take action because of their guiding credo that says 'We believe our first responsibility is to doctors nurses and patients, to mothers and fathers and all others who use our products and services'. Such values were not set by consultants. CSR consultancy adds to the existing capacity for social and environmental contribution, but, no matter how much money is on the table, good business ethics cannot be produced from a can by the PowerPoint-toting consultant. It has to be authentic, in the hearts and minds of those who own, control and lead the organization. Only then can CSR market advantage i.e. trust be fully realized.

## FURTHER READING

John Elkington, *Cannibals with Forks*, Capstone, 1997.

Collins and Porras, *Built to Last*, Random House, 1997.

Cohen and Prusak, *In Good Company*, Harvard Business School Press, 2001.

George Montbiot, *Captive State*, Macmillan, 2000.

Naomi Klein, *No Logo*, Flamingo, 2001.

Carmel McConnell, *Change Activist*, Momentum, 2001.

43

[6] Quoted in *The Times*, 24 February 2001.

# PART 2

## THE CLIENT-CONSULTANT RELATIONSHIP

# CHAPTER 5

## PSYCHOLOGICAL CONSIDERATIONS OF CONSULTING: THE CLIENT-CONSULTANT RELATIONSHIP

❛The messiness, contingency, sprawl, and indeed danger of the real managerial world ought to be the centrepiece of our thinking, not a footnote or an afterthought, not a concession to learner questions about relevant issues, not something we find merely amusing or annoying because it doesn't fit in with the neat prescriptions we'd like to make to leaders and managers.❜

Peter Vaill, 1991[1].

## INTRODUCTION

In the late 1970s, process consulting was king. The graduates of the first Organization Behaviour Program at Case Western University in Cleveland Ohio were making waves in the business world. They were the products of the 1960s – the age of Aquarius, the pill, communal living, drop-outs, protests, environmental awareness, tolerance, Haight-Ashbury, Carnaby Street, Bob Dylan, Indian mysticism, folk singers in coffee houses singing about finding oneself and saving the world, psychedelic drugs and marijuana-fuelled love-ins. Some of the children of the 1960s became the management consultants of the 1970s and their paradigm of personal development, insight-building t-group (therapy/encounter groups) participation invaded the corporate world and even Clinton's Oval Office. Large oil companies, for example, had organization development departments to consult internally. They funded such events as employees dancing around medicine wheels to bond as teams and speakers like Marilyn Ferguson[2] to talk to the managing directors. Speakers from California, decked out in long kaftans and gold chains invaded corporate America with advice from the enlightened. It was a time when a decade of 'new age' thinking invaded the business world in a way previously unheard of.

All of this was very much a product of its time, the legacy of a cohort of war babies and baby

---

[1] Vaill, Peter B, *Managing as a Performing Art*. Jossey-Bass. 1991.
[2] Ferguson, M, *The Aquarian Conspiracy*. J P Tarcher. 1987.

boomers born at the time of the rise of counselling psychology and the pursuit of individuation, the questioning of women's role in society, traditional roles in general and the pursuit of the house in suburbia with two cars in the garage. Carl Rogers' humanistic psychology encouraged people to discover who they really were underneath the façade created to respond to parental and societal constraints. National Training Laboratories' (NTL) behavioural science training groups encouraged people to experience who they really were and the impact they had on others.

People were encouraged to reveal a personal side of themselves in group situations, or to try new and different ways to facilitate personal interaction in the workplace. While some of this may have been of dubious benefit to the organization, it left a positive legacy of personal/professional development in the workplace that remains to this day – bringing humanistic and developmental psychology into mainstream business. The contribution of psychology/behavioural science in areas such as leadership and management development, workplace communication, teamwork development and employee assistance programs is undisputed.

The values of process consulting reflect those of this era – facilitating individuals, teams and whole organizations to discover what they would like their business to look like, the values, mission and vision of the organization – 'What do you stand for and what do you want to accomplish (in this life)'? The values are closely linked to organizational development, enabling a diagnosis of the internal and external processes that affect the organization's behaviour and performance.[3]

However, with new technology developments and the more profit-focused 1980s and 1990s, process consulting fell somewhat out of favour. The expert or technical consultant became all-important. In this model, according to Margulies:[3]

> '. . . the consultant is primarily concerned with bringing expertise to bear on a problem experienced by the client and in this regard . . . provides a service which the client does not have available'

While the role of process consultant has been distinguished by the close 'empathetic and symbiotic relationship with the client', the relationship between the expert consultant and client has almost been 'viewed as incidental' and the client is left with the responsibility of 'formulating a plan for the implementation of the proposed solutions'.[4] This may have been true in 1977 when these words were written, but today the expert consultant is expected to take projects through to completion and often this means installing computer systems like financial or Human Resources (HR) systems.

Margulies suggests that these two main types or styles of consulting are not as polarized as suggested in the past. In fact 'the role of the consultant is much more marginal and peripheral than is suggested by the process model and not as distant, uninvolved and task-oriented as suggested by the technical model'. A peripheral person is both in the organization system and outside it. Margulies calls it a 'boundary position' and notes that such positions tend to 'generate considerable personal stress, tension, and personal conflict'. How consultants choose to deal with their stress and tension can have an impact on their effectiveness. In addition, consultants must deal with the anxiety of their clients as well. This brings about speculation about the desirable or necessary psychological characteristics of the consultant.

The role of consultant can be a very isolated and even lonely one – being both 'part of' and 'not part of'. And even lonelier in the case of the independent consultant. Margulies suggests that personal development training for being a consultant should include what he terms

---

[3] Margulies, Neuton, Notes on the Marginality of the Consultants role in R J Lee and A M Freedman (Eds) *Consultation skills reading*, Virginia. NTL Institute, 1977.

[4] In Lee and Freedman, *Consultation Skills*, Prentice Hall & IBD, 1984.

'emotional muscle' and what could be called resilience. The consultant must be able to face and resolve the dilemmas that occur because of the marginal nature of the relationship with the client organization and do it in such a way that a rigid, polarized response to organizational issues is avoided. Therefore, it is essential that strong, creative, well-rounded, self-aware people take on the heavy demands that consulting requires.

## SETTING THE STAGE FOR PSYCHOLOGICAL UNDERSTANDING OF THE WORKPLACE

The title 'Consulting into the future: the key skills' might suggest that the future skill needs for consultants would be all new. However, in terms of looking at the psychological issues in consulting, we should return to some older understandings. We need to start consciously applying more of the older teachings, realizations and truths, and spreading the word among consultants that this has been a very neglected area.

We can take the definition of consulting as:

> ❛A helping process emerging from a personal relationship established between one or more persons trying to solve a problem or develop a plan (defined as the client) and one or more persons trying to help in these efforts (defined as the consultant)❜

The quality of the relationship between the client and consultant is one of the key factors influencing the success of the consulting effort.

While the legacy of the 1960s is still present, the historical legacy of organizations is quite different. Rothschild and Davies[5] suggest we look at the origins of organization theory to find some clues regarding the attitude to human considerations in the workplace. Max Weber, in the nineteenth century, built his model of the rational/hierarchical/bureaucratic organization on his observations of the Prussian Army. Thus the model for organizations in western society was not a model of holistic, emotional, life experience, but one which emphasized the notions of mind, reason, rationality, objectivity, scientific pursuit and masculinity.

After the Second World War, an industry arose (initially in the USA) based on knowledge of the development and maintenance of organizations,[6] and dividing that knowledge between:

1 **Management science** – The more tangible and quantifiable side of business (e.g. business decisions, finance, marketing, administration).

2 **Applied behavioural science** – The 'softer', psychologically-based side of business (e.g. human behaviour, leadership, group development, values and motivations).

Dealing with management science has always been the 'easier' or content-driven side of the organizational knowledge divide. It is the side that can be imparted by books, classroom instruction and example. Applied behavioural science or the psychological side of the business world has to be approached in a different way. While some of this knowledge can be imparted rationally, much has to be experienced to be learned. Insight into one's own behaviour is essential. Moreover, behavioural science is still the more 'unemphasized' part of consulting and the business world.

Clark and Salaman[7] state that the usually accepted roles or styles of consultancy are (still) embedded in a belief that organizations are rational and that the 'affairs of organizations are conducted legally, reliably, consistently, calculatingly and predictably'. However, there is much

[5] Rothschild and Davies, Organisations through the lens of gender: introduction to the special issue, *Human Relations*, vol. 47 No. 6 p 583–5890. 1994.
[6] Shultz, J, Historical overview of OD consulting, in Lee, R J and Freedman A M (Eds), Consultations Skills Reading, NTL Institute, Arlington, VA. 1984.
[7] Clark T and Salaman G, *Creating the 'Right' Impression: Towards Dramaturgy of Management Consultancy*. The Service Industries Journal, vol. 18, No. 1 (January 1998) p 18–38.

to suggest that the opposite is true and from business decisions that affect the public good (e.g. Enron and Andersen Consulting) to putting someone forward for promotion, mainly subjective and political considerations hold sway. Thus it is essential for consultants to understand and be able to deal with the non-rational, inconsistent, unpredictable, humanness of organizations.

Clarke and Salaman also feel that, because consulting is intangible and perishable (i.e. consulting does not produce a concrete product, but is an interaction solving a problem), the outcome is dependent on the quality of the interaction. Any interaction or relationship involves psychological issues, emotions, and motivations. If we think of other interactions in life, we can admit quickly that the quality of interaction is paramount. This chapter explores the psychological relationship between consultant and client, highlighting basic skills, models and techniques that can help the consultant manage that relationship.

The consulting relationship is a psychologically rich one to explore. Of particular interest are the issues of:

1   The discussibles and undiscussibles.

2   Power and conflict.

3   Achievement and self-image.

4   Affiliation needs.

5   Personality type.

6   Anxiety.

In all this, the aim is to enhance the relationship of the client and consultant through understanding and addressing, when appropriate, the psychological basis of their relationship, thus increasing the chances of the consulting project's success.

## A note on psychological models

In context, psychological models can help simplify the understanding of human behaviour – leading paradoxically to an ability to comprehend and deal with the complexity of life and human behaviour. Out of context they can give a false sense of control over life and can lead to fundamentalist thinking, as if one has 'found the answer'.[8] In other words, if one has models for psychological behaviour without the context of a knowledge of human development, life span development, human motivations and so on, they can become simplistic ways to label and to put people into boxes.

In some organizations, the introduction of models for understanding and labelling of people has led to less understanding. Instead of treating people as individuals, they become labelled 'Introverts' or 'Hold ups' or 'Plants'. Tobias makes the point that people assume that they know all about others because of the categories into which they fall and act towards them according to these assumptions. He feels that this misuse of psychological models and beliefs supplies only quick answers, relief from ambiguity, techniques of pseudo-authenticity and false and superficial comfort, and that perhaps the most important contribution psychology can make is to lead people away from the phoniness of simplistic techniques.

Keeping in mind some of the cautions of the above, we can explore some of the models and theories that have proven useful in organizational life and why they continue to help us to understand the relationship between consultant and client.

[8] Tobias, L L *Psychological Consulting to Management*. Brunner/Mazel, New York, NY. 1990.

# SHADOW ISSUES AND THE UNDISCUSSIBLES

In every part of life there are issues that are well known to all, issues that may be obvious to one party and not another and issues that are not in the awareness of anyone connected to a situation (shadow). Every organization has issues or aspects that it does not acknowledge. These can be beliefs about the organization, for example, an organization that has a certain image or belief about itself may be unwilling to acknowledge or address situations that run counter to that belief.

The issues that are not discussed, acknowledged or addressed can easily threaten the success of consulting projects or even the health or survival of the organization. For instance, in a large organization an affair between the CEO and a managing director (Mr X) was never acknowledged or openly discussed. Most people realized that there was a relationship; however, some seemed not to want to believe it. Half of the directors team quit in one year due to the ineffective management style of Mr X. This was not addressed because of the relationship between the CEO and Mr X. Many of the senior people left due to the situation that was developing in the team of managing directors – the CEO and Mr X were virtually running the company, making decisions and presenting them as *fait accompli* to the managing directors. All of these issues would have to be openly addressed if the situation were to be resolved. Interestingly, issues that are sexually related often will be classified as 'personal' and not within the organization's right to discuss them. The answer to this is 'Address any issues that affect the bottom line' – the affair itself was not the immediate issue – the fallout was.

Frequently, the only safe areas to discuss are the organization's goals, technology, structure, policies and procedures, products and financial resources. Those grey areas that are often not discussed include attitudes, perceptions and feelings about the formal systems, values, and informal interactions, including favouritism and group norms.

The Johari window[9] is a useful model to explore these issues with the client. Cope[10] has modified this well-known model to highlight discussibles and undiscussibles in the organization: those issues the client will discuss but the consultant will not, the issues the consultant will discuss but the client will not, and the issues neither or both will discuss. If there are issues that are not readily being discussed, it is the responsibility of the consultant to be aware of this and to encourage the client to explore them together. If there are issues that are not being discussed, there is no problem solving going on and no contingency plans being made. The success of any consultancy project is threatened (see box 'Our Sabotage' Fig. 5.1).

# POWER AND CONFLICT

One of the most frequently overlooked areas in the consulting relationship is that of power. Who has the power? Who is concerned about power? How will power needs affect the consulting relationship? How much should the consultant influence and control, and how much should be left in the hands of the client, even if some projects are not a success? Power struggles can be the result of the consultant and the client each trying to keep control and forgetting their roles in the relationship. Alternatively, perhaps they have never developed a trusting relationship which allows them to determine who helps who with what, or how much challenge the client wants and needs. Power issues can remain in the shadow area and be undiscussed and unaddressed, later manifesting themselves in anger and aggressiveness on the part of either or in passivity on the part of either.

[9] Luft, in Porter & Molir, B (Eds), *Reading Book for Human Relations Training*. NTL Institute, Alexandria, VA.

[10] Cope, Mick, The Seven C's of Consulting, Financial Times/Prentice Hall, London. 2000.

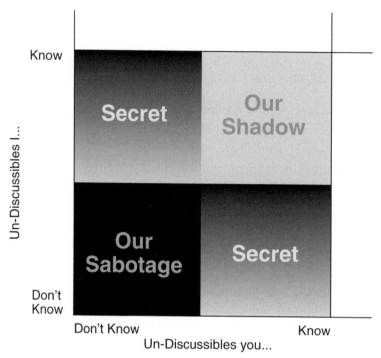

FIGURE 5.1: Shadow shadows

Also important is the way power and conflict are addressed in the client organization. Bullying and aggressiveness can be present in the organization to such an extent that many people feel demoralized. This can show itself in high staff turnover, lateness, chronic absenteeism, stress leave. The client may be underusing legitimate power within the organization, leaving a power vacuum, allowing these issues to continue. The consultant must address these issues and get to the root cause if they are to be resolved. He or she must be able to handle appropriately the often unpleasant issues of conflict and the misuse of power. Moreover, consultants must deal with not only the client's anxiety in such situations but also their own. Reducing the anxiety of all concerned can lead to a more effective consulting project.

A consultant to Finance Directors recently estimated that her clients spend at least 85 per cent of their time dealing with people dilemmas (most of which involve conflict of some kind) and not in dealing with finance strategy or financial issues. She also noted, however, that most people make attempts to avoid dealing with conflict and/or they are not skilled at managing situations that involve conflict, and so many people situations or dilemmas remain partially or wholly unresolved.

Conflict can have benefits and costs. These are usually associated with whether or not the conflict is recognized and dealt with in a way that produces positive consequences and outcomes. Hoffman, in literature from his organization, Concorde (1993),[11] stated that the beneficial outcomes of dealing well with conflict can include:

☐ focusing attention on the real problems

☐ preventing social stagnation

[11] Hoffman, B, Conflict, power, persuasion: Negotiating effectively, 2nd ed. Captus Press. 1993.

☐ encouraging growth and change

☐ increasing internal cohesion

On the other hand, not dealing well with conflict, or dealing with it by using dominance and imposition, withdrawal or avoidance can lead to cycles of violence or vengeance. In a workplace situation, this may involve:

☐ refusal to work with certain people

☐ not cooperating in supplying resources to another's project

☐ out and out sabotage of projects

Dealing with conflict, dealing with difference, or dealing with the frustration of not getting all that we want in a situation is a normal part of workplace existence. We can do it well or poorly; it is our choice. However, dealing with conflict is an essential managerial and consulting skill. We learn to do it in the same way that we learn to do many things: informally, for example through experience, family rules and cultural norms. It may or may not be appropriate to use those methods when faced with workplace conflict.

With the increasing emphasis on effective teamwork, and also effective project management, dealing with conflict in a skilled, caring and business-like manner is essential. One good tool for this work is the Thomas-Kilmann Conflict Mode Instrument.[12]

## ACHIEVEMENT AND SELF-IMAGE

How committed is the consultant to personal success? Is the success of the consulting project for the benefit of the client or for the consultant's own self-esteem (implying promotion opportunities within his or her consultancy)? Consultants must have an appropriate desire for achievement, i.e. they must be concerned about doing a good job for the client. They must never forget who owns the project. If the consultant's need for personal achievement outweighs concern for the good of the client, it may lead them to try to do the task alone, diagnosing the problems, imposing the solution they believe to be best, not checking with the client, making decisions that are the client's to make, getting angry at the client if they do not follow the consultant's advice and so forth.

The important issue in such a case is the personal awareness or lack thereof on the part of the consultant. If consultants are unaware of their need for achievement and the impact this has on the client organization, it can lead to power struggles between the client and the consultant. If these issues remain in the shadow area and are not discussed or acknowledged, they can lead to dismissal of the consultant or a failed project – a project that the organization does not really want or perhaps need, and that will not be supported by the organization in the long run.

Closely linked to achievement issues are the self-image issues of both the client and consultant. The client that hires consultants has every reason to believe that the consultants will do everything possible to help solve the stated problem. The client wants the success of the project to reflect favourably on him or herself and may be relying on the project's success for promotion or other rewards within the organization. The client also needs to see him or herself as capable of changing in a desired way and needs to be open to suggestions and collaboration. Likewise, consultants need to see themselves as capable of helping, but must balance this with not falling into the trap of becoming 'know it all' smug experts.

53

12 Thomas, K W & Kilmann, R H Thomas-Kilmann, Conflict Mode Instrument. XICOM, Inc. 1974.

## AFFILIATION NEEDS

Are the two parties, client and consultant, concerned with intimacy and understanding? The consultant must understand and know the client's perception of the problems, but too much empathy can lose the consultant's perspective and the client's respect. As discussed earlier, consultants maintain a position on the periphery of the client organization. They may be asked to attend social events and it may be quite appropriate to do so. However, these situations must not lead to the consultant engaging in behaviour that will alienate the client or lead to such a close relationship that the consultant is no longer seen to add an objective viewpoint.

Whether fair or not, the consultant has a certain distance and image to uphold to maintain the client's respect. This can be a problem if the consultant is away from home, in the client's home city, living in a hotel, away from family, home and friends. The only source of socializing may be members of the client organization, who may try to influence the consultant to see their version of events in the organization. Thus, consultants can run the risk of undermining their own ability to take a fair and considered view of organization events. Not only will they add to the difficulty of working with the client, but particularly to finding out what the issues are in the client organization.

## PERSONALITY TYPE

I refer the reader back to previous comments in this chapter about psychological models. It is essential that consultants be well trained in the use of psychological instruments, particularly if they have to do with personality type. In fact, a more broad-based psychological training is advised if a consultant is to use instruments effectively, sensitively and meaningfully in their work rather than a superficial manner. I will not go into any more detail on these as there are many courses and books available on this topic, a selection of which are at the end of the chapter.

There are many models available to give people an understanding of aspects of personality. The most widely used non-psychiatric instrument in the world today is the Myers-Briggs Type Indicator and it is particularly popular in organizations. There are also many other instruments that tell us about specific parts of the personality that help us to understand the style that people adopt, motivation and many other aspects that affect interaction in the workplace.

## 360 DEGREE FEEDBACK

The practice of giving formalized 360 degree feedback is a natural outcome of the early days and continuing work of National Training Laboratories group work in organizations. Here, members are encouraged to give and receive feedback about themselves and about their impact on others. The purpose of this was and is to have individuals gain more insight about themselves, their habitual ways of interacting with others and the ways they might affect others. It also encourages the open flow of communication between individuals. It can be an excellent way to encourage both personal and professional growth. The 360 degree instrument is a structured and often more business-oriented, non-threatening way of giving and receiving feedback and can have a positive impact on the ways that managers and executives interact with their direct reports, their peers and those that they report to. It also gives them more insight into wider patterns of 'people issues' in the workplace, specifically human interaction in the workplace, including management style and ways of managing conflict.

Specifically, through 360 degree feedback tools, individuals in the workplace are offered the opportunity to seek feedback for themselves on specific issues from their peers, their direct reports and their superiors.

There are several good products in the marketplace, for example, the LBQ[13] (Leadership Behaviour Questionnaire), that offer this structured, paper and pencil means of:

1   Collecting feedback in a semi-anonymous way.

2   'Theming' the feedback.

3   Providing a document that will aid in understanding the feedback.

This feedback can then be discussed with the individual in a single session. However, the preferred method is to use it in an ongoing coaching relationship. This can be with a coach or consultant who can offer ways of understanding the feedback and ways of using it in a constructive program of development for a single individual or members of a team. Personal and professional growth of both the individual members of a team and the team itself can be enhanced with skilful use of 360 degree tools.

The main message of the instruments is that a more self-aware employee will be more effective in his or her position due to having more information about his or her habitual ways of doing things. More information means more choice when it comes to evaluating how to handle situations. The professional that is unaware, has less choices regarding appropriate decisions that could be made when dealing with situations in the workplace. This method of collecting and feeding back data to individuals and team members is enhanced and encouraged by a more open, non-threatening environment in the workplace and also, in a circular fashion, encourages a more open and non-threatening environment. Furthermore, the ongoing use and acceptance of 360 degree instruments should, within that non-threatening work environment, encourage a general openness and acceptance of more open communication, and therefore more open access to information, leading to more effectiveness in terms of team interactions and workplace decision making.

How open and non-threatening the environment of a client organization is, can be assessed through a psychological audit. Essentially this is a method of 'diagnosing' the climate of the organization.

## PSYCHOLOGICAL SURVEYS OF THE WORKPLACE

An organization's 'psychological health' can be revealed through a psychological evaluation. This interview-based consulting method will identify a range of 'indicators' that can be used to assess whether an organization is an emotionally healthy place to work, which things are affecting personnel and how they are being affected.

1   The first stage is a series of in-depth qualitative interviews to identify the particular concerns within the organization. For example, the espoused and actually lived values and goals of the organization, the quality of the interaction between members of the organization, level of respect, type of discipline, the issues and pressures people face and how much support they receive, whether it is a 'blame culture', the degree of trust, taboo subjects, what is necessary in order to 'get ahead', the quality of leadership, the quality of dialogue, myths, prejudices and discrimination.

2   The second stage involves looking for themes, key issues and problems, and pinpointing

---

[13] Sashkin, M, *The Visionary Leader: Leader Behavior Questionnaire* (LBQ). Third Edition. Organisation Design and Development, Inc. King of Prussia, PA.

structural or cultural things that may affect the psychological health and development of organizational personnel, either negatively or positively.

3　The third stage involves making recommendations for solutions to problems and for the enhancement of psychologically positive things in the culture or structure of the organization.

4　The fourth stage would include getting the commitment of upper management to a psychologically healthy environment, having a program to change the environment of the organization in keeping with the recommendations and having a program that would ensure the permanent adoption of a psychologically healthy work environment by the employees.

## HOW STAGE OF LIFE AFFECTS MANAGING

The way a person in their 20s, 30s or 40s sees the managerial role may be very different according to the life stage they are in and what is important to them at that stage of life. The needs for managerial or personality development at these various times are diverse. There may also be a gap in understanding, for example, between what the 30-year old human resources (HR) manager sees as important and the 45-year old consultant. Knowledge of life span development would enable the consultant to better understand and work with those differences.

Research by Kakabadse, Kakabadse and Myers[14] confirms the role of life stage in managerial behaviour. They showed that there are differences between younger and older managers and that age is the key in shaping attitudes and behaviours of top managers. Older managers are people:

> ❛ . . . who have, over time, been held to account for their successes and errors and have turned numerous experiences into developmental opportunities. ❜

It is essential, therefore, for the consultant to have knowledge of the different goals and interests of the different client managers they will be working with.

## PSYCHOLOGICAL SERVICES

While this chapter has not gone into detail regarding psychological services, it is necessary for human resources professionals and managers to understand the following services:

☐ Employee Assistance Programme, Human Resources – what is their purpose in terms of the psychological development of employees? Are they used only as a way of dealing with problem employees?

☐ Does the organization deal with behaviour only or try to enhance the psychological 'growth' of the employee?

☐ Using in-company and external mentoring and coaching.

☐ Making sure your human resources staff can handle emotional crisises effectively and appropriately.

☐ Setting up training and follow-up coaching for HR personnel.

☐ Support and 'clinic-ing' groups within your organization for HR staff who handle employee problems

[14] Kakabadse, Kakabadse and Myers, *Essence of Leadership*, International Thompson Business Press, London. 1998.

## SUMMARY

In the author's experience it is not the day to day running of any organization that provides the biggest challenges or problems for consultants. It is the people aspect, which includes resolving issues of power and conflict, the needs of all individuals to have close nurturing relationships, anxiety – both the consultant's and the client's, achievement and self-image, different personality types working together, what people will and will not discuss. Some of these issues are also addressed in the chapters on Ethical Behaviour, Leadership and Spirituality, and Organization Politics. All of these issues have to do with how people think, behave and interact with one another – psychology. This is the rich but difficult 'stuff' of consulting, which we could only give an introduction to in this chapter.

Many consultants make the mistake of thinking that their job is only about the business content of any project they are engaged in. They find their immediate clients difficult at times. They find themselves frustrated with people who are the 'targets' of change, resisting seemingly great ideas, forgetting that they actually have to 'buy' changes or cooperate with each other. The consultants do not think that addressing that is part of their job. Or they feel out of their depth in addressing these issues because they involve anger, sexual behaviour, greed, lack of ethics and so on – very difficult issues. But these are the very issues that make projects and businesses fail. It is essential that consultants have both skill in human interaction and motivation as well as personal insight into their own impact and issues that cause them difficulty – or they will inevitably affect the success of their consulting work.

## FURTHER READING

Arnold, J, Cooper, C & Robertson, I. *Work Psychology*. Third Edition. Financial Times/Pitman Publishing. 1991.

Bridges, W. The character of organizations. Consulting Psychologists Press, Inc., Palo Alto, CA. 1992.

## RECOMMENDED READING

Kroeger, O & Theusen J. Type talk at work. Delacorte Press, New York, NY. 1992.

Lee, K. *Dealing with Conflict*. Management Quarterly, Part 8. July.

Myers, I B. Gifts Differing. Consulting Psychologists Press, Palo Alto, CA. 1980.

# CHAPTER 6

## THE BUILD MODEL OF CLIENT RELATIONSHIP MANAGEMENT

### INTRODUCTION

Just as a good film has a subtext that underpins its purpose, so has a good consultancy engagement – to develop a client relationship that offers a successful and sustainable partnership. The benefit for the consultant is a growth in the commercial value of that relationship and a reduced cost of sale. The value to the client is a consulting partnership founded on long-term value rather than the short-term transactional quick fix that drives so many engagements. This chapter offers a partnership model that will be of value to:

☐ **Consultants** – By helping them to understand the factors that underpin the development of a sustainable partnership and the steps that need to be taken to help the client migrate from a position of antipathy to advocacy.

☐ **Clients** – By helping them to understand why some consulting relationships work well, but others never seem to progress to a stage where they are happy to recommend the consultant to a colleague.

### THE LIFE CYCLE OF A CLIENT-CONSULTANT RELATIONSHIP

Any effective client-consultant relationship will share a number of common stages: meet the client, help with a problem, confirm that the issue is resolved and close the contract. This is a natural process of supportive change, one seen in everyday life. This natural life cycle can be broken in to seven distinct stages (Figure 6.1).

1  Identify and understand the client's needs.

2  Clarify what root cause or issues are to be addressed.

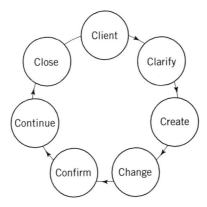

FIGURE 6.1: Client-consultant relationship life cycle

3  Create a solution to resolve the problem.

4  Manage the change process.

5  Confirm that the transition has taken place according to plan.

6  Ensure that the changes will continue once the project is complete.

7  Close the engagement and maintain the relationship.[1]

However, both client and consultant consistently underplay the close stage. Consider what happens often in the field where all the primary effort is placed on the early stages. Meeting the client, making the sale, creating a relationship, understanding the problem and then helping to develop a solution that meets the client needs. The problem is that in the rush and race to deal with the front end, the latter stages are forgotten. There is frequently little measurement after implementation, a failure to consider and deal with the factors that help the change to become sustainable and, finally, an almost complete absence of an effective close stage, which can be, intriguingly, the most important stage from a commercial perspective.

Look inside any organization and ask a simple question, 'Of the last five major change programmes, how many were closed?' The ramification of failing to close effectively is that an opportunity is lost to build on any success from the current engagement and to enhance the commercial nature of the partnership.

The net result is that a huge gap appears in the life cycle of the engagement (Figure 6.2). This gap will clearly cause operational problems because there is no apparent after action review to understand what has worked, what has not worked, and what (if any) problems need to be cleared up before departure. Importantly, from a commercial perspective, if there is no effective close, then the bridgehead to move to the client stage for the next possible engagement has been lost. Any re-entry is done from a cold position, where the previous engagement is conveniently ignored by the consultant (and often the client).

The ability to successfully build on the last engagement and to sell further client services is key to any fruitful (and profitable) client-consultant relationship. Frequently, people allocate time to find new clients and work to promote a product or service. However, the need to continually generate new leads and sales for the pipeline can be costly. The effort of constantly

[1] For further information about this framework, see the *The Seven C's of Consulting* by Mick Cope (Financial Times Prentice Hall, 1999). Additional information about this and other development frameworks can be found at www.wizoz.co.uk

FIGURE 6.2: Failure to close effectively

identifying new prospects can be daunting, whether a sole trader, small consultancy or a large multinational group. The alternate approach is to focus on the development of high value, long-term, profitable relationships. Where the client creates a pull in the market, instead of the consultant having to push for effective relationships.

In this chapter, a new framework is introduced that will help consultants to step back and look at how they build sustainable and successful relationships into their closure process. The focus is on a partnership model, rather than on short-term transactional selling. The build model sets out a full life relationships framework, which defines the journey that an effective client-consultant partnership might follow. It also offers advice on how to guide the client through the journey and thoughts about how the build framework might be applied within a consultancy.

## TRANSACTION VERSUS RELATIONAL SALES

When starting to consider the relational element of the consulting role, we are often faced with a negative view. Often the consultant is seen as a charlatan or trickster, with little moral backbone. This is supported by a suspicion that consultants just are out for the quick buck. Consulting can be seen as a get rich quick profession, where the emphasis is on billable time rather than delivering value through sustainable change.

Much of this poor image may be driven by the considerable demand on consultants to push for short-term revenue. They can be pressured to meet the utilization target, hit the yearly bonus or, for the freelancer, pay the mortgage. All these things conspire to drive a need for short-term revenue through transaction sales, compared to long-term profitability from an effective partnership.

However, all blame should not be placed on the consultant. The client too has certain foibles that contribute to the apparent corrupt behaviours. The client's constant pressure to deliver quick solutions. This is often directed by a need to satisfy this year's budget problems, to prove to the city or financial stakeholders that things are fine, or to meet the illusionary requirements of success that has been driven by yet another government quality target. There may be a degree of manipulation on the part of the client when they employ an external advisor in full knowledge that the problem cannot be solved. As a result, the consultant is there to be the bearer of bad news and to deflect any political blame from the client. Finally, there may be a tendency for self-depreciation in the senior team. A belief that the external agent will automatically have more knowledge and capability over and above any home grown talent. As such, the client is not always prepared to challenge the consultant when they offer the latest 'wiz-bang idea that is sure to solve all their problems'.

# THE BUILD MODEL

The foundations of the short-term consultancy approach is so deeply embedded in the systemic structure within industry that it will take a fundamental shift in how people and companies think, feel and behave to create a more balanced relationship. However, there are things that the consulting industry can do to try and redress the negative impression and to build a profession that is not the butt of the company joke factory. This is to shift from a short-term, transaction-based relationship to the desire to build long-term partnerships through the delivery of value through sustainable change. The build model offered below is not the answer, but it does set out a structural pattern that can be used to understand the nature of profitable partnerships and develop in-house strategies to move towards a long-term relationship.

The build process is based around the following four factors:

1  **Build levels** – The level indicates the commercial nature of the relationship with the customer. This will range from a customer who is generally aware of your product, through to someone who is fully engaged in a long-term buying relationship.

2  **Build dimensions** – The dimensions indicate how you help to facilitate a desire on the part of the client to enter into a partnership relationship. The key message is that any relational process is built around three elements: the buying behaviour; intellectual appreciation of the product; and an emotional appreciation of the consultant or their product.

3  **Build steps** – The steps indicate the differing stages needed to progress the client from stranger to valued partner.

4  **Build drivers** – The drivers indicate the specific action you can take to manage each step change and so help people move along the partnership journey.

## The five build levels

The build levels describe the journey that a client takes as they progress from someone who is broadly aware of the consultant's offering, but have no interest in a relationship, all the way through to a position where the client is fully engaged. At this level there is a clear partnership in place, to the extent that the client is a vocal advocate for the consultant's services, encouraging others to use them and their services.

The five build levels can be explained:

1  **Aware** – At this stage the client may be aware of the consultant and their offering, but there is no desire to commit to a purchase.

2  **Belief** – Here the potential client believes in the need for this type of product and decides to make a single purchase. This is the stage where many relational models might end, i.e. the sale has been made and money banked. However, one sale does not make a partnership. At transaction level, there is a high cost of sale and a willingness on the part of the client to switch to competitors who can offer a similar proposition.

3  **Conviction** – The customer is convinced that the consultant's product has real value. At this stage they have moved from a transaction model into a relationship with the

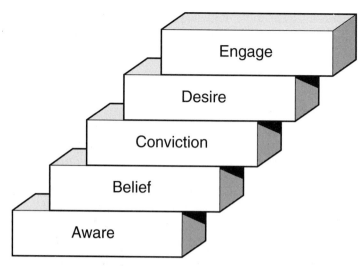

FIGURE 6.3: Build levels

consultant. There is a real conviction that this agent can help to deliver sustainable value and the client is happy to prolong the relationship.

4 **Desire** – There is a real desire on the part of the client to maintain a partnership relationship. They demonstrate this by defending the product or service against any opposition inside their company. The desire to develop a partnership can be so strong that the client seeks to understand more about the consultant's ideas and thus moves into the knowledge transfer stage.

5 **Engage** – At this stage, the customer and consultant are fully engaged in a connected partnership. In many cases, ownership of the partnership process has migrated from the consultant when the client becomes an advocate who actively promotes the consultant's propositions to others. This is similar to the football supporters who proclaim the benefits of their team to all and sundry.

Completion of the build model is when a sustainable and profitable partnership is established, not when the initial sale is made. If people see making a sale as the goal, then the end result is a short-term sales-based organization. If, however, they see the sale as only part of a desire to create long-term sustainable partners, then the sale is purely an indicator along the journey to build a relationship and not the primary goal.

## The build dimensions

There are three primary elements that help to foster a commercial relationship. The cognitive or 'head' element – how much the customer understands about the consulting product and its benefits; the affective or 'heart' element or how the client feels about it; and the behaviour or 'hand' factor, or how much effort the client expends on purchasing the product, i.e. what they do as well as what they say and feel.

The effective consultant makes sure that they understand the three dimensions and how they interact. More importantly, they will appreciate how it might be possible to give someone evidence to help them change their mind about something, but that it is much harder to pressure people to feel differently. At best, stories, metaphors, emotional leverage or personal

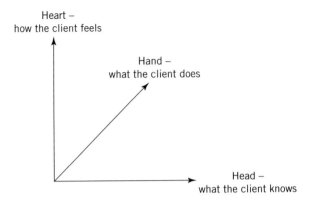

FIGURE 6.4: Build dimensions

disclosure can be used to help effect an emotional change. The reality is that in emotions, the actual process of feeling different is something outside the consultant's direct control.

When a trading relationship is developed it is feasible to offer the customer data and evidence so that they can discuss it. Nevertheless, any shift along the emotional or heart continuum will take place internally and is beyond the consultant's control.

It is important to develop a range of actions and behaviours that help the client move up the build levels. These actions will tend to consist of iteration around the head and heart dimensions (Figure 6.5).

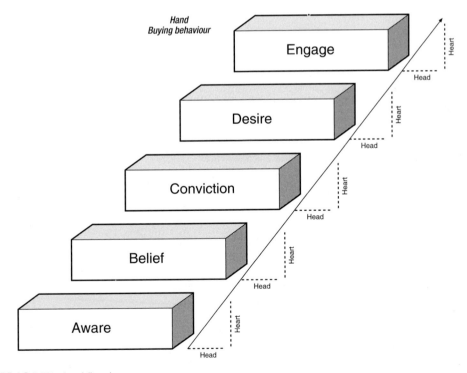

FIGURE 6.5: Build levels and dimensions

The first step might be a head action. Offer the client hard evidence about why they should listen to the proposition. This might be followed with a heart step. Give them time and space to reflect on the data. Once the client believes in the general idea, they can be offered hard tangible data about the value that can be derived from the relationship. This process can go on ad-infinitum until the optimum relational level is reached.

By understanding the factors that drive a change in how people think and feel, it is possible to build a series of actions that will help to manage migration up the build levels. Hence, an appreciation of the drivers at each level can enable the consultant to exert a greater degree of influence over the client's adoption journey.

## The build steps

If the goal is to get the customer to progress effortlessly through the five build levels, it helps to understand the steps they need to go through during the journey. The objective is to take them from a position where they might be fiercely opposed to the product or service, through to a position where they are keen market advocates. The journey might be one of a managed shift from 'anti' to 'educator'.

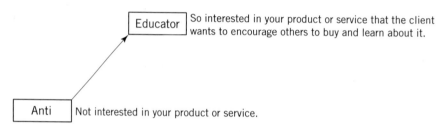

FIGURE 6.6: Build steps

However, the journey from anti to educator, albeit powerful, is rarely taken in a single step. To help the client make this shift, they will often have to go through a number of steps:

☐ **From anti towards the product to an ambivalent position** – The client does not really have a strong belief either way.

☐ **From ambivalent to believer** – The client accepts the general need, but is not necessarily convinced by the consultant's service.

☐ **From believer to buyer** – The client is prepared to make a single transaction purchase.

☐ **From buyer to customer** – An ongoing relationship has developed with the purchaser.

☐ **From customer to champion** – The customer will happily promote the consultant's proposition.

☐ **From champion to defender** – The client is such a strong advocate that they will counter any criticism against the product.

☐ **From defender to disciple** – The client's belief is such that they want to learn more about the product.

☐ **From disciple to expert** – The new knowledge puts the client in a commanding position as an authority figure.

☐ **From expert to educator** – The client has the capability and desire to help others make a similar journey.

There are a number of key points about the build steps:

1 There is no suggestion that all customers should be at the educator level. This would be very costly in terms of time and energy.

2 The key is to decide in advance what build level needs to be achieved with the client, and to apply the appropriate energy to guide them to the right position.

3 In some cases, it might make sense to regress the client down the build levels. Where the consultant has decided to exit a particular market, it is wise to pull people at the higher levels back down to a believe level.

4 In many instances, it is possible to leap-frog over the steps and jump several levels. However, this presents a risk. Namely, if the jump is made too fast, this may have happened because of an emotional purchase, which is not backed up by any logical appreciation of the product. In which case, the client might fall back down just as quickly, once the initial enthusiasm fades.

## The build drivers

Drivers are those actions that can help the client to progress up the build levels. Although they can be complex, it is conceivable to consider them in relation to the head and heart dimensions. In working with a client there is a choice. Is the best driver interaction an intellectual one, to offer the client sound logical data about why the engagement will work? Or is it an emotional interaction where the goal is to work with affective forces to help the client to become emotionally engaged in the product or service? Although any client interaction will consist of a balance of the two, in many cases one of the two dimensions can be amplified to achieve the necessary step to a new build level.

Each of the build steps is shown below with the driver that might be used to help step to the next level. Each step in turn is indicated as a head or heart action.

1 **Head: anti to ambivalent** – Offer evidence. Like the consumer who is opposed to any use of the product, the first logical step may be to offer logical evidence to demonstrate that no harm will come to them from association. Note, this is generic data not necessarily specific data about the consultant's product or idea.

2 **Heart: ambivalent to believe** – Reason to believe. The emotional shift from ambivalent to a believer indicates that the person believes in the need for the benefits associated with the service, but has not bought into the need to make a purchase. The risk of a client at this stage is that once they believe in the need, a competitor may come along and steal them. It is important not to lose sight of the next stage and ideally to move them to buyer as quickly as possible. Offer firm evidence why the service offers the best value in the market.

3 **Head: believe to buyer** – Offer value. The logical shift from a position where someone believes in the need for a product to buying the service is driven by the logical appreciation that they will derive a benefit. There might be a financial, emotional or rational payback resulting from the cost of sale. Interestingly, although the decision to buy might be driven by an emotional pull, generally the customer will be able to rationalize the decision.

4 **Heart: buyer to customer** – Make it personal. The buyer stage might be viewed as a transactional position. This is where cost will take precedence over the nature of the relationship as a buying determinant. The shift to a customer level comes once buying is personal and relationship-based. At this stage, the buyer has to want to come back, instead of purchasing from one of the competitors. The cost becomes less of a logical decision criteria. Rather, the nature of the relationship becomes more dominant. An indication of this can be found in the fact that up to 80 per cent of repeat client purchases are driven by the nature of the relationship rather than the quality of the previous project.

5 **Head: customer to champion** – Personal payback. The logical shift from customer to champion is a subtle but important one. This is the point where the client is prepared to tell others in their organization about their experience and its value. The benefit of this is that the client helps to increase market penetration and starts to reduce the cost of sale. The customer will often do this because they perceive some sort of personal payback from promoting the service. This may take the form of brand association or political power.

6 **Heart: champion to defender** – Stakeholder. The emotional shift from champion to defender is manifested by the willingness of the client to act as protector in cases where other people criticize the proposition. Frequently, the drive for this may be because the client has a personal stake in the ideas associated with the offering and view any attack as a personal criticism of their decision to support the idea.

7 **Head: defender to disciple** – Lead through learning. At this level, the customer sees sense in learning more about the proposition and so takes on a disciple or committed student role. Their goal may be to acquire knowledge and deploy it for personal or business gain.

8 **Heart: disciple to expert** – Re-frame. The step from disciple to expert is where the learner is able to take the ideas associated with the product and use them in a new way or direction. They add value by re-framing the base concept and present it to the market in a different form. They have internalized the learning and may start to present it using their own maps. The benefit is that this indicates fundamental buy-in – the risk is if they get it wrong!

9 **Head: expert to educator** – Recognition. The final stage, from expert to educator, is where the client has acquired so much expertise that they are selling the proposition to their peers. At this level, the cost of sale has been almost eliminated and the client is acting as a market advocate. There is often a need to shift the nature of the relationship from teacher or guide to that of a professional peer, where the client's value and expertise is openly acknowledged.

### Full build framework

By linking these four factors (build levels, dimensions, steps and drivers), the build framework can be developed. It is not offered as a rigid solution to support development of a client partnership, rather it is a mental framework that can be used to understand the nature of the client relationship and what is needed to enhance the commercial value.

## BUILD APPLICATION

The build framework offers a broad model to help understand the nature of a partnership relationship and how to manage it more effectively. The following actions provide more specific ways that the model can help to manage clients using a partnership approach.

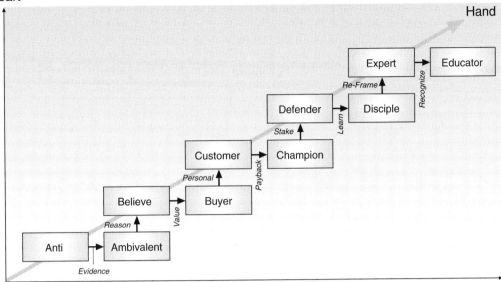

FIGURE 6.7: Full build framework

1 **Client segmentation** – Consider the two build maps in Figure 6.8. Company A might be viewed as successful. All of the key clients are buying their products and there are some emotional relationships in place. However, the cluster concentration is at the lower level. Although the company might be generating income now, one has to question where the income will come from in the future. Moreover, with such a cluster at the buyer level, what happens if a competitor surfaces who is able to provide comparable service at lower cost? Will the buyer base switch and therefore cut the income flow overnight? Company B appears to have less income with a smaller cluster at buyer and customer, yet they do have strong supporters for their product within the customer base. They have people who want to learn more about what the company does, so that they can be seen to associate with the consultant's brand and products. The focus for this company could be to build on this cluster model by maintaining the top end penetration and to try and generate more income by leveraging the existing brand leaders.

2 **Investment decision** – An alternative suggestion is to use the build model to drive investment decisions for the sales and marketing budgets. By understanding where the client base is on the framework, it becomes easier to judge where the various budgets need to be allocated. With a high level of anti-ambivalents, the spend could be on broad advertising and client contact programs to get people to understand the basic value of the product. If the focus is at the buyer level, money might need to be allocated on a customer relationship exercise. Where the concentration is champion-defender, more effort could be placed upon developing client education sessions, to help clients to appreciate the nature of the product being offered.

3 **Referral management** – The most successful market pitch is often one backed up by client referral. Clearly, referrals from someone at champion, expert or educator level will help

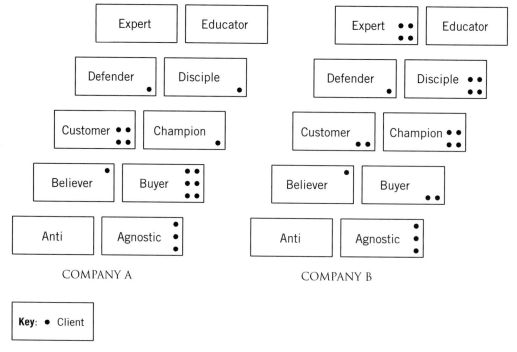

FIGURE 6.8: Build maps

to generate work in another part of the business or with another client. However, the converse can be true. A client who is less than enamoured with the current offering, maybe at anti or ambivalent level, can be quite detrimental or even devastating if they are exposed to a new prospect. Map the current client base against the build model and it becomes easier to actively identify those people who need to be ring-fenced and contained within a protective wall, and those who should be encouraged to share their views.

4   **Calling plan management** – The calling plan is possibly one of the most important aspects of any partnership process, but one that may fall by the wayside when other pressures come along. This is often because it is seen as an addendum to the process and not an integral part. If someone thinks that they are just 'keeping in touch' with the client, then it is easy to put it off until tomorrow. However, if the call can be seen to elevate the client within the build model, then clear value can be ascribed to each call. In addition to this valuation, the build model also facilitates a process where the effectiveness of each contact call can be measured.

5   **Account management** – Once the client base is clearly segmented along the build levels, it becomes possible to develop an aligned account management structure. For example, to have one person manage clients that range from ambivalent to expert is not practical. It might make more sense to cluster expertise around different groups. Allocate the client groups who sit at the lower end to account managers who are more experienced at short-term sales relationships. This way their expertise is drawn upon to get the people who are anti to at least a buyer level. At this point, it may be wise to hand over to an account

manager more focused on running long-term relationships. This person may be tasked to shift people from customer to champion. Finally, perhaps hand over to a more experienced member of the team who can take the client to expert level. This can be achieved by virtue of their deep understanding of the product and services offered by the company. On the other hand, it can be structured in a different way, where account managers are tasked to take the client from anti to expert and support them along the way. The goal is to build an account management structure that best fits the desire to migrate clients up the build levels and so reduce the cost of sale.

6 **People development and evaluation** – Any partnership process depends upon the capability and performance of the consultant. An understanding of the nature of the build process and how different capabilities are required along the way, enables the ability to manage and migrate people up the build levels to be improved. For example, there are a number of different capabilities required to step people along the different build stages. The anti to ambivalent stage often needs an evidential-based process, where clear facts and figures are offered to help the potential client appreciate the utilitarian value of the proposition. This capability to operate at a factual and granular level is different to the buyer to customer stage, where relational skills might be required to become emotionally closer to the client. A full comprehension of the differences between the stages facilitates an assessment of whether people have such a capability and allows the development of strategies to enhance their skill base.

7 **Client process automation** – Once the consultancy team has a clear partnership framework in place, it is possible to understand what elements can be automated. For example, at the anti to ambivalent to believer stage, to what extent can the delivery of scenarios that map your product or service benefits to the potential client market sector be automated? Can you find ways to ensure that potential clients are continuously made aware of the benefits of your service through viral marketing?

8 **Identify future decision makers** – One common goal for any consultant is to reach those people who command the most influence. However, it is clearly not always feasible to do this. Sometimes work takes place at a defined level in the organization and there is little chance to get the senior team involved. In this case it helps to identify who the key stakeholders or power brokers are at this level and target these people as potential future champions or experts.

## SUMMARY

1 The build model is designed to help people to choose how they develop a successful partnership. It gives an understanding of how to progress people through the various levels on the build framework, and perhaps to take someone who is an anti all the way through to the educator level.

2 It is a rare occasion when a client can be taken through all levels of the framework in one engagement. The ultimate goal of the build framework is to ensure that when the current engagement is closed, the client is helped to appreciate the value that has been delivered. If the client comprehends and appreciates the value at an emotional and cognitive level, it is possible to step them up a level on the build model. For example, if the client started

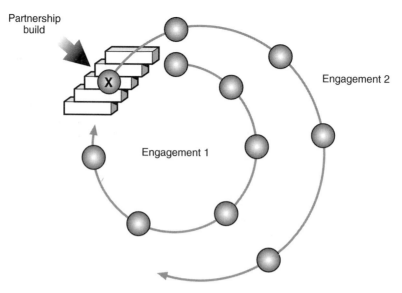

FIGURE 6.9: Spiral build process

the current engagement as a buyer, aspire to get them onto the customer level; if they started the existing engagement at champion, use the project as an opportunity to migrate them to defender level. There is no optimum approach, the goal is to be aware of the client's current level, the level the client should be migrated to, and what action will help the client to make the shift.

3 The important thing to stress is that the closure stage is not the point to say goodbye, it is the time to say hello. By saying hello, it makes complete sense for the client and the consultant to reflect upon their relationship and to jointly decide if they want to move towards a partnership, one that will create shared success for both parties.

> This is not the end – it is not even the beginning of the end –
> but it is perhaps the end of the beginning.
> Winston Churchill (1874–1965) Speech in November 1942.

# PART 3

CONSULTING: THE KEY SKILLS

# CHAPTER 7

## CREATING SPACE FOR ORGANIZATIONAL CHANGE – NEW INTERVENTIONS

### INTRODUCTION

In 1987, Schein[1] distinguished three forms of consultant-client relationship: purchase of expertise; doctor-patient, and process consulting. All of these are still important today and are likely to remain so.

This chapter concentrates on approaches for process consulting, where the role of the consultant is to be expert, not in the specifics of the client's problem, or in diagnosis of 'illness' and prescription of appropriate remedies, but rather in the process of change, in helping the client to address their own issues.

From the theories of 'open space technology' to 'Neuro-Linguistic Programming' and storytelling to painting, consultants and their clients are pushing the limits of traditional approaches, combining and adapting methods from areas such as religion, theatre, education and psychotherapy and applying them to the organizational context.

In this chapter a selection of approaches is surveyed that well illustrate the various alternatives, are interesting and useful and have some track record of success.

The various approaches considered, while relatively new in the context of organizational consulting, are not new in themselves – each has some history in a particular context. The brief descriptions are intended to introduce you to the various possibilities, give a taste of how they might help you and your clients, and encourage you to find out more.

### WHY DO WE NEED THESE APPROACHES AND WHY NOW?

Consultants working with organizations already have a rich repertoire of approaches, and the new methods surveyed here are a valuable complement, rather than substitute. Nonetheless,

[1] E H Schein, *Process Consultation II*, Addison-Wesley, 1987.

there are good reasons why we must continue to expand our range of interventions and indeed vary our basic approach.

Few consulting interventions are properly evaluated, but surveys suggest that typically 80–90 per cent of projects fail to deliver expected benefits. Given the outcome of many mediations, consultants may question the approach they take – whether it is appropriate and whether the theoretical process bears much relation to reality.

For example, a typical structure for a consulting project of the 1970s and 1980s would follow a top down, rational-objective and linear process. This would involve analysis of market, competitors and so on; elaboration of alternative competitive strategies and a careful, objective choice between them; and finally implementation of whatever was needed – people, systems – to deliver this blueprint.

However, this process may not have borne much relation to reality. For instance, there is now widespread recognition that strategy is in large part driven by who is in power, and is a social and political construct.[2] In any event, lengthy cycles of planning and implementation are risky. For example, events may move too fast for the organization to respond, or technology may evolve faster than the time taken to evaluate it.

In actuality, organizations and change are 'messy'. They do not conform to tidy plans, but are driven by people and their relationships. Two areas much discussed in recent years are chaos and emotion, and it seems that consulting must embrace these if it is to help organizations to change. The approaches examined here are characterized by a holistic and integrative style that explicitly recognizes the multifaceted, complex, non-linear and, above all, human aspects of change in organizations.

In addition to consultants seeking new ways of working with clients, people from other fields are moving into consulting and bringing their own experience, values and approaches with them. There are many new entrants, ranging from individuals – the result of redundancies, early retirement or simply changes in career plans – to organizations – groups previously occupied with a particular business or social activity, now offering consultancy services.

For instance, in recent years organizations such as BT (telecoms), IBM (computers), Hyder (utilities), theatres and Findhorn (spiritual community) have all begun to offer consultancy services. This provides a compelling reason for the proliferation and differentiation of consultancy offerings. However, the most important factor may be the increased sophistication of clients and the complexity of the issues that they face.

This is driven partly by information and knowledge. The most obvious development of recent years has been the internet, although other factors may be more important in practice. There has been an explosion in the number of Master of Business Administration degrees (MBA) and other management courses, themselves increasingly international in terms of participants, location, and the examples used. Both managers and consultants are increasingly mobile, expected to change their role or employer every few years.

One view is that as change becomes more frequent it is change that becomes the norm. Successful organizations are those that can change more effectively than their competitors. In this case, the greatest value that consultants can add is to develop the capability of the organization to change in the future.

---

[2] K E Weick, *Sensemaking in Organizations*, Sage, 1995.

## CASE STUDY

The director of research and development at a large pharmaceutical company invited consultants to help him to reduce the time from the initial research to the launch of a new drug.

Traditionally, he might have asked for a report and recommendations, and commissioned consultants to help with implementation or simply ordered his staff to make this or that change. Instead, over three years, his staff worked on the problem themselves and implemented improvements as they went, while two consultants operated part-time as group facilitators and gave one-to-one coaching to certain managers.

When asked why he had followed this approach, the director was quite clear. He wanted:

☐ His staff to become a team, able to deal with problems as they arose.

☐ To transfer knowledge, experience and skills from the consultants.

☐ His team to be able to manage change for themselves.

In the director's view, an approach based on coaching and facilitation, while it might take longer, would be more successful in outcome – providing real and lasting change.

In the example above, the client wanted help with the process. Explicitly help on how his staff would work together on the problem. The new interventions cast the consultant in the role of an expert in process rather than in content. The role of the consultant is to design and facilitate a process, which allows the client to work on a particular issue. The consultant's role is not to solve a particular problem, but instead to give the support to enable the clients to solve it for themselves.

## NEW INTERVENTIONS

### A simple typology of new interventions

At the risk of oversimplifying, the approaches described in this chapter can be divided into three groups:

1  Those which provide a framework or process for an intervention – a sequence or structure.

2  Philosophies or conceptual frameworks, which do not prescribe particular methods but provide an underpinning set of values and assumptions or beliefs.

3  Specific tools and techniques.

In practice, any consulting mediation is likely to be a mixture of these. Over time, any approach becomes both richer and more complex and attracts supporters and critics who describe it differently. However, the descriptions below provide a useful introduction.

## FRAMEWORK APPROACHES

Several approaches to working with groups – such as creative problem solving[3] and synectics[4] – have become relatively well known recently. These offer an invaluable bridge between more traditional and innovative approaches to consulting. In brief, these methods follow the pattern:

[3] D J Treffinger, S G Isaksen, and K B Dorval, *Creative Problem Solving – An Introduction*, (revised edition), Center For Creative Learning, 1994.
[4] J Ceserani and P Greatwood, *Innovation and Creativity*, Kogan Page, 1995.

- [ ] Scope the problem.

- [ ] Understand the current situation.

- [ ] Develop a view of the desired future state.

- [ ] Explore and choose paths to get from the current to the future state.

- [ ] Develop an implementation plan.

A limitation of these structured approaches is that they may perpetuate the split between thinking and doing, whereas in practice implementation informs and shapes initial ideas – an iterative rather than linear process. Nevertheless, they offer:

- [ ] A coherent, well-proven and documented process for consultants and clients to follow.

- [ ] Language which is familiar and comfortable to those with a business background.

- [ ] A solid framework for particular techniques or processes.

## Large group interventions

An alternative to highly structured work by small groups is to get everyone involved in a particular issue in one place, at the same time, and to provide minimal structure so that they self-organize to collectively solve the problem.

Various approaches exist from the relatively less structured Open Space Technology[5] to the more structured, Real Time Strategic Change.[6]

The originator of Open Space Technology, Harrison Owen, stresses the participative, self-organizing nature of large group interventions (LGIs) and warns against their use when the solution to a problem is known.[5]

LGIs are most appropriate when:

- [ ] The answer, for example the vision for the new organization, is unclear.

- [ ] Fast change is imperative.

- [ ] Passion and energy about the change or the future is important.

Herein may lie the reasons why some organizations are reluctant to use LGIs. They give power to the wider group, they do not follow a tidy, pre-ordained sequence and they are uncomfortable for leaders who believe they know all of the answers.

Furthermore, participants in LGIs may find it difficult to return to a more conventional way of working after the event. Alternatively, they may not be able to successfully transfer the good ideas developed in the hothouse atmosphere of the event, back into their organization. This can actually worsen or create tensions, and bring disillusionment.

The key to a successful use of LGIs is in the preparation, particularly in the relationship between consultant and commissioning client. This is true of all the approaches looked at in this chapter.

These frameworks may be considered the backbone of the new consultancy interventions toolkit. Philosophies or conceptual frameworks provide underpinning philosophies or 'ways of thinking'.

[5] H Owen, *Open Space Technology: A User's Guide*, Berrett-Koehler, 1997.
[6] B B Bunker and B T Alban, *Large Group Interventions: Engaging the Whole System for Rapid Change*, Jossey-Bass, 1997.

# PHILOSOPHIES OR CONCEPTUAL FRAMEWORK APPROACHES

## Chaos theory and systems thinking

These approaches have their origins in the study of the natural world. However, they have become increasingly important in the field of organizational change and have been developed to the point of offering specific tools and techniques.[7,8]

Their greatest value may be in drawing our attention to several key points about the real world:

- ☐ Events, people and so on are parts of a system where the parts interact.

- ☐ Events may have multiple causes and consequences and simple cause and effect thinking may be too limited.

- ☐ These causes and consequences may themselves be remote in time and location and are, therefore, difficult to identify.

- ☐ Events and outcomes are unlikely to be completely predictable.

- ☐ Any analysis we make, our understanding of events, must necessarily be a limited model of reality.

The implications of this are far-reaching. Most obviously, it suggests that consultants should adopt a participative and creative approach, which allows for joint construction of shared meaning and is flexible in allowing outcomes to emerge and change. More or less explicitly, the various approaches in this chapter assume this philosophy, rather than one based on belief in absolute truth and expertise.

## Appreciative inquiry

Appreciative Inquiry (AI)[9] has at its heart a simple yet potentially powerful premise: that it is better to focus on understanding and developing strengths and positive points than to be driven by fixing problems and shortcomings.

Where much consulting is problem-oriented and assumes bad intent and resistance to change on the part of staff, AI begins by asking what is good and right and assumes positive intent. In other words, it is much easier to effect change by doing more of what works than to set out to fix problems.

AI is best established in North America and has yet to become established in Europe where it is too early to properly judge its impact. However, we can see that AI rests on a very fundamental set of beliefs, and its European success may depend on how acceptable these are to a particular organization.

# TOOLS AND TECHNIQUES APPROACHES

There are many approaches that offer specific ways of intervening to facilitate change and the following provide an illustrative selection. For the most part the approaches do not offer a comprehensive framework or underlying philosophy and might therefore be better used as part of a larger change process.

---

[7] P Senge *et al. The Fifth Discipline Fieldbook*, Nicholas Brealey, 1994.

[8] B Oshry, *Seeing Systems: Unlocking the Mysteries of Organisational Life*, Berrett-Koehler, 1995.

[9] D L Cooperrider and D Whitney, *Appreciative Inquiry*, Berrett-Koehler, 1999.

## Ceremony

Perhaps the most common forms of ceremony are marriage and burial. In organizational settings too, we see ceremony in areas such as induction, promotion or the familiar 'leaving drinks'. In all of these cases, the functions of ceremony are to:

- ☐ Provide a safe framework at a time of uncertainty.
- ☐ Mark a transition.
- ☐ Celebrate or appreciate.
- ☐ Give a sense of completion.

The value of ceremony in organizational change is obvious. However, overt use of ceremony in organizational change is infrequent, possibly because it involves emotion which, for many, is still seen as something to keep away from the workplace.

Recently the expression 'emotional intelligence at work'[10] has become commonplace. It reminds us that people do have emotions, which are likely to be as important at work as elsewhere, and that any organizational change process that ignores these is naive and incomplete.

## CASE STUDY

One practical example of appropriate ceremony use comes from the large consulting organizations themselves. When two of these merged in the mid 1980s, one produced a book made up entirely of informal photographs of day-to-day life in the office in the year preceding the merger. Its purpose was to recognize and honour how things had been, so that partners and staff could let go of their previous firm – see it as different rather than better.

This was reinforced by the metaphorical value of the book – something to shut and put on the shelf, instead of carrying around.

## Storytelling

At its most basic, storytelling is simply narration. Most consultant communications, such as reports, can be regarded as telling a story. In organizations, we often hear stories about particular people or events which, frequently repeated, have the effect of teaching how to succeed or fail, how to behave and not. Any new recruit will quickly hear such stories and pick up the culture of their new employer.

Stories tend to evolve naturally, perhaps as a way for humans to make sense of the world around them. Certainly, stories have an extraordinary value in transmitting and sharing ideas, across people and over time. Their importance in organizations is well documented.[11,12] For the consultant, an interesting question is 'Can we deliberately evolve and use stories to bring about and sustain change?'

One form of storytelling is the analogy – the 'moral tale' if you like. Here, a seemingly irrelevant or fictional story actually embeds an important lesson. In fable, for example, we have stories such as 'Little Red Riding Hood'.

Some consultants and their clients have used storytelling in a deliberate way – constructing stories and choosing which ones to repeat.[13,14] It is perhaps too early to assess this properly, however these case histories above suggest that it does work.

[10] D Goleman, *Emotional Intelligence*, Bloomsbury, 1995.
[11] E H Schein, *Organizational Culture and Leadership*, (second edition), Jossey-Bass, 1992.
[12] K E Weick, *op. cit*, 1995.
[13] M Parker, *Creating Shared Vision*, Dialog International Ltd., 1990.
[14] H Owen, *Spirit: Transformation and Development in Organizations*, Berrett-Koehler, 1987.

## Metaphor

Perhaps the most obvious examples of metaphor are in artistic fields, for instance, painting or theatre. A particular piece can transmit meaning far beyond the limits of the written word. It can allow the artist to express themselves in a way they cannot otherwise, and the observer can project their own meaning onto the piece.

Metaphor has much to offer as an instrument of organizational change. Consider the following examples.

> ## CASE STUDY
>
> A senior group of railway engineering managers built a model of the channel tunnel (some years before it was built) out of sand. Over the course of one day, the previously disparate group developed a new understanding of both the technical and people issues and started to work as a collaborative, creative project team.

> ## CASE STUDY
>
> A group of directors from several organizations met to develop a 'blue sky' vision of their business. In previous meetings it had proved difficult to move beyond minor adaptations of the current situation, or to get any sense of how the public, government or other stakeholders would see them.
>
> Using a mix of painting and drama they drew a picture of how they saw things and used role-play to portray different stakeholders.
>
> By using unfamiliar methods, the directors were able to develop new perspectives unconstrained by their usual ways of thinking. As important as any final view of the future were the discussions – the sharing of knowledge and assumptions.

## Theatre

One use of theatre will be familiar to many in organizations: role-play and simulation of real-life situations are often used as part of training courses. However, other approaches, derived from theatre, also have much to offer.

The repertoire of theatre games has such varied uses as group energizers, team-building exercises and stimulating creative thinking.[15,16] Another use is the opportunity to play out a scenario, perhaps as a form of ceremony or rehearsal.

Perhaps the most interesting is the use of theatre to provide a metaphor. For example, a leadership team may be invited to watch or act part of a Shakespeare play and to discuss how the politics and power play relates to their own organization.[17]

A critical and much-discussed need for organizations is to engage people, to bring intentions alive, to raise passions. Multi-sensory and dynamic, theatre and music may be just the tools for this job.

## Neuro-Linguistic Programming (NLP)

Two of the most striking features of NLP,[18] on first approaching it, are the breadth of what it covers and the difficulty of properly defining it. For instance, NLP offers frameworks, philosophical principles and specific tools. Therefore, it does not fit easily into our typology.

[15] E S Foster, *Energizers and Icebreakers*, Educational Media Corporation, 1989.

[16] E D Platts, *Playful Self-Discovery*, Findhorn Press, 1996.

[17] Work carried out through Cranfield University, UK by Richard Olivier, Visiting Fellow, Cranfield School of Management and Theatre director, Globe Theatre, London, England.

[18] R Bandler and J Grinder, *Frogs into Princes*, Real People Press, 1979.

NLP can be described as a set of frameworks for understanding and influencing how people think and act, derived from studying individuals who are exceptionally good in a certain field, and NLP seeks to learn 'How do they do that?'

NLP originated in the US in the 1970s and quickly became popular with two groups:

1 **Therapists** – Who could immediately apply it to their work.

2 **Salespeople** – Who tried to use an improved understanding of how people think to sell to customers – perhaps by manipulating them.

Not surprisingly, NLP has many vociferous advocates and critics. Recently there has been growth in the area of 'NLP in business'. However, this consists generally of NLP trainers, therapists and Human Resource professionals applying NLP to personal issues which happen to arise in the workplace. For example, difficulty in making decisions, lack of self-confidence or interpersonal conflict.

Nonetheless, many NLP techniques can be translated from personal to group and business issues. A particularly striking use of NLP principles is to release creativity in groups by giving them new perspectives.

## CASE STUDY

The marketing managers of a telecommunications company were meeting to form a shared vision and to agree new ways of working – to become a real team that contributed to their organization. Grand words, but what to do in practice? Especially difficult because the individuals in the group were already in cliques and did not trust each other.

The consultant stood up and had them follow her into the corridor, and very deliberately shut the door, saying 'Let's go someplace else and figure out some practical actions. This team is really good at that. That team in there is stuck, let's leave them to it'.

Then the consultant walked them into another conference room and shut the door, inviting them by saying 'You know when you coach one of your staff – sometimes you just ask questions, sometimes you give advice or whatever. I bet you are all really good staff managers, and other people find it really useful to have your perspective. Imagine, now, that you're coaching that other group in that other room'.

The consultant continued, 'I want you to come up with some practical actions they can take to improve their teamwork and make a contribution to their company. And I mean practical – if they can't write it straight into their 'to-do' list, it won't happen'.

The group found this both useful and energizing and, over the following days, did some work which they had only expected to achieve several meetings later.

A major theme in NLP is to be clear on desired outcomes or goals. In the following account, challenging a group about its aims served to build a team with the energy to act.

## CASE STUDY

Two groups were charged with implementing new IT systems to handle accounts and alumni records in a British university. After some months they had made little progress – the work within the IT department was done but there was no involvement by users. The IT managers just could not get anyone interested.

At a meeting, the consultant was struck by two things. First, the groups sat at separate tables, with no interaction, each visibly dominated by the IT project manager. Second, the majority of the team members — including department heads, the bursar and vice-chancellor — were in effect mentally elsewhere.

The consultant asked the obvious question: 'Why do you want to do this?'. The IT managers explained that Year 2000 compliance required an upgrade to systems, and as the systems were so old, they were being replaced.

The consultant asked again: 'Why do you want to do this? I understand that Year 2000 compliance is an issue, and that you're going to have new systems. But so what? If this is just a system upgrade, why are you all here? Apart from Year 2000 compliance, why else is this important?'

Tentatively, someone said, 'Well, if we had decent alumni records we could raise more donations, and offer would-be students a network'. And another volunteered, 'If we had good accounts, we could better manage the money we have, and attract extra grants'. Yet more: 'And if we had more money, and better alumni records, we could attract better students' . . . 'and lecturers' . . . 'and form alliances with overseas universities' . . . 'and be a leading university'.

From a group of uninterested individuals they had started to form a team with a shared purpose.

## PUTTING THE PIECES TOGETHER

The approaches described above can be used in various ways and individual consultants will have their own ways of working. However, it is essential that consultants adapt their approach to the specific client need.

One criticism of some consultants is that they always use the same method or bring the same solution. For instance, there is a risk that an IT consultant will see all problems as IT ones. Similarly, there is a possibility that consultants using new interventions such as those explained, may always use the same ones.

It is desirable for consultants to draw on a range of approaches, mixing and matching as appropriate. The following case study illustrates many of the approaches described above and how they may be combined in the context of organizational change.

## CASE STUDY

Following a merger, a leading international management consultancy wanted to:

☐ Take stock of the management development provision and focus on some important areas.

☐ Have a clear, coherent vision for management development in the new organization, shared by the team members.

☐ Create a single management development team with common ways of working.

Most importantly, the client wanted the group to change from an essentially passive provider of training to one that took the lead in developing the organization and individual staff. In effect, was more strategic and proactive and did not wait for instructions or permission.

There were some 65 management development staff spread over five countries, ranging from a few junior administrators to many senior and experienced facilitators and directors. For various reasons, the new management development team had to be up and running with their new focus and ways of working within a month.

Working as a joint client and consultant group, a four-day event with the following outline structure was designed:

| DAY 1 | DAY 2 | DAY 3 | DAY 4 |
|---|---|---|---|
| Honouring and letting go of the past | Our future | Ideas into action | Beginning |
| ☐ Opening event context, objectives and scope-setting | ☐ Opening event context, objectives and scope-setting | ☐ Opening event context, objectives and scope-setting | ☐ Opening event context, objectives and scope-setting |
| ☐ Open space: harvesting concerns and ambitions | ☐ Evolving a shared vision | ☐ From vision to action – our future timeline | ☐ Consolidation and integration |
| ☐ Our past timeline – honouring the past and harvesting learning and 'wants to take with us' | ☐ Evening news and community theatre: 'Our vision in action' | ☐ Celebration | ☐ Beginning |
| ☐ Evening news and community theatre: 'Our story' | | | |

At one level this was a very conventional process – 'Where are we now? Where do we want to be? How do we get there?' However, within this simple framework the event used many different approaches according to what was best suited to each part of the session.

Most obviously, with 65 people gathered in one large room over four days, it was a large group intervention (LGI). At many points during the event there were questions about what to do next, how to split into sub-groups and so on. The consistent response of the facilitators was to ask the group to organize itself – to demonstrate that they had to make their own choices.

The first major session followed the structure of Open Space. Individuals were invited to post their concerns on a wall, and then to form groups around those concerns they considered most important. Each group was asked to discuss and report back on both its fears and what elements it wanted to keep.

Building in the notion of appreciative inquiry (AI), the event continued with an appreciation of how things were pre-merger: what was good, what should be left behind, and what should be brought forward in some way. The process was borrowed from NLP: individuals were invited to imagine a timeline stretching from the past, through the present and into the future (the new organization) and to walk along it in a mood of quiet reflection.

In the evening, sub-groups prepared and put on short plays that told stories about how life was in the old organizations.

Days two and three followed a similar pattern: self-organized groups used a variety of methods from creative approaches and NLP to define their agenda and to work on specific problems.

Day four could have been seen as the end of the event. Instead, it was framed as the beginning of the new organization. To that end, participants were given some time to invest as they wished – typically in first meetings of their new work teams. They then performed a short ceremony as a circle of 65, where each person was able to say how they felt, what they hoped for and what they would do to contribute to the new group.

Although fairly simple on paper, in practice the event was highly charged in terms of energy and emotion – anger, grief, joy and so on – and was described by participants as a 'hothouse' and 'emotional roller coaster'.

This is perhaps the best illustration of how using new interventions made a difference: the event evoked a personal engagement too often missing in conventional approaches.

# SUMMARY

In recent years, there have been important changes in the relationship between clients and consultants. Longer term relationships and ways of working, which are closer to joint exploration and learning than to the traditional expert and doctor-patient models, have developed.

This translates into what consultants and clients actually do day to day. From traditional 'write a report' style consulting, interventions are now likely to be all-embracing in terms of issues and participation, dealing with both personal and business issues, integrating a range of approaches, and flexible rather than rigid.

This chapter is based on anecdotal evidence, personal experience and a relatively limited number of books and other publications. It is not clear how common the interventions mentioned here are, however the approaches introduced are particularly useful when conventional methods prove inadequate.

There is a risk that consultants and their clients may be seduced by the novelty of new approaches, blame certain approaches for failure of a particular change, or 'surf' from one approach to the other without ensuring that activity actually results in change.[19]

It might be said that, for consultants to facilitate change successfully, they must first attend to their client's intent, to their own intent in working with the client, then to their relationship, and only then to particular approaches. With the right intent and relationship, much is possible. Without these, tools and techniques are just activity.

The successful consultant of the future will be the one who can develop relationships based on trust, is able to understand and balance complex issues, who can be both open to and learn from others, and has a high degree of personal strength. They will be familiar with and able to use a range of approaches according to need.

Development of these new consultants offers challenges both for learners and developers. Development involves more than attending courses and also includes work experience, ideally with a process and support for learning on the job, such as mentoring or coaching.

The traditional model of apprenticeship is relevant here. The role of the 'master' becomes more to encourage, challenge and inspire and less to transmit knowledge and control compliance with procedure. Consulting may come to be recognized as a craft, combining theory, research and experience, according to the individual artisan's sense of what they are working with.

---

[19] E C Shapiro, *Fad Surfing in the Boardroom*, Capstone Publishing, 1996.

# CHAPTER 8

## COACHING FOR CHANGE AND HARMONY

### INTRODUCTION

‘It's not so much that we're afraid of change
or so in love with the old ways,
or in between that we fear . . .
It's like being between trapezes.
It's Linus when his blanket is in the dryer.
There's nothing to hold on to.’

Marilyn Ferguson, 'Women's Voices: Quotations by Women',
www.womenshistory.about.com/library/qu/blquferg.htm, 5 February 2000.

Organizations, teams and individuals need to regularly re-evaluate their ways of interaction within their environment. This helps to preserve or find a new place, a new contribution or new values in a global environment, which is also undergoing a dynamic deep-rooted and constant change.

The amount, nature, frequency and rhythm of change-related demands are becoming more intense and more rapid. This is happening both on a personal as well as on a professional level. It is necessary to know how to respond to multiple changes, whether the changes are beneficial or not and whether the results of those changes create additional value or prevent a reduction of existing value.

Moreover, these changes also impact the organizational stakeholders – those parties who either affect or who are affected by an organization's actions, behaviour and policies, and the external environment. Thus, there is a need to assist and enable organizations and individuals to embrace the process of change in a more comfortable, harmonious and efficient way. In addition, initiating new changes in a conscious, well thought out manner, when appropriate, is becoming essential. Effective coaching enables people and organizations to readily incorporate and adapt to problematic aspects of change as well as building capability for the initiation of change.

This chapter explores strategies for effective use of coaching by discussing two approaches based upon different but complementary principles, namely coaching by experts and co-coaching. The purpose of coaching, how coaches are used and their potential benefits are explored.

# REASONS FOR COACHING

‹ There is nothing more difficult to plan,
more doubtful of success,
no more dangerous to manage,
than the creation of a new order of things ›

Niccolo Machiavelli, *The Prince*, translated by Luigi Ricci,
NAL, 1998, originally written in 1513.

There are many, varied and often multiple reasons why organizations adopt a coaching initiative (Table 8.1). Some programs are initiated by company policies and some by individuals. Whatever the reason for coaching, the assumption is that coaching needs to meet the requirements of both individual and organization. A survey of UK organizations reveals that the use of one–to-one coaching in some form has risen from 50 per cent to 70 per cent.[1] In practice, coaching tends to focus, most frequently, on the ability to improve management skills and capabilities and to manage adaptive or transformational change.

| COACHING FOR | FOCUS ON |
|---|---|
| Executives | Role model and boardroom behaviour. |
| Achievement | Fast-track, tailored and discrete development of individuals and teams for high achievement and performance. |
| Development | Investment for the future – development of a cadre of future leaders; growth and career progression with clear individual and commercial benefits. |
| Supporting change | Groom for particular change and challenges (e.g. mergers and acquisitions, restructuring, re-engineering). |
| Performance improvement | Improve individual and/or team performance (e.g. improve the capability of leadership and line management). |
| Visioning | New business issues and personal growth. |
| Managing crisis | Change and transition. |
| Problem solving | Address problematic behaviour and/or deficit in interpersonal and leadership capabilities. Overcome and remove personal blocks. |
| Transition | Assist individuals to develop into a new role, new responsibility and/or new context after restructuring. |
| Integration | Assist individual rapid assimilation of a new role, organization and culture. |
| Balance | Assist individuals to achieve work/home balance. |
| Harmony | Assist individuals to achieve harmony and/or spirituality in the workplace by supporting integration and alignment of individual's and organization's goals. |

TABLE 8.1: Reasons for coaching

[1] Quo Group, 'Selection and Development Review', British Psychological Society, February 2001.

In general, coaching is meant to be a practical, goal-focused form of personal, one-on-one or one-to-team learning. It provides those being coached with important feedback that they would not normally receive about personal behaviour, performance, career and organizational issues. Moreover, coaching repositions the individual in the centre of those factors that contribute to his or her effectiveness. Therefore, the onus is on the individual to take an active role during the coaching process.

## WHY COACHING FOR CHANGE AND HARMONY?

‹ Because self-awareness and looking inward is where all change begins ›
Brandt, 'Corporate Pioneers Explore Spirituality', *HR Magazine*, pp. 82–7, April 1996.

In the environment of rapid socio-technological change and global market forces, most organizations are in a process of continual reshaping. As a result, individuals in organizations have a need to embrace changes and to reflect upon them as a journey to the inner self, in their search for meaning in a newly created organizational reality.

If these individuals occupy senior management roles, this has to take place at two levels. First, defining their own individual search for meaning and, second, translating these meanings for others within their sphere of influence. This is to provide an organizational purpose that can guide the behaviour, ethics, systems and nature of individuals and create a deeper meaning with other stakeholders and the environment.

The individual's internalized purpose can impart a more harmonious alignment with the organizational purpose. In turn, this presents a more effective way forward than the often separate individual's journey and the 'bottom-line' aim of the private sector or 'managing with less' target in public sector organizations. Coaching can provide coachees with capabilities and skills to handle challenges and changes within their role, in addition to anticipation of a future role. As such, coaching can be remedial or developmental.

In order to achieve success, organizations need clarity of purpose and values, and individuals who internalize this intention can easily align themselves and are more likely to find inner harmony than if change is forced upon them. Therefore, the harmonizing is of considerable importance. Coaching can assist in the synchronization of purpose and values for both the organization and the individuals and assist in defining these goals and enabling their realization. Coaching may be internally provided by one's manager, peer specialist (e.g. HR professional) or by an external expert. In order to illustrate benefits from different approaches to coaching we can examine now the designs of coaching by external expert and co-coaching.

## AN EXAMPLE OF EFFECTIVE COACHING BY EXTERNAL EXPERTS

This example illustrates a method utilized by an International Financial Company (IFC) to develop employees' capabilities to cope with transformational changes.

### Background

The IFC was a single channel business, servicing its customers through branch offices. In the course of organic growth, considerable effort was made to develop a high performing management. In the 1990s, branch customers fell steadily in the UK and all competition had expanded into other channels of client services. At the strategic meeting for planning multi-channel service procedures, senior managers realized that they were unprepared to manage fundamental change. Hence, the decision was taken to employ external coaching to facilitate the process for anticipated change on a voluntary basis for all senior managers.

## Human Resources role and selection of coaches

Senior Human Resources (HR) professionals were assigned to the management team. They helped to develop strategies and had a role in the selection of coaches. The HR department was responsible for monitoring the coaching impact against 360 degree feedback and personal development plans. Given no previous experience of coaching, the HR department tendered for a service provision and the criteria for selection included: credentials, track record and reputation. In addition, matching coaching experience and style with the coached person's needs was undertaken.

## Coaching provision

The prime coaching emphasis was on fostering capabilities for change. Hence, coaching was more oriented towards the coached person's future role and position than the current job. In other words, coaching was primarily focused on pulling out potential, commitment and expertise rather than on improving existing skills, knowledge and experience. However, both strategies were in operation. Furthermore, coaching was used to identify high potential individuals and groom them for the future, to assist some individuals to accept new roles after merger, and for some to achieve harmony in the new workplace.

## Evaluation

Coaching was not evaluated against the bottom line impact, but against 360 degree feedback and personal development plans (PDPs). Moreover, a staff survey revealed that managers viewed coaching as an important development tool. It enabled considerable high performance in a time of change, and enabled individuals to understand the new reality and find harmony in the workplace. Considering the voluntary nature of the initiative and the expressed demand, coaching was judged to be an effective tool for change.

# AN EXAMPLE OF EFFECTIVE CO-COACHING WITHIN AN ORGANIZATION

An alternative approach to expert coaching can be explored through a review of a combined health service organization (HSO) and corporate sector manufacturing organization (MO). A co-coaching program was designed to incorporate many of the requirements for successful coaching and to minimize the risks associated with a conventional expert and/or boss/subordinate coaching arrangement. These risks mainly concern the role conflict that may occur in conditions of disclosure of weakness to a boss or authority figure. This may have distinct managerial as well as developmental implications for the individuals being coached.

The purpose of the co-coaching program was to accelerate the development of managerial capability for middle managers who had clear potential for additional responsibility and promotion. In pursuit of these goals, the program sought to provide participants with competency-based feedback about strengths and development needs in the workplace, together with the development of feedback and coaching skills. This was achieved through the creation of co-coaching pairs that, once established, would continue to work together for a 12-month period following the initial workshop.

Overall the approach was concerned with providing a supportive environment that encourages participants to pursue an open, confidential coaching relationship and to feel able to experiment with new ideas, behaviours and future commitments and most importantly provide 'fellow travellers on this journey toward wisdom'.[2]

Although from a mentoring perspective, Bell (2000) mentions the issue of 'readiness', this concept has equally valid application in a coaching context. The issue of readiness includes the process of 'levelling the learning field', which Bell describes as stripping the relationship of any nuances of mentor power or command. The creation of rapport in the relationship is accomplished by allowing the learning process to be superordinate, removing the mask of managerial supremacy.

In a co-coaching context this has been achieved through the use of explicit ground rules that stress empathy, authenticity, respect for others, and learning from experience. In our example, participants on the program were encouraged to work on understanding what these words mean for the everyday practice of coaching.

We will now explain co-coaching in more detail.

## CO-COACHING: WHAT IS IT?

The co-coaching process is principally about forming a mutually supportive relationship, usually with a managerial peer. The relationship may be within an organization or across several organizations, but is usually in different disciplines. The principle is that the co-coaching pairs are at roughly the same level with each other. This allows both parties to benefit from each other's different experiences, but minimizes the disadvantages associated with boss-subordinate coaching. Nevertheless, this form of coaching can and should be complementary to the process outlined here.

The co-coaching system applies a progressively acquired skill to each member of the co-coaching pair in a circular fashion, using the following broad sequence:

- ☐ Identification of important/priority issues for development.
- ☐ Making sense of information.
- ☐ Reaching conclusions and making decisions.
- ☐ Developing new ways of seeing situations, people and issues.
- ☐ Building on strengths and minimizing weaknesses.

This approach has some similarities with the 'developmental alliance' identified by Hay (1995).[3] The following describes some underlying values, which have been found to permeate the successful co-coaching process:

- ☐ Growth and development are natural human drives.
- ☐ We are all capable of taking charge of our own development.
- ☐ We are capable of helping other people to think through and make their own decisions.

Hay provides a useful conceptual distinction between coaching, counselling and a developmental alliance. She says that coaching is diametrically opposed to a developmental

[2] C Bell, 'Mentoring as partnership' in M Goldsmith, L Lyons and A Freas (Eds.), *Coaching for Leadership*, Jossey Bass Wiley, 2000.
[3] J Hay, *Transformational Mentoring*, McGraw Hill, 1995.

alliance, insofar as the developmental alliance is person-led, long term and broad focus, while coaching is organization-led, short term and with a specific focus. Although primarily a 'coaching' orientation as defined by Hay, co-coaching includes a person-centred method to find opportunities for growth and development. Within co-coaching there is a much greater emphasis upon building a relationship as a basis for skill development and learning.

In consideration of co-coaching, it is useful to differentiate between various approaches in helping people:

☐ **Telling** – An individual gives assistance by telling the other person what to do. This technique is largely problem-centred and excludes the other person from the problem-solving process. It is often used where there is clearly defined knowledge and/or skills transfer and the recipient lacks knowledge or skill in the particular domain.

☐ **Advising** – An individual assists by giving advice. This is usually problem-centred and includes the advice recipient in the problem-solving process. The advisor will often generate possible options and help the other person to select a particular solution. The risk with this approach is that the advisor will only offer solutions within their own area of knowledge and expertise; solutions that are unlikely to violate the other person's expectations.

☐ **Manipulating** – This method appears to be centred towards the individual, but actually excludes him or her. In this situation, the manipulating individual may influence the person or the situation and even provide a solution. However, this takes place without the other person being aware of what has happened or understanding the process of achieving a solution.

Co-coaching is an approach which seeks to reconcile the need to acquire and develop short-term knowledge or skills with personal insights about the process of acquisition and the implications for future contexts. Co-coaching also affords an opportunity to give as well as to receive coaching in a spirit of reciprocity and trust.

## Coaching through a co-coaching process

All of the above approaches to help people can be appropriate means of development, depending upon circumstances. The choice of the right technique requires consideration of a number of factors, including the level of current skills, the managerial context, previous experience, the specific needs of the person to be coached and the time and resources available.

# CO-COACHING PROGRAM STRUCTURE

The co-coaching program consists of a substantial amount of pre-work. This involves a 360 degree competency-based questionnaire and a range of personality inventories. These questionnaires and inventories help to reveal how participants in the program are perceived at work and, to some degree, to see how they perceive themselves in terms of personality preferences and work style. The participants summarize this pre-work and use the insights gained to inform the process of forming the co-coaching pairs, through the active presentation of themselves to others in the group.

The basic structure of the program is organized around four stages: contracting, exploring, understanding and action. In practice, this is often a cyclical process; as new issues are uncovered it may be necessary to start the process again from the beginning, sometimes re-contracting to take account of a different set of circumstances.

☐ **Contracting** – This stage outlines the reason for having the coaching session, what both parties hope to achieve, ground rules, respective roles and any limitations of involvement, confidentiality issues and the frequency of the meetings. This stage is also about creating the environment for coaching, establishing rapport, putting the other person at their ease, building trust and encouraging openness.

☐ **Exploring** – Involves trying to get a full and broad picture of what is or has been happening. Exploring what information the participants have and from what source, trying to establish what they think and feel about their current and past experiences. This usually entails some understanding of the context within which each party in the co-coaching process is working. There is some initial focus on specific issues and an attempt to challenge perceptions and underlying assumptions that may appear inconsistent or inaccurate.

☐ **Understanding** – Following the exploration of the problem, parties to co-coaching work to communicate to the other person their point of view. This is after successful probing, when they feel that they understand the cause of an issue or a concern facing them and are ready to confirm that understanding. The effect for the other party is a reaffirmation or change in perception and understanding as a result of feedback, interpretation and challenge.

☐ **Action** – The actions taken by participants after the co-coaching are the tangible results of the process. However, the work environment may not provide the support and encouragement for outcomes from the co-coaching sessions. It is key to incorporate some clear guidelines if positive actions are to be achieved from the process. These guidelines should include:

☐ A clear specification of outcomes.

☐ Creative generation of ideas for action.

☐ Clear identification of support resources.

☐ The need to draw up an action plan, usually with specific objectives, success criteria and time limits.

These stages each contain a set of sub-processes that will need to be repeated at every co-coaching meeting. However, as the relationship develops, different stages may be emphasized.

## CO-COACHING AND MOVING ON

The co-coaching process is intended to last for 12 months and both parties prepare for the final separation as part of the operation. The co-coaching partners agree to meet at regular intervals throughout the year and the stages from contracting through to action is completed either in individual sessions or over two or three meetings. In the course of moving on, both co-coaches have an opportunity to consider the whole procedure of forming, developing and building independence in their partner and therefore acquire an exemplar coaching process skill for future application and learning.

## THE BENEFITS OF CO-COACHING

The benefits of the co-coaching approach, mainly concern relationship aspects of the process:

☐ Receiving an alternative perspective from a skilled colleague who is always on your side.

☐ A reasonably safe environment in which to work out problems.

☐ A means of self-development which is largely within your control.

☐ A model for an authentic relationship based upon trust and confidentiality.

## CO-COACHING OUTPUTS

Participants in the co-coaching process develop improved feedback and coaching skills, as well as many personal insights. These serve as potential benefits to all future subordinates and peers the participants may subsequently coach. Most importantly, participants have experienced an approach to coaching that has a philosophical foundation in the acknowledgement of the concurrent individual and organizational needs. The method recognizes the necessity to reconcile these through a development process based on equitable treatment and shared values.

With regards to evaluation, a number of longitudinal approaches are used. These include 360 degree pre and post-competency based appraisal, line management appraisal, peer review and rate of progress in the organization. These measures are used in benchmarked exercises within organizations, where comparisons are made between the more conventional and the co-coaching approach. The early results tend to suggest that the co-coaching process whereby pairs are on the same level, works best in *conjunction* with a traditional boss-subordinate coaching model. This works well, particularly amongst high potential participants who need both coaching support from a member of the senior management, while developing coaching skills in a climate as free as possible of implicit assumptions about an individual coachee's role in the hierarchy.

## COACHING AND CO-COACHING SKILLS: TOWARDS RECONCILING CHANGE AND HARMONY

> ❛Today's leader is a people developer and relationship builder who asks 'how can I help this person become more valuable as an individual as well as to all of us? Today's leader is a coach.❜
>
> D Sethi, 'Coaching from below' in M Goldsmith, L Lyons and A Freas (Eds.), *op. cit.*, 2000.

Coaching is required by many managers who need to address immediate issues and build capability to perform in the future. Whether coaching is for immediate performance in the short term or in the long term, the coaching experience requires a clear process, an authentic relationship and a climate characterized by reciprocity and trust.

The idea of a partnership for learning is an important aspect of the coaching technique. This process starts with rapport between those individuals involved in the coaching. The partnership moves through the use of empathy towards advice and feedback, finally developing autonomy and independence in the coachee. The creation of a safe climate for effective coaching is critical. Moreover, productive coaching requires skill, self-discipline and mutual trust.[4] Both the expert coaching and co-coaching role require some common key skills, in addition to the fundamental needs of those who require to be coached and some shared processes.

A skill set believed to be essential for effective coaching, in both the expert coaching and co-coaching model, is presented in Table 8.2. Coaches need to deal with contextual realities by

---

[4] D Sethi, 'Coaching from below', in M Goldsmith, L Lyons and A Freas (Eds.), *op. cit.*, 2000.

understanding the personality and motivations involved. By doing this, they will be able to mitigate potential negative attitudes and practices of power that are subsumed within the social fabric of organizational structure and to keep their work at a professional level.

☐ Active listening.

☐ Effective questioning.

☐ Building and maintaining rapport.

☐ Articulating empathy and distance.

☐ Providing feedback.

☐ Providing insights and perspective.

☐ Allowing the coached to explore and make sense of new reality.

☐ Focusing on and linking content with process.

☐ Mature reflection.

☐ Reading non-verbal behaviour.

☐ Defining and analysing the coachee's intention, behaviour and impact.

☐ Reframing.

☐ Goal setting.

☐ Establishing commitment in those coached.

TABLE 8.2: Coaching and co-coaching key skills

In addition to the well-designed coaching program and skilful coach, the potential coachee has to see the need for coaching intervention and be committed to the coaching procedure. Key needs for coachees are presented in Table 8.3.

☐ Desire to learn.

☐ Ability for self-reflection.

☐ Self-assessment of own needs.

☐ Desire to receive feedback.

☐ Ability to trust and to be open.

☐ Commitment to coaching intervention.

TABLE 8.3: Key characteristics for those coached and co-coached

Although coaching is an open-ended process, which analyses the present situation, defines the performance goal, elicits personal and extra-personal resources, and implements a plan for achieving the goal and evaluates these achievements, it also has some key core processes. These provide a framework within which coaching takes place. Some common, key coaching practices are presented in Table 8.4.

☐ Explore the current predicament in terms of personal reactions, needs and possibilities.

☐ Set specific goals and aims for the coaching process.

☐ Identify the options to achieve a realistic goal.

☐ Commit to a timed action plan to attain the goal.

☐ Evaluate achievements.

TABLE 8.4: Key processes in expert and co-coaching models

All coaching models' strategies embrace, in varying degrees the concepts of assessment, visioning, exploration or strategizing, action or performing and reflection and evaluating, in order to enable understanding and change. The self-reflecting nature of coaching makes it essential for coachees and co-coachees to seek insights into how their own assumptions and views are constructed, and to define and understand perceived challenges or issues before they are addressed.

## SUMMARY

1   This chapter has considered the process of coaching within an organization from the perspective of a fundamental need to reconcile change with harmony. This brief overview has identified the need to base any coaching endeavour upon a relationship characterized by trust and reciprocity.

2   The differences between mentoring and coaching can sometimes be blurred to benefit understanding and to capitalize on the need to base short-term skill formation and development upon high integrity work-based relationships.

3   There are necessary but insufficient elements within a traditional coaching relationship, and two approaches to coaching can comfortably co-exist to aid both the organization and the individual.

4   The context for coaching has to allow for the open exploration of developmental issues, together with the capability of constructive evaluation. It is only with the combination of these two elements that coaching for change and harmony is likely to happen. Coaching and co-coaching address some fundamental human needs to learn and to develop socially. Both provide a deeply rewarding and personal way for the knowledge to be shared and co-created.

# CHAPTER 9

# BEYOND MANAGEMENT DEVELOPMENT: FACILITATING GROUNDED, EXPERIENTIAL LEARNING

## INTRODUCTION

Individuals and organizations seek new knowledge, insight, perspectives and practices, and consultants and management development specialists are used to satisfy this urge. Continuous learning is now fundamental to organizations' success in our increasingly global, competitive and turbulent world. The ability of all consultants, not only management development specialists, to transfer their expertise to members of client organizations is also becoming a key factor in commercial success. Helping individuals and organizations to learn and develop is not solely the remit of management development initiatives, but is intrinsic to culture change and corporate transformation processes – any consultant attempting to bring about significant change will need these skills in the future.

Despite their undoubted importance in fostering and disseminating knowledge, management development initiatives, especially classroom-based courses and programs, have a history of promising more than they deliver. They often fail to bring about the tangible changes in organizational actions required for success. It seems that many individuals absorb little, retain less and apply very little indeed.

Questions have long been raised about the efficacy of management development courses. The criticisms have focused on their intangible nature and hard to measure effects. One response has been attempts to assess the quality and value of the courses through feedback questionnaires, endearingly called 'happy sheets' by trainers, and post-course appraisal interviews with line mangers and human resources professionals. Another has been to introduce follow-up projects and reviews to embed the learning and translate it more directly to the workplace. Relatively little, though, has changed in terms of how most training events and courses are conceived and structured as a learning experience for managers. For the most part, management development initiatives tend to be disconnected from the organizational reality of the participants. They also emphasize teaching and the performance of the trainer, often at the expense of learning.

Some organizations and human resource specialists are embracing the possibilities offered by the internet. Many management development curricula now incorporate newer, more flexible, and cheaper, web-based approaches, placing the onus for learning on the individual.

However, classroom-based courses still remain an important component of the overall learning process for individuals. For the most part, managers work, make decisions and interact with others in their own and other organizations: managerial work is essentially social in nature. Live, facilitated group events are vital to develop awareness, judgement and interpersonal skills. Moreover, the input from and interaction with outsiders and colleagues are especially valuable in creating fundamental shifts in mind-set and approach that enable organizational renewal. The intimacy and sharing of experience generated by classroom-based courses also foster creativity, innovation and the exploration of new ways in which the organization might work. In their typical form, management development courses are ill-suited to today's manager. Yet they are vital in rapidly changing markets and in increasingly collaborative and networked organizational forms. They cannot be abandoned, but must be reconceived to make them more meaningful and to serve the needs of the managers of today. Consultants and management development specialists will have to rise to the challenge or find their role and value questioned.

This chapter addresses the role and nature of formal classroom-based courses and programs, the centre-piece of most training and development initiatives within organizations. Specifically, this chapter:

☐ Analyses typical management development approaches and highlights some shortcomings.

☐ Proposes an approach to classroom-based in-house learning that is embedded in the context and reality of the organization, and focuses attention on experience and reflection.

☐ Describes how such an approach was used successfully to develop and facilitate a number of master-classes for a global systems consultancy.

☐ Sets out some practical guidelines for the creation and facilitation of grounded, experiential learning events or programmes.

## MANAGEMENT DEVELOPMENT: IMPLICIT ASSUMPTION AND HIDDEN SHORTCOMINGS

About a decade ago, management education came under the spotlight.[1] There was a perception that managers were under-trained and under-educated, and the potential implications for organizations' ability to compete in world markets led to efforts to increase management training, and education in general.

More, however, has not necessarily meant better. The training and education of managers or other professional groups has become quite a distinct genre, characterized by short modules on well-defined subjects, small class sizes, high levels of trainer input, interaction and participation, and many exercises, examples and project work. The emphasis is on practical techniques, succinct models and easy to apply prescriptions. In many ways, management development is more akin to being taught at nursery school than to university education.

[1] G Salaman and J Butler, 'Why Managers Won't Learn', *Management Development and Education*, Vol. 21 (3), pp. 183–191, 1990.

The management development style described above evolved in response to a number of obvious, and some more deep-rooted, factors. At a very basic level, managers have work pressures that do not permit them to take, frequently at any rate, extended periods of time away from the workplace to peruse and ponder. Both managers and training providers feel the need to cram as much into a short period as possible. Managers want to get the most from the limited time for training. Training providers want to demonstrate the value they add, and so justify their fees. Quality in some circumstances may fall victim to quantity.

Management development courses also have to cope with differing motivations of attendees. Some experienced management trainers categorize attendees into three groups:

1  Learners, who are genuinely interested in the subject and in learning, and are prepared to work and contribute on the courses.

2  Holiday-makers, who regard going on courses as a form of vacation and consequently as a way of getting out of work and relaxing – if they learn something it's a bonus.

3  Prisoners, who have been sent on the course by their managers, and who generally think they have nothing to learn and that it is a waste of their time.

If these are truly the motivations of attendees, then management development courses are justifiably closer to nursery school classes than university lectures. Trainers use short input sessions, animation and performance, discussions and interaction, exercises and practical examples to hold the course together. The learners are actively involved and absorb the input, the holiday-makers are entertained and the prisoners are co-opted and given one or two ideas to take back to the workplace.

Clearly, the skill in engaging a disparate audience is and remains vital. An over-emphasis on style over substance, and simplicity of prescription over richness of explanation, however, can ultimately be detrimental even if it is initially appreciated. According to Huczynski,[2] management gurus and development specialists promote the acceptance and continuity of management fads. They take academic research and concepts and the practices of leading organizations, and translate these into themes, methodologies and courses accessible to managers. In doing so, they reduce the complexity, remove the caveats and recast tendencies into predictions. Management gurus and development specialists play on a set of perceived managerial needs:

☐ Managers are not academics. They regard knowledge as instrumental in achieving their goals, and hence seek prescriptions rather than general understanding.

☐ Managers value predictability and the clarity offered by cause and effect linkages in relation to actions.

☐ Managers are expected to be in control of activities, results and the people who work for them, and so they value tools and techniques through which they can exert or demonstrate adequate control.

☐ Managers operate within a social environment where their status, authority and career prospects are shaped by their ability to project confidence and to be versed in the latest management thinking and practices.

☐ Managers are individuals needing differing levels of security, recognition, support and legitimacy, and look to externally validated knowledge and practices to fill these needs.

96

[2] A A Huczynski, *Management Gurus: What makes them and how to become one*, Routledge, 1993.

These needs have been used to craft ever more attractive and succinct messages, as management gurus and consulting firms have competed for managers' attention. Successful experiences in a few organizations and limited research findings have often been packaged as universal truths, disconnected from organizational contexts. As fads such as Total Quality Management (TQM), Business Process Re-engineering (BPR), Empowerment, the Learning Organization, and the dot.coms have waxed and waned, the promise of new knowledge and lasting solutions has often fizzled out in disillusionment.

Rather than moderate their claims or provide depth and richness in their expositions, gurus and development specialists have tended to improve their delivery and performance. Clark[3] argues that consultancy is essentially an intangible and difficult to define service. Consequently, consultants need to draw upon symbolic means to project competence and value. Management gurus, in particular, use theatrical techniques of energy, drama, suspense, and counterpoint to convert the audience to the gurus' way of thinking and to restructure managers' ways of thinking. Central to the popular management development process is the performance of the trainer and the impression it creates in the minds of attendees, sometimes overshadowing the substantive knowledge or techniques covered in the course itself.

Bold, abstract messages, however polished the delivery, are less likely to appeal to managers in the future. The creation and application of unique knowledge in a customer-focused way are seen as central to growth and prosperity. Uncertainty, complexity and discontinuities are normal and are embraced as opportunities. Control is being replaced with collaboration, and management increasingly resembles facilitation. For many, the collapse of the dot.com bubble at the start of the century brought about a realization that there are no 'silver bullets' or magic formulas for commercial success. The need for depth and the appreciation of nuances in a subject are being recognized.

As Salaman and Butler[4] point out, the emphasis on performance can impede learning. It promotes passive reception, with little effort demanded of attendees to see for themselves the relevance, application and practicality of concepts presented. Short exercises, where attendees mechanically apply techniques, are rarely challenging or stretching. They frequently facilitate problem solving by rote, or single loop learning,[5] but generally fail to promote a searching examination of individuals' own thought processes and preconceptions. Learning is more superficial: understanding and appreciation are replaced by acceptance and awareness.

The prevailing approach also does little to address the resistance to learning implied by the label 'prisoners'. The training needs analysis, the course development and the delivery are undertaken largely by management development specialists, usually supervised by Human Resources (HR) professionals. Senior line managers occasionally put in a guest appearance, but otherwise delegate responsibility for the development of core skills and competencies. Whether prompted by arrogance, prior disillusionment or a perception of irrelevance, resistance to learning is a cause for concern, especially where the learning is intended to bring about change in a working environment. The preaching of generic, pre-packaged concepts by outsiders disconnects recipients of management development courses from their organizational environment.

This disconnection manifests itself at many levels:

☐ The subjects discussed are shaped and structured according to external parameters, such as academic fields or professional disciplines.

☐ Examples and problems discussed are generic and stylized.

---

[3] T Clark, *Managing Consultants: Consultancy as the Management of Impressions*, Open University Press, 1995.

[4] G Salaman and J Butler, *op. cit.*, 1990.

[5] C Argyris, 'Double Loop Learning in Organizations', Harvard Business Review, Sept–Oct, 115–125, 1977.

☐ Values advocated in courses may be at odds with experienced organizational values expressed through hierarchies and power structure.

☐ Best practices may not be aligned to internal, and often tacit, recipes for personal and organizational success.

☐ Organizational routines, expectations and constraints are finessed.

☐ Political tensions and cultural assumptions are side-stepped.

☐ Real-life issues and concerns of attendees are barely touched upon.

The context in which people work is avoided or missing from most management development courses. The nuances of how an organization works or what makes it successful in its particular environment are brushed over by general statements and assertions. Individuals who have succeeded by 'learning the ropes' may, rightly, not want to jeopardize their prospects by taking on dubious, pseudo-academic strictures. Yet continuous learning and change appear fundamental to organizational life in the future.

# GROUNDED, EXPERIENTIAL LEARNING

There have been numerous positive developments over the last decade or so, and there are some undoubtedly good examples of management development courses.[6] Management training is now far more accessible and informed. Business schools offer a wide range of in-house and open courses, and have injected research-based knowledge and rigour into the content of these courses. In general, management development specialists try to engage with attendees, are more skilled presenters and communicators, and are more sensitive to the pressures and concerns of managers. Training needs analyses are conducted more thoroughly to assess key issues and learning requirements. Senior managers are becoming more supportive of and involved in development initiatives.

The Grounded, Experiential Learning approach builds on and extends these positive developments in three complementary ways (see Table 9.1).

Key to the design of an event seeking to facilitate Grounded, Experiential Learning is the 'learning cycle'. The learning cycle refers to the process by which individuals, teams and organizations learn; namely experience stimuli in the form of ideas, observations, thoughts and actions, make sense of their experiences and consequently modify their behaviours.[7] There are four main sources of input or stimulus for learning:

1 **Concepts/ideas** – The frameworks and (action) theories individuals use to plan actions or make sense of events; they are the building blocks of mental models or paradigms used to shape, usually subconsciously, everyday life.

2 **Implications/applications** – The actions, prediction or routines emanating from individuals' theories of the world.

3 **Experiences/actions** – Arise as individuals immerse themselves in the 'doing' of a task or living/acting out of a situation.

4 **Reflections/synthesis** – The outcomes of reviewing what has been done and experienced.

Structured learning is best facilitated and consolidated if inputs are linked systematically, and if individual learning styles and dispositions are accommodated. The learning cycle is illustrated in Figure 9.1.

[6] K Patching, *Management And Organisation Development: beyond arrows, boxes and circles*, Macmillan Press Ltd, 1999.
[7] D Kolb, *Experiential Learning*, Prentice Hall Inc., 1984.

| 1 LEARNING | The approach redresses the current imbalance between teaching and learning: |
|---|---|
| | ☐ The role of the trainer(s), consultants or faculty is to facilitate a learning experience rather than to teach a pre-defined course or subject. |
| | ☐ The experiential, tacit knowledge of participants is acknowledged and valued, as well as the formal or codified knowledge inherent in theories and/or best practices. |
| | ☐ The course is designed to foster personal discovery, realization, reflection and self-assessment. |
| 2 GROUNDED | The approach grounds or embeds the learning experience within the organizational reality of the participants: |
| | ☐ The development and facilitation of the event is a joint effort and a shared responsibility between external consultants and respected line managers. |
| | ☐ The course content is a combination of concepts, principles and external best practices, and internal strategies, policies and procedures. |
| | ☐ Organization-specific case studies provide the specific context for exploring and applying new ideas and concepts. |
| 3 EXPERIENTIAL | The approach emphasizes action and experience over passive absorption: |
| | ☐ Numerous opportunities are provided to live out, and observe, meaningful situations through role-plays and business simulations. |
| | ☐ Feedback is offered by peers and facilitators on individuals' actions in role-plays and simulations. |
| | ☐ Individuals are encouraged to reflect upon their experiences and their own, previously unconscious, biases, assumptions and predispositions |

TABLE 9.1: Grounded, experiential learning

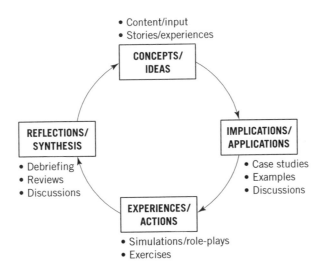

- Content/input
- Stories/experiences

**CONCEPTS/IDEAS**

**IMPLICATIONS/APPLICATIONS**
- Case studies
- Examples
- Discussions

**EXPERIENCES/ACTIONS**
- Simulations/role-plays
- Exercises

**REFLECTIONS/SYNTHESIS**
- Debriefing
- Reviews
- Discussions

FIGURE 9.1: The learning cycle

Unlike other management development approaches, the Grounded, Experiential Learning approach places far more emphasis on experiences/actions and reflections/synthesis. The concepts and ideas covered in a course only have a significant and lasting effect in a work environment if they are assimilated and integrated into participants' ways of thinking and acting. New insights, techniques and knowledge need to fuse with existing knowledge and routines. This sense-making process is fundamental to learning, and is both triggered by action and is retrospective in nature. The notion of sense-making is best captured by the phrase: 'How do I know what I mean until I see what I say?'[8]

Experiencing even a simulated situation, as participant or observer, has a more profound effect than hearing stories or abstract principles. Basing simulations on organization-specific case studies further narrows the gap between the abstract concepts and ideas, and the reality of organizational life. Individuals are presented with possible scenarios, are expected to draw on both new and existing skills and deal with a live situation. Rich, constructive feedback, from both facilitators and peers, highlights unnoticed tendencies and helps to make sense of, and integrate, the concepts and ideas discussed. The involvement of senior managers in offering suggestions, addressing misconceptions and translating the ideas into the work context, with all its imperfections and constraints, helps to embed the learning. Abstract notions are made meaningful, relevant and easily grasped. The approach shares many of the advantages of on-the-job coaching or mentoring, advocated by some as the most effective form of learning.[9,10] Yet, it provides greater focus, intensity and structure, and importantly a risk-free environment.

The Grounded, Experiential Learning method places the onus on the participants to extract as much from the course as possible, rather than have development specialists cram it with content. It is the participants who perform in, or more accurately live out, simulated situations, not the facilitators. There are no pat answers offered, but detailed debriefs of complex simulations. Time is allowed for personal reflection. Previously vague thoughts crystallize and become connected into more meaningful wholes. Participants gain a deeper understanding of what they knew already, as well as what they learn from the inputs, discussions, and simulations. The facilitators provide input as in conventional courses, and they may play roles. More importantly, the facilitators help to make sense of the concepts in a real world setting and share their expertise, knowledge and perspectives with that of the participants. In many ways they role model the nurturing and leadership behaviours that are the hallmark of future managers.

## GROUNDED, EXPERIENTIAL LEARNING IN PRACTICE

One highly successful global consultancy, specializing in the development and implementation of IT systems, has benefited from the grounded experiential learning approach. Critical to the company's future commercial success were the skills and competencies of its project, program and engagement managers to handle its increasingly complex, multinational assignments.

In 2000, Syscon (the name has been changed for reasons of confidentiality) was involved in a wide range of systems development and implementation, including the customization of applications, bespoke developments and internet solutions. Increasingly, Syscon was being asked to implement worldwide Enterprise Resource Planning (ERP) solutions, to undertake Enterprise Application Integration (EAI) programs integrating legacy systems to web-based portals or pages, and to help set up dot.com companies from scratch. Despite being highly

[8] K Weick, *Sensemaking in Organizations*, Sage, 1995.
[9] A Mumford, *Management Development: Strategies for Action*, Institute of Personnel Management, 1993.
[10] N Dixon, *The Organizational Learning Cycle: How We Can Learn Collectively*, McGraw Hill, 1994.

competent in managing discrete IT implementation projects, many of the project managers asked to take on these complex programs lacked the necessary capabilities. Syscon senior management sensed that their project managers needed to 'raise their games' significantly to address the cultural, political and organizational challenges of spearheading major transformation programs.

Syscon developed a global 'Competencies Matrix' linked to the complexity of projects and programs, drawing on the experience and insight of senior managers, and defined a set of skills and competencies required to manage complex Syscon programs. A project/program management (PM) master-class was developed jointly by Syscon and specialist external support including the author. The class was piloted in May 2000, modified slightly, and rolled out from September 2000 on a global basis.

The week long PM master-class is currently offered at a rate of about ten classes per year. It is jointly facilitated by external consultants and senior Syscon managers within the operating regions. The learning cycle underpins the master-class, with each element of the cycle addressed, as far as practicable, within each of the sessions. While addressing a wide range of substantive subject areas, around one-third of the class time is dedicated to running and debriefing simulations. A Syscon case study in four parts provides the context for many of the challenging and complex business simulations and a mechanism for integrating the various subject areas into a cohesive whole. Particular attention is paid to creating a stimulating, risk-free and supportive environment. This encourages participants to share their experience and to contribute to the discussions and group learning throughout the class. Participants consistently comment that the most learning occurs through the simulations.

The PM master-class has far exceeded the expectations of Syscon senior management and participants. It has:

☐ Given many participants a new perspective on their role and a deeper understanding of how to support or bring about major strategic change.

☐ Changed their approach to dealing with senior managers in client organizations and to working in partnership with client staff and other consultancies, which has contributed to greater success on their programs.

☐ Initiated a shift in mind-set and attitudes that has made participants more tolerant of uncertainty, more embracing of change and more aware of wider business influences.

☐ Made participants more flexible and responsive – more adept at improvising and drawing on a repertoire of skills, rather than applying a familiar but rigid approach.

The success of the PM master-class inspired the development of a similar class for client managers (CMs) responsible for the marketing of consulting services and the relationship with key clients. The subject areas were tailored to the needs of CMs and new case studies drafted, but the class format and style were retained. The CM master-class piloted in December 2001, and is being rolled out across Europe initially. As before, the CM master-class met the expectations of Syscon senior management and participants, and received particular praise for its thought-provoking simulations. For many, the class has highlighted the need to be more subtle, more attentive and more flexible in their dealing with clients.

The success of the Grounded, Experiential Learning approach within Syscon is all the more remarkable given the background and seniority of the participants. As medical staff will tell you, doctors make the worst patients. Similarly, talented consultants often make reluctant course participants and find it difficult to critically examine their own shortcomings.[11] Despite a wealth of experience and mounting external distractions, participants remain engaged throughout the class. Most are taken by surprise by its intensity and the extent to which it stirs emotions, stimulates thoughts and causes them to question taken for granted assumptions. Some find the detailed feedback uncomfortable until they appreciate the richness and depth it offers in terms of learning opportunities. Senior management regards the significant investment, both in direct costs and foregone income, as well worthwhile.

# CREATING GROUNDED, EXPERIENTIAL LEARNING PROGRAMS

The Grounded, Experiential Learning approach is distinct from conventional management development, but is not esoteric, nor is it unproven. Those who have experienced it sing its praises and wonder: 'Why isn't more training done this way?' Success, though, comes at a price. Paradoxically, the concept of facilitating a learning experience that puts the responsibility on participants to be involved, to share and to actively learn, requires more skills and effort on the part of the facilitators. Embedding the learning within the context and culture of the organization also places a notable responsibility on the organization's senior managers.

Three areas merit specific attention by those wanting to apply the approach.

## 1 Shifting from teaching to facilitating

The design of a course, the subjects covered and the pre-prepared slides and other materials are necessary as a store of knowledge and a guide to action, but should not become an indispensable crutch or rigid format. Mechanical adherence to agendas, timetables and prescribed content can inhibit interaction, thought and creativity, and can even take on the aura of a strait-jacket. Facilitation is essentially a helping relationship, enabling others to gain for themselves a better appreciation of, or insight into, a situation or issue. Facilitators need to focus their attention on the participants, not the content. Although disconcerting and sometimes draining, facilitators should try to make the process more responsive, open to question, and inclusive:

☐ Responsiveness relates to addressing the subjects, issues and concerns of the participants, as fully as time and expertise allows.

☐ Openness to question is intended to accommodate differing views as participants share their constructions of reality and how the organization works.

☐ Inclusiveness relates to incorporating participants' concepts and experiences into the course, thereby helping to integrate and fuse the concepts, knowledge and insights offered by the facilitators with those held by participants and more widely in the organization.

A learning experience is essentially co-created and unpredictable. Clearly, the facilitators should be confident and fluent in the subject areas, and up to speed with the latest research and advances in theory. They should also be able to communicate and explain concepts and ideas. Yet, they should not privilege their knowledge, but regard it as partial and always subject to revision. The role is one of offering alternative perspectives, re-framing issues and shaping conceptions. Facilitators should pay attention to how their ideas are being received and interpreted:

☐ Concepts and ideas, recast in relation to their work situations, provide vital clues in piecing together participants' mind-sets, interpretations and learning processes.

[11] C Argyris, 'Teaching Smart People How To Learn', *Harvard Business Review*, May–June, pp. 99–109, 1991.

☐ Disagreement hints at the perceived tensions between theory and experience, external best practices and internal routines.

☐ The articulation of lessons learned by participants helps the facilitators to adjust the time allocated to specific subjects, discussions, simulations and debriefs, making the whole learning experience more relevant and powerful.

Facilitators and consultants who presume the superiority of their paradigm and insist on proving that they are right in the face of resistance or disagreement with more explanations and references, are at best winning Pyrrhic victories.

## 2 Grounding the learning experience

The external facilitators or consultants play only one part. Grounding the event or program requires senior management involvement beyond defining the key skills and competencies to be addressed:

☐ Developing organization-specific case studies that are interesting and realistic requires effort and the willingness on the part of the organization to expose possible shortcomings in individuals and practices.

☐ Credible managers have to be prepared to facilitate fully the learning experience alongside external consultants or specialists, and to adapt their behaviour in favour of a supportive, mentoring role.

☐ The internal and external perspectives have to be woven into a seamless whole, enabled by continuity in senior management participation.

The challenges are many, from securing senior managers' undivided attention during the event to overcoming some senior managers' tendency to perform, to exercise authority and to demonstrate competence and control of the situation, behaviours that have made them successful in their careers.

## 3 Facilitating and making sense of lived experiences

Business simulations and role-plays are very powerful and sometimes threatening vehicles for learning. Run well, simulations enable participants to 'live out', and so experience firsthand, the situation, with some of the emotion and stress involved. They create an intensity and immediacy that is matched by few other learning media. Simulations have to be handled effectively and sensitively, if participants are to experiment, reflect and learn in what they perceive to be a risk-free environment. If participants feel they are role-play victims, unable to exert any control or achieve their objectives, the potential for learning is destroyed.

The learning objectives for each simulation should be clearly defined in advance:

☐ The case study, exercise or scenario should be constructed to draw out key themes, concepts and issues discussed during the formal sessions.

☐ Participants should be briefed, preferably in writing, about the context, purpose and focus of the role-plays or simulations.

☐ Participants should be reminded of the relevant learning objectives, and that they are in a risk-free environment, especially where the simulation results in a significant amount of feedback (implied criticism).

The process for the role-plays or simulations should be structured, and the role-plays separated from the other parts of the event. Facilitators may, in role, play difficult clients or managers, and it is important to make a clear distinction between the facilitator and the character in the simulation. Particular attention should be paid to:

☐ Making it clear when the facilitators are in or out of role, through the use of jackets or other symbols (i.e. wearing them in role, taking them off to mark coming out of role).

☐ Entries and exits by 'role-players', and clapping to mark the end of a simulation.

☐ Guidelines for debriefing by observers and facilitators alike, in particular to focus on positive points and constructive suggestions, and to use the character's name, not the name of the individual playing the role.

The roles to be played by facilitators should be prepared, making the simulation more realistic and believable, and making it easier to draw out key points or issues. In playing their roles, facilitators should:

☐ Actively solicit information or steer the discussion, while still accommodating the natural flow of the interaction.

☐ Remain in role even when participants start laughing or deviating from the simulation script or scenario – by taking it seriously, the facilitator makes it easier for the participants to carry through the simulation.

☐ Voice thoughts and views that would normally not be spoken in order to surface issues and facilitate the debriefing.

Facilitators should follow a consistent format when debriefing the simulations:

☐ Recap on the learning objectives, and the specific context and requirements of the simulation.

☐ Allow some time for those in the simulation to shift back mentally into being participants, collect their thoughts and reflect on their experiences, and for the other participants who have observed to review their notes.

☐ Recount chronologically the salient moments of the simulation, drawing on the notes and contributions of the observers, and analyse the flow of the interaction, highlighting possible connections between and implications of words and actions.

☐ Strike a balance between praising and reinforcing things done well, and pointing out areas for improvement.

☐ Refer specifically to models and concepts discussed during the event, and provide feedback on specific learning objectives, focusing attention on the relevance of the concepts, not on the realism of the simulation.

☐ Formally close the simulation and debrief.

A key skill of the facilitator is to help participants make sense of their experiences, integrating the different elements of the learning cycle into a significant whole. In doing so, the facilitators enable participants to make the shift from relative unreality to relative reality. Debriefed simulations are new scripts, giving participants the confidence and route map to initiate tangible actions once they are back in the workplace.

## SUMMARY

1 In an environment where rapid and continuous learning is a competitive necessity, the ability to transfer knowledge and expertise is highly prized. The techniques and approaches that have served well in the past need to be brought into line with the demands of the present. In particular, we need to put learning at the centre of our efforts to bring about personal and organizational development.

2 However convinced we are in the universality of our approach and methods, we need to embrace the ambiguity and nuance of organizational life. However sound our theories and concepts, we need to tune into tacit knowledge. However compelling our metaphors and stories and well crafted our exercises, we need to give prominence to experience.

3 This chapter has sought to:

☐ Demonstrate how typical management development approaches over-emphasize prescription, performance and generic, formal knowledge.

☐ Show how a Grounded, Experiential Learning approach redresses the current imbalance and better facilitates deeper and more organization-centric learning.

☐ Describe how the approach was used successful for a global systems consultancy.

☐ Set out some practical guidelines for the creation of grounded, experiential learning events or programs.

4 The challenge, as consultants and management development specialists, is to acquire the skills and competencies to support clients in the multitude of circumstances that call for learning.

# CHAPTER 10

## COPING WITH ORGANIZATIONAL POLITICS

### INTRODUCTION

This chapter aims to examine the impact that office politics has on consultants and the consultancy assignment. It is organized into two main sections:

1 **Analysis of the political landscape** – Both from a corporate and an individual perspective.

2 **Action** – To enable the consultant to run assignments successfully within the political constraints of the organization.

However, it is vital first to set out a definition of office politics and to understand when and why it is important for the consultant. Most people, when asked to describe office politics, will use negative language. Manipulating, manoeuvring, string pulling, game playing, back-stabbing, bitching, buck-passing, bullying, sucking up, stamping down, claiming success, to name but a few. Office politics is one of the most talked about dimensions of working life. It is blamed for many of the injustices and wrongdoings we encounter in the workplace. Moreover, it is usually something that *other* people do!

But is it always negative? Certainly, most dictionary definitions carry the pejorative and sinister connotations. Office politics is something devious and underhand. It is about advancing your own agenda at the expense of both others' and the organization's goals. It is about stitching up enemies, making yourself look good, and getting the lion's share of power and glory. So does this mean that all we have to look forward to at work is an unending diet of watching our backs and 'dog eat dog'? What does office politics really involve?

According to one definition it is the covert, rather than the overt, way of getting things done. Certainly, the assumption that office politics is informal rather than formal is well accepted. Thus, it is the information you will not find in the company manual. More than that, office politics implies the acquisition and utilization of power to achieve objectives. This practice can be both constructive and destructive. It can be driven by selfless concern for the general corporate good or by purely selfish motives: on the one hand public spirited, on the other, entirely self-seeking.

In summary, we define office politics as the informal, rather than the formal way of getting results, which can be both constructive and destructive (but most people associate the phrase with negative behaviours).

When and where does the consultant have to be on the look-out for office politics? Let us take one step back, examine the origins and deduce whether these factors still apply. The word 'politics' is derived from the ancient Greek word *polis*, which means city state – the organizational structure introduced to help create some order in a society with many diverse, and sometimes conflicting, interests. If we consider the parallels in business today, in all but the smallest organizations there are inevitably people, teams and departments with a range of different interests, agendas and perspectives. Immediately a question presents itself to the shrewd consultant: are all organizations political? Try this test. Think about an organization where you have consulted and answer the following questions:

- ☐ Are budgets tight?

- ☐ Are there more jobs at the bottom of the corporate ladder than at the top?

- ☐ Do some people appear to have more influence than their official status seems to merit – and certainly more than others of identical grade?

- ☐ Are some individuals always better informed about what is going on than others?

- ☐ Do people have different interests – both corporate and personal?

- ☐ Does decision making tend to take place through informal channels?

If the answer to any of these questions – let alone all of them – is yes, then the organization *is* political. It is a rare company that fails to score at least five out of six. Office politics is a fact of life.

Furthermore, research findings are clear: the people who get on in organizations (either as employees or as external advisors) are adept at handling the politics. They understand that all organizations are political systems. Perhaps more importantly, they know how to work them: if you want to sell business, gain approval of your recommendations, enlist support in the implementation process, you need to be proactive. In these circumstances, it is surprising that the term, office politics, continues to have negative connotations. More often than not, it is a label reserved for behaviours which are underhand, manipulative or damaging to others. Constructive office politicians are described differently – perhaps as effective strategists, skilful influencers or even powerful leaders.

## ANALYSIS

The first step of the consulting process is to understand the political dimension. Some individuals are naturals: they understand instinctively where the power lies, they are aware of the dynamics between people and they know how to influence things so that their way prevails. Those of us who are less fortunate or are less intimate with the company as external consultants, need to conduct at least some basic analysis to form a clear picture of the political landscape. This needs to happen at two levels: the corporate and the individual.

## Corporate level analysis

In order to establish the corporate political landscape, the consultant should establish the answers to these basic questions:

☐ What is the level of politicking (irrespective of whether it is largely constructive or destructive)?

☐ What type of culture is it?

In terms of the level of politicking, there are a number of signs that would indicate a highly political environment:

☐ **Excessive competition at the top** – This is likely to create competition lower down in the organization and may also indicate disagreement about the direction of the company. Conflicts of interest and personality are likely to be common.

☐ **Ambiguous goals** – In this sort of situation, you find people redefining the goals to suit their own purposes. Managers are well placed to empire build, and conflicts tend to arise between departments.

☐ **Complex structures** – Any organization structure that creates ambiguity or dual accountability is likely also to provoke a higher level of political activity – both constructive and destructive – purely because of the set up. There is a risk of ambiguity, and success will require a great deal of negotiation and cooperation. It is common, therefore, to find individuals vying for power and influence.

☐ **High level of change** – Office politics increases in situations where policy and procedures are not clearly laid out. When there is a high degree of change, it is often not possible, nor desirable, to keep rewriting manuals. This triggers political behaviour as rival factions struggle for ascendancy.

☐ **Refusal by powerful people to change** – When those in influential positions refuse to toe the corporate line, this can spark political battles throughout the organization. This sort of situation will be characterized by lip-service, rivalry between different teams, and destructive game playing in the boardroom.

☐ **No clear definition of performance** – Where it is unclear what you need to do to get on or even to get a favourable appraisal, the chances of politicking will be high. It will be necessary to draw attention to yourself, to play up successes and divert failures and to ingratiate yourself with your bosses. Clear remuneration and reward systems, along with honest and clear career planning, reduce this type of behaviour.

☐ **Punishment culture** – When the organization is tough on poor performers, or likes to publicize failures as a warning to others, it becomes very common for people to cover their tracks carefully to ensure that nothing that goes wrong can be traced back to them.

☐ **Limited resources** – When teams have to compete for head count and budget, they will need to exert political influence in order to ensure that their work is regarded as an organizational priority.

The way in which the consultant should adapt their approach if the organization is highly political is addressed towards the end of this chapter. However, at the analysis stage, it is vital to examine whether the politics in the organization are largely constructive or destructive and, to some extent, this can be revealed by conducting the second phase of the analysis and establishing the type of culture. Goffee and Jones[1] categorize all cultures into the following basic types:

- ☐ Networked.
- ☐ Mercenary.
- ☐ Communal.
- ☐ Fragmented.

☐ **Networked** – The networked culture is characterized by a high degree of sociability, empathy and trust. People genuinely like each other and spend a great deal of time in one another's company – both in work and out of it. Communications are face to face and an open door policy is likely. Patience, tolerance and openness are all highly valued.

☐ **Mercenary** – By contrast, the mercenary culture is focused on achieving goals and is often quite a ruthless environment. Pace and performance are highly valued and winning vitally important. The mercenary culture secures business success by driving people internally, through setting high targets and rewarding accordingly. More emphasis is placed on action than reflection.

☐ **Communal** – The communal culture is both highly sociable and highly focused on business results. People are passionate about the business – and about each other. There are few barriers and communication channels are plenty and open. The edges between work and non-work life can be blurred, in extreme cases merging into one. Work becomes a way of life and people are united in achieving common goals.

☐ **Fragmented** – Finally, people within a fragmented culture are neither sociable towards one another, nor do they wholeheartedly support the organization. Instead, they work largely for themselves, by themselves. Absence from the office is commonplace and associated with busyness – with the client, on the road or on a project working from home. People often relate more to their profession than they do to a particular company.

There are a number of ways in which a consultant, even if new to the organization, can establish what type of culture they are dealing with. One approach relates to the greatest luxury at the disposal of the consultant – research. Whether it is qualitative or quantitative, face to face or systems/paper-based, highly structured or more fluid, the consultant has the ultimate licence to establish what sort of culture they are dealing with. In fact, any consultant should make it a part of their professional etiquette to conduct a robust diagnosis of the culture – without it the project is unlikely to be successful. It is vital to establish:

- ☐ What is really good about the organization?
- ☐ What is valued around here?
- ☐ What drives people?
- ☐ How do people behave towards one another?
- ☐ What are the main problems and why?
- ☐ What is the predominant leadership style?

The answers to these questions will give vital clues about the type of organization the consultant is dealing with. In addition, examine corporate governance and the organization

[1] Goffee and Jones, *The Character of Corporation: How Your Company's Culture Can Make or Break Your Business*, HarperCollins, 1998.

structure, establish to what extent the power is devolved through the organization and find out how decisions are made, and by whom. For instance, partnership structures, where there may be many clients, any of whom can sign off a piece of work, are likely to be fragmented; whereas a company, which involves all its senior management team and seems to have no sense of urgency, is probably networked. On the cynical assumption that 'What gets measured gets done', it is often also valuable to analyse the impact of performance management systems and/or reward mechanisms.

Finally, research can frequently unearth an organization's true, rather than its espoused, values. This will enable any consultant to examine their own ethical framework and question whether it is an organization with whom they want to work.

## Individual level analysis

Having analysed the political landscape from an organizational perspective, it is important to turn to the individuals. This too is a complex assessment, with many factors having a bearing. It is perhaps helpful to explore two dimensions – the client's role and their personality.

**Role** – As a consultant, it is vital to establish the who's who of corporate life. This has to take into consideration both official hierarchies and reporting lines, and informal networks and power bases. Effective consultants have an instinct for knowing who needs to know what and how they should be handled. They understand the informal roles that people fulfil, a number of which are listed below:

☐ **Budget holders** – Budget holders hold budgets! It is therefore essential to understand exactly who fulfils this role in a company and to form an effective and transparent relationship with them. Understanding the individuals, the reporting lines, and the sign-off processes will help to ensure that there are no awkward misunderstandings.

☐ **Approvers** – These people represent the final approval point. It is likely that they are at director level and may or may not be the budget holder. Having said that, companies can vary hugely. There are organizations that delegate authority significantly, so that a relatively junior person in the Human Resources (HR) or Information Technology (IT) department, for instance, has freedom to give the OK.

☐ **Opinion formers** – These people seem to exert a degree of influence over what happens in the organization, irrespective of their formal position. These people are important and you should aim to develop close relationships with them. This does not mean you have to kowtow to them and agree with everything they say, but it is useful for you to know the way they are thinking, and why. Involve them in your research, enlist their support going forward. The allegiance of opinion formers will help to lend credibility to you as a consultant and will help you to gain critical mass more quickly. It is also useful for you to have their ear, so that you are able to influence them.

☐ **Business users** – These are the people who will ultimately have to live with the solutions you recommend. Successful consultants recognize the need not only to involve them in the research phase, but throughout the entire programme – right through to implementation.

☐ **Gatekeepers** – Gatekeepers seem to control the information flows in a company. Again, this may not be a function of their official role, but more to do with their belief that 'information is power' – and that power is there for the taking. They open and close channels of communication, they control the speed with which information is revealed, and they filter/translate the details according to the message they need to convey. Be aware of their existence and of their potential power. Use them wisely. Do not tell them things if you think they will misuse the information. However, do seek information from them.

☐ **Repositories** – These people have a wealth of knowledge and information, built up either through experience or by keeping a constant ear to the ground. Do not hesitate to consult them. Their information might help to inform your decision-making process and stop you from reinventing the wheel.

☐ **Cliques** – These informal groupings inevitably develop in any organization. They may be united by common interest – officially or unofficially. They may be 'allies' or 'enemies' – either of each other, or of the consulting process. It is crucial to understand where the divisions lie, their relative power and what they feel about you.

☐ **Assessors** – Assessors, both expert and non-expert, will assess everything you do. They may not be particularly welcome. Nor do they often appear to be particularly helpful. Nevertheless, they will have a view and you will need to handle them carefully.

**What are these people like?** – Having identified the roles that people fulfil, it is necessary to analyse them as politicians. Given our earlier conclusion – that politics can be both constructive and destructive – it is important to understand where the individuals stand on this continuum. The matrix below categorizes people into four basic types, depending on their motives (are they constructive or destructive?) and their skill or competence (see Figure 10.1).

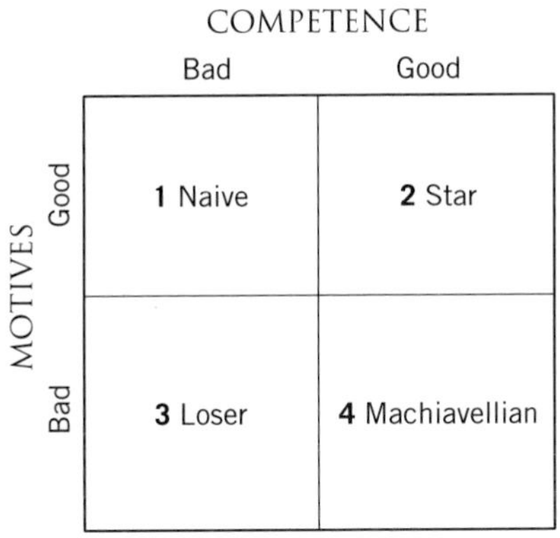

COMPETENCE

| | Bad | Good |
|---|---|---|
| **Good** | 1 Naive | 2 Star |
| **Bad** | 3 Loser | 4 Machiavellian |

MOTIVES

FIGURE 10.1: Political types

Boxes 1 and 2 in Figure 10.1 contain people driven by altruistic motives. Stars possess the political skill required to operate effectively in an organizational context. They are often both competent and admired, whereas naives are well-intentioned, but do not have the political skill to achieve their objectives. They may be perceived as irritants, innocents, militants or well-meaning incompetents.

In boxes 3 and 4 there are people driven by suspect motives – politicians in the most negative sense of the word. Four hundred and fifty years after its publication, Niccolo Machiavelli's tract *The Prince* remains the most chilling application of the belief that the end justifies the means. Frustrated by the constant political turbulence of the times he lived in, Machiavelli's advice to governments reflected his conviction that the political status quo must be protected at any cost. 'Machiavellian', therefore, is the description reserved for those people, driven by 'bad' motives, who are adept at understanding and interpreting situations, and making what they want to happen.

Losers are more likely to be described as politicians, since their activities are less subtle and their motives easier to read. They may be prone to misjudging situations or acting in a way that is transparently self-seeking. They certainly do not possess the political nous of the Machiavellian and are, consequently, less effective at making things happen.

# ACTION

## Mapping

In order to maximize the chances of successfully handling the politics within a client organization, a consultant needs to map it all out. Create a wall chart, mind-map™ or database, which clearly sets out the key people within the organization and their preferences/styles, the structure and divisions, the allies and adversaries, and so on. Overlay this with a robust analysis of the organizational culture and use your consultancy skills to assess what the picture looks like. Return to it frequently – ideally keep it visible. This map will help you to think through the implications of decisions, recommendations and changes.

## Types of culture

According to Holmes,[2] the way you consult in the different types of culture must be equally different. In a networked organization, he considers it important to 'make friends' throughout the organization and to be helpful to people when they need it. Loyalty is key and it is vital not to talk down the organization or the people within it.

By contrast, in a mercenary culture, the methodology has to be very different. Making things happen, focusing on results and linking up with the one or two people who have real power at that particular point in time are all important tactics. This is typically the type of organization where the consultant can expect, and should deal with, a high degree of politicking.

In a communal culture, Holmes feels you should 'join the family'. Passion, client focus and belief are vital. The consultant needs to get to know people intimately, share in their successes and empathize when things do not go so well. Politicking is frowned on in this sort of organization.

Finally, in a fragmented culture, you need to demonstrate your expertise clearly. Consulting in this sort of environment is not about making friends. Instead, it is an opportunity to work with the best, shine individually as a consultant and do some logical, rational and not intuitive, analysis. These people are all about giving advice and being expert and may expect the same from you, therefore a more consultative, questioning approach is unlikely to go down well.

Once you have conducted your analysis and understand both the type of organization and individuals you are dealing with, it is important to anticipate likely reactions and think through the implications of everything you do. On a grand scale, this applies to your project or program plans. Many consultants become absorbed by the rational side of planning and forget the emotional and political dimensions. Do not plan only what to do, but think through how to communicate and influence. Be aware of any potential resistance and create a strategy

[2] Holmes, *The Chameleon Consultant: Culturally Intelligent Consulting*, Gower Publishing, 2002.

to deal with it. Build it into the plan, with measures and milestones and, if feasible, share this sensitively with your main sponsor.

At a tactical level, it is important to try to avoid 'shooting from the hip'. If you have the luxury of a few moments, anticipate what the likely reactions will be on as wide a scale as possible. Use your map as a checklist to ensure that you have allowed for all conceivable actualities.

## Required qualities

To handle the politics well, you need to be both energetic and sensitive. It is all too easy to believe that situations will go away or sort themselves out – but invariably they do not. So be proactive and take decisive action. Resist procrastination and avoidance. However, once you have decided to be proactive and handle the politics, you must do so sensitively. Evaluate the personalities you are dealing with and how they are best handled. Think through the ideal sequence of your actions – who needs to know first, and why? Be very careful about committing anything sensitive to paper, not necessarily from any ethical standpoint, but more because it is very easy for others to abuse or misuse written material. Often writing is also less effective. However, paradoxically, many people lean towards impersonal communications media for sensitive issues, because they would prefer not to tackle them face to face.

## Review

It is also important to review regularly and carry out a 'political stock take'. Where are you? What are people feeling? How has the political map changed since you started your consultancy assignment? Do you now have more allies than adversaries than at the outset? Make time for this and do it properly. If politics is not something that comes naturally to you, you may choose to nominate someone in your team or company to challenge you and act as a political sounding board. One thing is certain, if you understand and handle the political dimension of the consultancy assignment, you are much more likely to achieve a good result. And the alternative? At best, a well-researched, expensive, consultancy report, which is filed away, never to be returned to. At worst, lost business and an irretrievably damaged reputation.

## SUMMARY

Office politics can be defined as the informal, rather than the formal way of getting results.[3] This can involve both constructive and destructive behaviours, but most people associate politics with more negative connotations. No matter what the consultant thinks about office politics personally, however, it is vital to the success of any project for them to understand and handle the political dimension effectively.

The analysis needs to happen at corporate and individual levels.

As far as the corporate level is concerned, the consultant needs to determine the degree of politicking taking place and the type of culture present in the organization. This will provide vital clues in terms of how best to handle the situations that arise throughout the consultancy assignment.

At an individual level, it is important to assess who the key players are – as a function of their formal and informal roles – and work out how best to handle them. How do they like to be influenced? What motivates them? How do they prefer to be communicated with? In this

[3] For further reading on this subject, refer to Clarke, J, Office Politics, Spiro Press, 1999.

analysis, role and personality both have a significant bearing. As far as their political activities are concerned, the consultant needs to be clear just what their motives are and how good they are at manipulating – or influencing – situations to get what they want.

Fortunately, the consultant has at his or her disposal the greatest luxury – that of research. Conducted in an appropriate way, this phase of the project should unearth political and cultural information, which will help the consultant to get it right. Mapping out the who's who, overlaying this with a picture of the organizational culture and building this into the project plan will all help the consultant to make recommendations which are more likely to be implemented – and bring enduring change.

# CHAPTER 11

## CHALLENGING PARTNERSHIPS: CONSULTANCY SKILLS FOR SUSTAINING COLLABORATION BETWEEN DIVERSE PARTNERS

### INTRODUCTION

This chapter describes some of the challenges and pitfalls of being a consultant to a partnership of different organizations and countries in the non-profit sector, and the methods used to enable highly diverse individuals to work together effectively.

Currently, consultancy is increasingly about working across many different boundaries. These boundaries are multi-dimensional and complex. Consultants may find themselves helping clients to address complex organizational, inter-personal and political issues. They and their clients will need the skills to manage expectations, which arise from diverse social and organizational roles and cultures. Leadership and teamwork across these boundaries require specific methods and skills. Without them, the boundaries can become barriers that are as multi-layered and complex as the opportunities they offer.

Some of the questions that this chapter will explore include:

- [ ] What is meant by 'effective partnership'?

- [ ] How can you build cross-sectoral dialogue in diverse partnerships?

- [ ] What methods encourage learning and teamwork between stakeholders?

- [ ] How can a partnership work when partners have unequal power and resources?

- [ ] What are the leadership skills and characteristics needed to build on the best from each stakeholder?

The first part of this chapter tells the story of two contrasting partnership projects, describing what worked and what did not work so well in each. These stories are designed to illustrate the qualities of effective partnership and their associated methods and skills. The second part analyses these experiences and the consultancy methods and resources used in each, in order to highlight the personal attributes and skills needed by consultants to sustain their positive cross-boundary work or practice.

## TWO PARTNERSHIPS

In the mediaeval town hall of Siena, Italy, two paintings hang on opposite sides of the wall to illustrate good and bad government. In one, the scales of justice are balanced and peace and prosperity abound. In the other, injustice and exploitation are accompanied with poverty and deprivation and conflict.

The mythical qualities of these pictures inspired the following two contrasting stories, which show the challenges of building productive partnerships. The stories are taken from real experience. They are about consulting to a partnership that worked and a partnership that did not work so well. The insights offered arose as much from unresolved conflict and frustrated expectations as from achievement of goals and significant positive results.

No amount of skill can guarantee positive results. The stories demonstrate methods and approaches, but are not recipes for success. The contrast between them emphasizes the leadership challenges and consultancy skills, as well as sounding a note of warning about the limitations of a consultant's influence.

## PROJECT 1: A PARTNERSHIP THAT WORKED

### The project

When Anne invited a consultant to work with her to draw up a funding proposal for a European partnership project the consultant felt torn. The funding program was highly competitive, rigid and bureaucratic. Funding awards were low. On the other hand, the consultant had both enjoyed the experience of previous consultancy to Anne, a local government equality manager. This offered another opportunity to work with a client with whom she had an established professional relationship and many shared values.

The funding program invited proposals to develop innovative methods for 'gender mainstreaming' – Eurospeak for evaluating and addressing the different impact of decision making on women and on men. Anne and the consultant put a three-year proposal together, and Anne selected and approached partners, an evaluator and a project manager. The bid was successful – one of two accepted from the UK – and work began.

The project design was innovative in its ambition to create joint learning outcomes, rather than an exchange of information about practice developed by individual partners. While Anne as the project leader was formally accountable, the consultant was given lead responsibility for keeping the work of the partnership on track and for ensuring that overall objectives were met.

### The challenges

Meetings between partners were the main vehicles for partnership work. They had to be carefully designed and facilitated, to allow a balance between 'reporting' on activities carried out by partner organizations in their local context, and joint work to develop new approaches and perspectives. Above all, they had to ensure and demonstrate that partners were working towards overall project objectives. The consultant designed the meetings in advance, coached the project leader throughout, and facilitated key sessions. As the project progressed, the consultant involved the project manager and evaluator in planning and facilitating meetings, and more of a team approach developed.

Pressure to demonstrate results was intense. The funding program was under threat of closure, and the administrators were anxious to make the case to continue the program. Partners were under pressure to justify taking time out to work on an external project. Their organizations were happy to sign up to the partnership but considered that additional work on 'gender equality' was low priority.

In practice, there was tension throughout between the objectives brought by individual partners and the results they were signed up to produce. Partners had no trouble developing local initiatives for gender mainstreaming. Finding a way to demonstrate how the partnership project made this possible, was more of a challenge.

This tension was reflected in discussion at the first meeting of partners. The essence of the project was to develop and promote gender equality 'mainstreaming' within local multi-agency partnerships. However, it was soon discovered that each partner had their own unique way of interpreting the project objectives and the key terms of 'mainstreaming' and 'partnership'.

The consultants established that while no one knew exactly what the term 'gender mainstreaming' meant, and each had different concepts of 'partnership', all saw the project as an opportunity to advance their work on women's equality. After lengthy discussion, the consultants adapted a revised working title for the project, which reflected the shared vision for the project established during the first meeting: 'Effective Local Partnerships'.

## Valuing diversity within shared vision

At the first meeting, establishing a shared vision between such diverse partners in a short space of time was challenging. Differences of culture and approach were so marked that it seemed vital to the consultants to take time to name and explore them, as the first step towards creating common ground. Partners brought with them a history of mistrust arising from negative experiences of cross sectoral collaboration in local contexts, and there was a real danger that they might reenact this in relation to each other.

The consultants spent time at the beginning of the session identifying differences of approach and how these related to local organizational context, and the roles of individual partners. When the time came to draw up an agreed set of criteria to evaluate local initiatives, partners moved spontaneously from advocating their own approach to seeking a formula which embraced multiple strategies for implementing gender equality. This established a basis for collaboration within the partnership and became a model for local partnerships.

## Identifying uniqueness as a basis for innovation

As the project developed, it was a constant challenge to maintain a balance between the uniqueness of each partners' local work and creating a joint product, which the partnership could call its own. To achieve this, each meeting allowed space for individual reports, in which partners were asked to demonstrate how local initiatives contributed to overall project objectives.

At the second meeting, partners acted as co-consultants to each other, identifying and selecting elements of good practice to adapt and try out in their own context. This caused confusion initially, as country groups were reluctant to split up, and language barriers made communication difficult. It did help each partner to identify which aspects of their working practice they valued and how it was adapted to local context. It also sharpened awareness of what they had to offer each other, and of what they had to learn from each other within the partnership.

## Affirmation as a basis for dialogue

At the third meeting, one of the partners remarked on the value she experienced of taking time out to reflect together on their practice, and acknowledge and evaluate what they had achieved. She and others stated that they felt their work was affirmed within the project in a way that they had not experienced in their own organizations. The process of naming each other's achievements had given them an opportunity to experience how their work was valued through the eyes of others, and this had given them a new sense of the value of their own work.

## Partnership as an environment for innovation and learning

As partners got to know and trust each other, they became more open to learning from each other and began to introduce and try out aspects of each other's practice. The partnership became an environment for mutual inspiration and learning, and partners sustained each other as change agents as they implemented change and new initiatives within their work practice and organizations.

Several partners reported that they had begun to introduce working methods used within the partnership meetings into their own meetings with local partners. They found that those methods allowed more room for dialogue, and encouraged strategic thinking.

Furthermore, partners referred to ways that they had been inspired by each other to try out new ideas and to become more adventurous in their practice. In Italy, for example, cross-sectoral partnerships were forged for the first time between regional members of a national trade union confederation and local women's organizations. In Ireland, a local Trade Union Centre for the unemployed began to work on a national level. In South Holland, women's organizations began to address diversity by taking measures to increase participation of black and minority ethnic women.

## Demonstrating results

Further challenges arose in the final year of the project, when the partnership had to demonstrate it had produced a product of its own, independently of local results. An editorial team drafted a case study describing the working methods of the overall partnership, and a tool-kit for others wishing to use the methods developed.

The partnership agreed to promote the method through which they had built their own 'learning partnership' as their product.

The toolkit and the case studies describing methods and results achieved by local and the transnational partnership are available from MargaretPage@maya.consultancy.demon.co.uk or on www.maya-consultancy.demon.co.uk.

# PROJECT 2: A PARTNERSHIP THAT DID NOT WORK SO WELL

## The project

This project was also the result of a successful bid to a European Union funding program. The proposal was put together by a consultant and the lead partner over a period of a year. Its objective was to develop new consultancy methods to address challenges identified by partner organizations in attracting and sustaining women in leadership roles. Once the project began, the consultant and lead partner both became partners in the project. The consultant's leadership role was informal and developed in the latter part of the project.

The other partners were individuals representing local government, confederations of small businesses, a university, a management development network for women managers and small consultancy firms. Countries represented were Spain, Italy, the UK, and Ireland. All had special expertise in developing women's leadership and promoting women's equality in or through their organizations. These countries had been approached informally and had signed up their organizations to join the project.

## The challenges

The budget approved was lower than the bid and partners had to be asked to scale down their activities and submit a new proposal in order to take part. In the time lag since submission of the proposal, organizational priorities and personnel had changed; participants had to renegotiate and resell the project within their organizations. At this point, several partners withdrew. This was a demoralizing start to the project.

Within each country consultant partners worked in pairs with client organizations to diagnose problems, design and pilot consultancy interventions and evaluate results. The project leader provided a time frame for delivery, but was not available to support partners in their development work. Consultants struggled to develop and negotiate authorization for work programs within their client organizations. Resentment quickly built up as partners felt they lacked the support they needed to overcome the obstacles they were meeting within their client organizations. The emphasis on financial controls by the funder and lead organization furthered this resentment. Late payments and inefficient project management furthered these insecurities.

In this challenging environment, communication between partners in different countries was minimal. Meetings of the international partnership took place and partners attended; however these were conflictual or indifferent. Consultants' insecurity was expressed as indifference or hostility and focused on the project leader. While partners gave the required progress reports, they showed little curiosity about each other's work.

## Project results

Despite these difficulties, individual client and consultant pairs did achieve significant results within each country. A range of innovative consultancy and training tools were developed. A publication was written and disseminated, describing the challenges identified by each organization, the methods developed and results achieved.

However, in contrast to partners in Project 1, partners in Project 2 stated that they experienced the differences within the international partnership as too great to learn from. No shared vision was created, and partners did not identify common ground, develop relationships of trust, inspire or sustain each other as change agents.

## Project leadership

The project leader was concerned with delivering results, and satisfying the funder that objectives had been met. However there were no consultancy resources to facilitate building of relationships between partners or to enable learning from diversity. In the absence of these resources and under pressure from the challenging project environment, good will turned to hostility. The consultant's attempts to facilitate collaboration produced no results. While the project catalysed useful and innovative local initiatives, the increased value of cross-sectional and international partnership was not realized.

# KEY CONSULTANCY METHODS AND SKILLS

What were the challenges in Projects 1 and 2 for the consultant?

☐ **Commitment increased potential for achieving but also for conflict** – Individual participants in both projects were highly committed and value driven. All considered themselves in some sense to be change agents, introducing and asserting the value of new practices within organizations. Each had different models and strategies for bringing about the changes associated with project objectives. This diversity and commitment brought potential for creativity – but also raised the stakes and potential for conflict.

☐ **External pressures were played out between partners** – The issues that the projects addressed were not a priority and did not attract resources within the organizations concerned. Yet those responsible for administering the funding were under pressure to demonstrate results, and passed these pressures on in their requirements of the projects they funded. These external pressures were sometimes played out in relationships between partners and project leaders. Both control and facilitation were needed to enable partners to deliver. It was difficult for one individual to enact both kinds of leadership. In Project 1, consultants working alongside the lead partner could exercise these different kinds of leadership; in Project 2, facilitative leadership was not taken up by partners who were preoccupied with their own challenges.

☐ **Diversity between partners was an asset which was not always realized** – For the partnership to work, diversity between partners had to be experienced as an asset, a resource for learning and innovation. However, under pressure, partners sometimes experienced these differences as too great to be useful; a deficit rather than an asset. Relationships had to be built, within the limited time available, to enable partners to overcome mistrust arising from differences in culture, working practices, political ideology, and a history of conflict relationships between the organizations they represented. In both projects, the consultancy task was to design and facilitate a process to enable learning from diversity. This process needed to be sufficiently flexible to work with the priorities and concerns brought by partners, and to meet tight program objectives.

☐ **Consultant and client dialogue sustained partnership dialogue** – Many of the pressures experienced by partners within their professional environments were acted out between lead partners and consultants. These relationships were emotionally charged, frequently explosive and needed to be nurtured with sophisticated relational and interpersonal skills. Where collaboration could not be sustained between lead partners and consultants, dialogue within the wider partnership also broke down and learning between partners was minimal. Common ground could not be built in the absence of trust and motivation. In Project 1, consultancy resources had been made available to work alongside the project leader to facilitate learning between partners. This enabled relationships to be built and practice developed which generated 'learning partnership'. In Project 2, these resources were not available and learning partnership did not develop.

What key consultancy methods and skills used in the partnership worked to create a project environment within which partners could support and learn from each other, and then use this learning within their organizations? Were there skills that could have enabled the partnership in Project 2 to work better? Or are there certain environments where skills, however sophisticated, simply cannot be used?

First impressions always influence how people relate to one another. Typically, there are unspoken assumptions between partners about unequal power and access to resources which need to be brought out into the open. Differences need to be addressed and understood in order for partners to begin to work together. A first step, therefore, is to facilitate a discussion in which partners share what is specific and unique about their work, and identify the differences between them – differences of language, culture, historical and political context, sector, position in their organizations, and level of experience. Each partner's interpretation of the project objectives must be explored, in addition to how these have been shaped by the context in which they are working.

The task of agreeing a common framework for the project work may seem daunting, yet watersheds do occur where the participants seem to relinquish their partisanship and cease to advocate their own approach. Instead, they recognize the value of each other's approaches, and that multiple approaches will be more effective than any single one. The process of naming differences and affirming the unique qualities of each project establishes the possibility of collaboration – a common project can begin.

The methods and skills described here are not usually the ones that consultants first think about:

☐ Developing self-awareness as a tool to tap into mutual perceptions and how these might open up or close down opportunities for learning and collaboration.

☐ Naming the unique qualities of experience, skill and knowledge brought by each partner, and enabling each partner to speak from base, before attempting to create a common language.

☐ Acknowledging context specific meaning brought to concepts that are apparently shared.

☐ Naming differences in power and approach between partners and exploring how previous experience influenced mutual perceptions.

Skills such as these provide an affirming environment in which partners will feel valued, and this is key to a reciprocal learning process. However, using these skills is neither straightforward nor easy: powerful emotional needs often come into the consultancy frame. A core consultancy skill is, therefore, the ability to hold open the tension between the consultant's own needs and desires and those of their clients; between individual needs and the needs of the project. Consultants need to develop their ability to see self through others' eyes, while also keeping a project's objectives in mind.

Every business environment has its own ways of working, values and priorities. These take shape in relation to national and sectoral context, and build the expectations brought by the business's individual members to partnership initiatives. Yet, what happens to the individuals who have come together from these different 'worlds' and developed a new shared language and set of practices of their own after a project has ended?

In the 'partnership that worked', partners said at the end of the project that they would miss 'the new country' they had created. In this world they felt their work was valued and their contribution recognized. They had come to a shared understanding and framework to comprehend the challenges and had developed new practice to address them.

In both projects, consultants helped individual partners to focus on how to 'translate' their new knowledge and practice into a language and form that would be recognized and valued by stakeholders in their own work contexts. Individual partners helped each other to use political skills to promote the work of the partnership within each of their organizations. They struggled with how to assert the value of these new ways of working in their organizations, and with how to introduce new work practices. Once they had done so, there were issues about how to accredit the joint project work that had been done. This was crucial to affirm the added value of the partnership, but sometimes clashed with the individual need to have their work rewarded.

Much, inevitably, got lost in the process of 'translation'. In the product-oriented business environments in which partners were operating, it was difficult to find a way to find the words to represent the joint reflective process that had been crucial to the learning partnerships. The language of individual reward seemed to conflict with the more subtle process of cross-fertilization through which individual partners had developed new practice. Consultants and partners became skilful 'bicultural' practitioners, operating with different systems of meaning as they travelled between project and organizational environments, bringing knowledge and experience from each one to the next, engaging with colleagues in reflection on experience and testing acting on new knowledge as they developed new practice.

Maintaining a sense of connection, without losing touch with a feeling of separate role and identity can take on a particular edge when working in cross-cultural projects – whether culture refers to national, sectoral or differences relating to communities of identity. In these projects, individual partners arrived exhausted at their partnership meetings: they were looking for recognition and affirmation missing from their work environments, for care rather than challenge. Consultants had to create an environment where these individual needs were met sufficiently for the work of the partnership to begin. Care for the individual had to be balanced with care for the needs of the partnership. To achieve this, the consultants worked with their own inner world material – deciding when and how to bring their own feelings into the consultancy role. Sometimes, by sharing their own responses, they were able to engage partners in more in-depth analysis of blocks to collaboration. At other times, by sharing vulnerability and self-doubt, new and unexpected directions were taken which proved productive for the project. Occasionally sharing was not possible and in these cases consultants drew from awareness of their own responses to prepare an effective intervention.

The key skills the consultants used in this area were:

☐ **Self-awareness** – Working with one's own and the client's inner world as they are expressed within the consultancy frame.

☐ **Relational skills** – Introducing self-awareness into client/consultant relationships in the context of political and organizational tasks and goals – and across thresholds.

☐ **Maintaining dialogue** – Between two individuals in order to sustain creative collaboration.

A dialogue relies on people retaining a sense of their own uniqueness and difference, yet staying open to connection with the other. This sense of both connection and separateness between two unique individuals is hard to hold onto. It can break down when difference seems too great for connection or becomes threatening. High levels of trust were also needed when consultants and clients traversed the thresholds between different worlds and played strategically to their different cultures and values systems. Individual practitioners had to manage their self-image and the presentation of their partnership work strategically as they moved between multiple political frames. They had to pay attention to the impact of their actions on relationships with partners as they did so, and develop ways of talking about mutual perceptions and expectations as part of their practice to sustain the partnership.

## SUMMARY

Managers and consultants can develop and use the following skills on the job by becoming 'reflective practitioners'. Think about yourself conducting an enquiry into your own practice, using enquiry skills.

1   Develop critical self-awareness. Observe patterns in your interactions with others, notice how your desires and feelings influence your approach. Analyse how these patterns enhance or block collaboration and experiment with ways of acting differently in relation to others.

2   Check your observations out with clients and colleagues. Explore with them how you each experience your interactions and how they enhance or block the quality of your business collaboration.

3   Hold onto a sense of your own separateness and the unique and diverse qualities brought by each of your colleagues and clients to your collaboration. Notice when dialogue breaks down and what triggers it – practice naming your differences as a basis for repair and for moving back into dialogue.

4   Design cycles of reflection on experience into practical work with clients. Use these to enable clients to develop skills for learning from their own experience, to build relationships designed for learning, to maintain person-to-person dialogue, and to repair dialogue when it breaks down.

5   Be strategic. Cultivate awareness of the special quality of value base of the 'environment' you create with your clients and colleagues. How do the values, the working methods, qualities of interaction and languages used differ from those used in the organizations and environments within which your clients have to apply the new knowledge and practice that you are generating? Develop strategy. How can you help each other to 'translate' what you have developed together into a form that can be used in these different environments? Keep a note of what gets lost in translation and the effect of this on your collaboration.

6   Use political skills to demonstrate the value of your working methods and results. Protect the positive outcomes of the working methods you have developed in these other environments. Can you honour and accredit the quality of relationship and collaboration

that you have developed between you as you move between these environments? Again, keep a note of what gets lost in translation – and the effect of this on your collaboration.

8 Challenge and confront when necessary. Prevent undermining and give credit to you and your colleagues' and clients' achievements. Be a change agent!

9 Hone your survival skills and be aware that individual strategies may undermine collaborative relationships.

## REFERENCES

J Benjamin, *Like Subjects, Love Objects, essays on recognition and sexual difference*, Yale University Press, 1995.

M Lugones, 'Playfulness, 'World'-Travelling, and Loving Perception', first published in *Hypatia 2*, Vol. 2, Summer 1987; reprinted as chapter 17, pp. 275–290 in Diana T Meyers (ed.) *Feminist Social Thought: A Reader*, Routledge, 1997.

J Marshall, 'Living Life as Inquiry', *Systemic Practice and Action Research*, Vol. 12, Issue 2, pp. 155–171, April 1999.

W Torbert, *The Power of Balance: Transforming Self, Society, and Scientific Inquiry*, Sage, 1991.

# CHAPTER 12

# ETHICAL CONSULTING: IS THERE A RIGHT WAY?

## INTRODUCTION

Companies, large and small, have a problem. When it comes to telling the public or their people about anything, they are usually believed to be engaging in clever public relations rather than telling the truth. The same is true for national government or governmental agencies. And also for supposedly worthy groups, such as scientists or doctors.

This cynicism is deep-rooted and does not operate only at an organizational or group level. It is true for individuals and work teams who may, for example, question their manager's own interest, manifested by communications or behaviours. Indeed, managers themselves talk about their own work-based ethical standards and the pressure exerted on these by their organization – represented by their boss, senior management, shareholders or any of the other entities that constitute 'The Organization'.

There is little difference for the external consultant. Consultants talk of their company's focus on the bottom line, which drives them to operate in ways that they may normally avoid. Some consultancy cultures develop values that only recognize targets and results in the business. Consequently, operating in an ethical manner or providing support for colleagues to do likewise, is often unrecognized. Additionally, some consultants may cite external forces, market pressure and competitor activity, claiming that these considerations cause behaviours that challenge their own ethical position. However, before consultants working as sole operators reward themselves too loudly, one should remember that they are not free of these pressures. In a business world where their income wholly depends on their own activity, they too are subject to the challenges of securing assignments, meeting clients' requirements, responding to competitor activity, and delivering solutions on budget, which may create tension between their own ethical standards and the business demands. Perhaps we should remember that this occurs in a sector not wholly free of externally perceived and generally accepted unethical practices.

Is the business world in which consultants operate becoming increasingly unethical? It is hard to say whether there has been an increase in unethical business behaviour over the past few years, although it seems like it. Part of this may be because of increased public awareness of the subject, which causes more media reporting and increases public awareness and interest. It is also partly due to the repeated ethical conflicts we see in business activity from restructuring, with significant lay-offs, accompanied by high executive compensation. Or indeed, hidden multi-million dollar fraud, or the artificially high medicine prices to maintain profit at the expense of others' illness and death. We should not forget that this construct of 'bad business' translates to literature, TV and film. Business owners, senior executives and professionals (scientists and doctors of medicine) are often portrayed as the villains, the people engaged in bad practice.

To what extent are we free from the impact of the vilification of business? Try the short test in Table 12.1. Respond to the statements as honestly as you can. Remember, you might not need to be honest – it depends on your purpose.

The purpose of this chapter is three-fold. First, it is about consulting beyond cynicism, it is about saying that we, as consultants, are equipped to address the variety of ethical problems and dilemmas that confront us. And that we can do this while remaining true to our own standards. Second, it is also about recognizing that the interest of society in business ethical matters is not just a passing passion but here to stay, it is a fixed element of the human condition. Finally, it is about realizing that being seen and known to operate in an ethical manner is not just good practice, it is also good for business in the twenty-first century.

## BACK TO BASICS ON BUSINESS ETHICS

Let us just go back to basics for a moment. For some, the term 'business ethics' is difficult and has led to many musings on the possibility and impossibility of its existence. This is, in a way, because the subject itself is seen to originate within the tension between moral philosophy and pragmatic managerial practice. Even if we move from possibility to reality, there is still the challenge to identify and agree on what constitutes unethical business behaviour. Furthermore, in the process of identification, where is our stance? Does it exist in the highly persuasive arena of nostalgia informing values, or modernization challenging our nostalgic and inherited value sets?

The purpose of this chapter is not to wander into the philosophical debate about what business ethics are, it is simply to recognize that the term is slippery and subject to much ongoing discussion. Some reject this discussion in the face of real world activity: 'We are too busy worrying about real problems to take this academic sophistry seriously'. It is a case of the ivory tower meets the law of the jungle. Therefore if we leave the philosophical debate to others, what are we left with? This basic position is summed up by the assumption that business ethics is about human behaviour in the organizational context. Within this definition, we have to see human behaviour as consistent with norms and standards agreed by society. For consultants, this means managing and influencing their own and others' ethical conduct within the business context.

In short, this is about individuals recognizing issues, making judgements and decisions (based on generally agreed standards and norms) and behaving ethically. This would be simple, were it not for a variety of factors that can make it difficult to distinguish between right and wrong. We have already mentioned the divide between the philosopher and the business realist, and

| | STRONGLY AGREE | AGREE | DISAGREE | STRONGLY DISAGREE |
|---|---|---|---|---|
| My business is about maximizing the bottom line. | 1 | 2 | 3 | 4 |
| In my experiences, the more financially successful a consultant is, the more unethical their behaviour. | 1 | 2 | 3 | 4 |
| Personal ethical standards are frequently compromised in business practice. | 1 | 2 | 3 | 4 |
| The business world has its own rules. | 1 | 2 | 3 | 4 |
| As a consultant there are frequent occasions where I believe one thing but say another. | 1 | 2 | 3 | 4 |
| In the business context, if it is legal it is right – it is that simple. | 1 | 2 | 3 | 4 |
| Most people are out to further their own interests. | 1 | 2 | 3 | 4 |
| The consultancy world is like a game – and I am here to win. | 1 | 2 | 3 | 4 |
| In the business context, you need to distance your personal values when making decisions. | 1 | 2 | 3 | 4 |
| The competition will do virtually anything to win a contract. | 1 | 2 | 3 | 4 |

**Explanation**

Add your score, and compare your total with the following comments:

| Score | Comment |
|---|---|
| 1–8 | This indicates a high degree of business cynicism, which is likely to impact on your decision making, and is probably based on the idea that 'the business of business is business'. |
| 9–17 | While indicating some degree of cynicism, this shows that you are not wholly operating in a world of work isolated from the values, norms and standards of society and translated into the business context. Make sure that you think through carefully the ethical issues, perhaps using the decision-making wheel. |
| 18–32 | This indicates a healthy degree of awareness (on the cynicism scale), while allowing the appropriate application of values, norms and standards to explore issues from an ethical perspective. |
| 33–40 | While a highly laudable position, this score sounds a bell of caution. It might be that you do not easily recognize issues that challenge the business or colleagues ethically. This is because your own value structure is high. |

TABLE 12.1: Checking the baseline

also the tension between nostalgia and the challenge of the now. A short reflection on the ethical decision-making wheel in Figure 12.2 will reveal some of the other problematic factors. These elements serve to inform many of the behaviours in which consultants engage and the decisions that need to be taken. But first a brief consideration of the philosophical platforms will be of value.

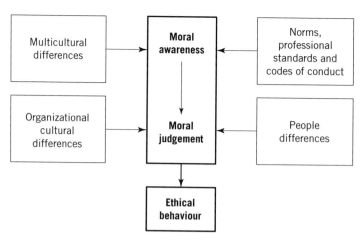

FIGURE 12.1 Individual ethical decision making and behaviour

## Our philosophical platform

This forms the background to the diagram (Figure 12.1), in a sense the 'white of the page'. There are, broadly speaking, three types of moral theory: duty-based, consequential and virtue theory.

☐ **Duty-based theory** – Assumes that there are certain ways in which we should or should not behave; it is therefore our duty to behave in these ways regardless of the consequences. In a business context, this approach can raise questions. For example, from a Christian perspective (which is duty-based), humans were created in the image of God. This suggests an inherent dignity in every person that must be respected as an act of duty. What then happens when organizations require people to carry out work of no purpose, or that is dangerous or alienating, or damages their self-esteem?

☐ **Consequential** – Consequential theory puts this around the other way. Here right or wrong is determined not by the intention of the actor or actors, but by the consequence. The duty-based approach sees lies or white lies as wrong, but what happens when they deliver a new sale, keep people in jobs, cover a mistake that a client might find unsettling? Utilitarianism (a consequential approach) is based on the assumption that the right action in any circumstance is the one producing the greatest overall happiness. In business terms, this translates into the belief that delivering against promises is seen as good practice. However, the same approach allows us to calculate the probable happiness outcome whether the promise was broken or kept. Thus, a large client organization that has paid an invoice twice will hardly notice the loss (small to them), while the consultant, who receives the double payment, gains a windfall and the balance on the happiness scale.

☐ **Virtue theory** – Focuses on character. From this viewpoint, we would be interested in how individuals spend their lives and how they intend to continue. It is about cultivating the virtues to flourish as a person. It has increasingly become the method applied most to business situations to help people, managers in particular, make sense of the wide range of ethical dilemmas they confront. At an organizational level, the belief is that business is a social activity whose purpose is to provide essential and desirable goods and services to make life easier. Therefore, sacrificing profit for reasons of social or environmental responsibility is what business should be about – enriching society and enriching shareholders. Virtue theory is also about how the organization operates internally. Investing in employees' ongoing development or in becoming a caring organization might be seen as 'theft' by the other approaches, but here it is seen as laudable.

## Professional standards and codes of conduct

Many organizations attempt to shape employees' behaviours through formal written structures, such as a vision, mission statement and corporate values. However, there are some who produce codes of ethical conduct. There are differences of opinion about the effectiveness of such codes. Some claim that their existence does indeed reduce the frequency of unethical behaviour. Nevertheless, since the nature of these statements vary, it is hard to define what exactly is meant by a 'formal' code. Furthermore, it is questioned whether employees actually read – let alone understand – such documents. Finally, there is good evidence that the existence of codes can cause, rather than alleviate, ethical problems. This is particularly the case where organizations espouse one approved type of behaviour and demonstrate another. For example, an organization that highlights the virtue of cooperative working within the ethical code, but rewards people on the basis of individual performance.

Professional bodies also have codes of conduct. This applies to the variety of bodies and societies of which consultants are likely to be members. Leaving aside the question of who reads them (let alone who remembers their content), there are other questions relating to purpose. Are these codes created for the purpose of public relations and to enhance the significance of the society in the eyes of the general public? Do they exist to create a professional elite, or do they provide their membership with an additional marketing tool to allay the fears of actual or potential clients? It is, of course, possible that the purpose of the code is to benefit clients and protect the profession from the abuse of unethical practitioners.

## Multicultural differences

Just what do societies or cultures ethically agree upon? Within a single society, culture has been defined as the way a group of people solve its problems. For a variety of reasons – historical, geographic, climatic and economic – cultures have produced specific solutions for specific problems. This occurs at an international level, between the United Kingdom and the United States or between Germany and Japan; and at a national level, between London and Liverpool or New York and San Francisco. Similarly, cultural differences take place in other groupings: religious, racial, North/South divide or even sporting allegiance. In the context of business, these differences call for an awareness that they exist and the desire for knowledge to understand them. Within this there is a decision to be made. As a multinational, we might claim that our managers, employees and business practices are exposing 'these different cultures' to Western values, so that they might think differently and benefit from greater independence and new business opportunities. Or we might adhere to a belief that local culture should be understood to prevent a violation of its ethical norms – 'show respect for it and work with it, not against it'. This is the debate between cultural imperialism and cultural relativism, and while it may seem to operate at a higher level than the usual consultancy assignment, it is not unknown. Clients, for example, may wish to develop and implement global value sets, or to align the European offices with the values already developed and living in Chicago.

Cross-cultural differences in ethical attitudes towards decision-making amongst managers and consultants are not well understood. It is accepted, however, that real cultural differences exist between collectivism and individualism, and on uncertainty avoidance, which in turn inform the ethical decisions taken by individuals. It is also interesting to note that ethical differences between varying national groups are less than expected and that managers, whatever their nationality, tend to see other national management groupings as less ethical than themselves.

## Organizational cultural differences

Organizations differ in culture. This is demonstrated within sectors, across internal divisions, and across national boundaries for multinationals. There is evidence to suggest that one difference is cultural strength. In strong cultures, the norms and standards that shape behaviour are known by all, or at least by most. The strength of this may even transcend the national boundaries crossed by the organization. Weak cultures, on the other hand, allow sub-groups to develop their own norms and standards, creating significantly different ways of behaving or thinking across departments and divisions. It is important to recognize that the place an organization holds on this continuum does not indicate 'good or bad'. Nonetheless, these differences exist and they will inform the ethical decision making of individual employees. This is one of the factors that must be read by both internal and external consultants if they are to operate effectively, making the appropriate decisions within such contexts.

In addition, other organizational features inform the ethical norms – 'The way we do things around here'. These include leadership, structure (authority and responsibility) and the internal systems, such as selection or reward.

To these formal features we also need to add the informal aspects of the organization. These may be less visible but certainly no less powerful. They include the symbolic individuals within the organization who represent role models and who show other employees how to behave. Increasingly, the evidence concerning organizational myth and story demonstrates the power of such discourse to maintain and shape culture for both existing employees and newcomers. Usually, at the heart of each story, sits the moral that expresses an actual corporate value and how this conflicts with espoused values.

## Different people, different decisions

People are different. In the decision-making process, an individual needs to be aware that a moral dilemma exists before being able to make a judgement. This does not happen automatically and different people will identify different situations as having or not having an ethical dimension. It seems that moral awareness can be increased through a variety of signalling activities. These activities fall into three categories:

1  An individual feels that others will be harmed by something.

2  He or she believes that colleagues will see the ethical dilemma in an issue.

3  The issue is framed or described by words that have moral properties (integrity, cheating, lying).

For both managers and consultants, this is useful. It provides ways to signal moral issues to a client and encourages them into open forum in order to address issues before they become a significant problem.

Awareness is just the first step towards acting. Between awareness and action is the decision of how to act. There is a variety of moral development and decision-making theory, but here we will simply register that a cognitive process takes place that enables an individual to process the data and head to a decision. We also have to realize that this process is not a well trodden path, which always leads to the same destination. Initially people will check the terrain, to see what the cues indicate. We have considered some of these cues, including the philosophical platform, the cultural context, the organizational values and systems, role models and standards and norms. These factors will influence the final decision and are of fundamental importance.

As a consultant, these elements will inform our decision-making processes. This reinforces the importance of being morally aware. Moreover, as consultants, be aware that we are one of these factors. For our clients and colleagues, we have the ability, because of our role and status, to influence moral judgements and ethical behaviours.

## TREADING THE ETHICAL PATH

The key question still remains – 'Is there a right way?' How can a consultant operate, using a consistent approach, to decide what is right and to do the right thing? We can outline an approach that will support ethical decision making for consultants operating in the business context.

Figure 12.2 represents a wheel, to remind us that the process is not linear, but that it should be capable of iterative application. The more serious the decision, the more times it may be appropriate to travel around the wheel.

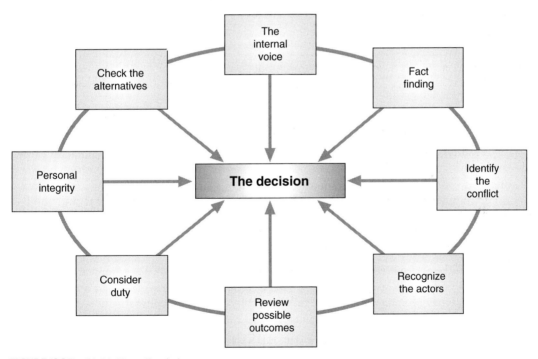

FIGURE 12.2 The ethical decision-making wheel

### Features of the ethical decision-making wheel

☐ **The internal voice** – While this approach is based mostly on a rational process, a good place to start is within oneself. When confronted with an issue, request or consultancy problem, does it make 'me' feel uneasy or uncomfortable? It may be impossible to frame

131

the reasons, but if it feels as though warning bells are ringing, take note. Consider the issue in more detail, do not simply avoid the subject at this stage.

☐ **Fact finding** – Recognizing that it is often impractical to gather all the available data relating to a particular situation is no reason to give up. Frequently, people move to the decision and the action without taking the time to gather the information.

☐ **Identify the conflict** – What ethical issues are associated with the subject or what values are held in conflict? Usually there are a variety of issues, which arise from a single subject – do not be tempted to stop at the first one you think of. A couple of useful activities to help this process are to apply the three philosophical theories and consider the subject from their perspective. What does duty-based, consequential or virtue theory lead you to identify?

☐ **Recognize the actors** – Actors include the parties affected by the decision, but also those making the decision and those who are otherwise involved as stakeholders. Often, this process of actor recognition creates a complex web of relationships where identifying who benefits and who is harmed sheds more light on the issue. Where the opportunity exists, it may be useful to explore preferred options with the different groups that are involved.

☐ **Review possible outcomes** – Having identified the actors, it is fruitful to consider the outcome identified for each on the basis of different decisions. This is, in part, drawn from the consequential theory and provides additional insight to the ethical dilemma. This should be a prioritizing activity, which identifies the main positive and negative outcomes, rather than every possible result. In the business context, it is also important to try to gain some idea of three other outcome elements: the duration of the outcomes' impact, the result of a secret decision becoming known, and the meaning the decision will be given within the organization.

☐ **Consider duty** – This is based on the duty-based theory and questions values or standards, which cause a person to behave in a particular way. Where does duty lie?

☐ **Personal integrity** – This uses virtue theory and asks questions about character at two levels. First, there is the character of the community of consultants, of which you are a member – how would they respond to the dilemma with which you are faced? What would happen if consultant colleagues heard about the decision you made; would you feel pleased or embarrassed? And second, there is your own character. How would you feel about yourself if you made this or that decision? In the end, will people see you and will you see yourself, as a person of integrity?

☐ **Check the alternatives** – How many potential actions are there in response to this case? Is it possible to think more creatively? What is the cost in terms of harm and benefit of inaction? It may be an opportunity to talk the subject over with colleagues or with the client.

## IS THE ETHICAL PATH GOOD FOR BUSINESS?

Do ethics and business mix? One way to attempt to measure this relationship, explores the link between socially responsible organizations and financial performance. It has to be said that the evidence is unclear. Where the evidence seems positive, it may be because financially secure organizations are able to devote more resource to social issues. Alternatively, because of the involvement in social issues and the consequent building of relationships with all stakeholders, an organization may enhance its financial performance.

Amongst the consultancy community, it is clear that some practices and some sole operators market themselves on the basis of their ethical approach to work. In this sense they build a character for themselves, akin to the virtue theory idea, which creates a positive market reputation and the recognition that they operate with integrity for the benefit of their clients. Although, we could question which sub-groups within the client organizations receive this benefit, that would indicate a certain cynicism and miss the key point. This is the belief amongst such consultancies and consultants that there is a need to distinguish themselves from the rest of the community on the basis of their ethical approach.

It is far better to consider the foundation of a good consultancy business in the twenty-first century as being concerned with a quality of service and product that meets the needs of clients and shows a responsible approach to the community of stakeholders and society in general, rather than simply being about the bottom line.

## SUMMARY

In summary, there are a number of points that consultants working with today's organizations for tomorrow's world can extract from this consideration of business ethics. Briefly they are:

☐ *Ethical conduct.* We cannot escape the fact that working within the business community we will be confronted with situations that confront our own ethical standards. This is true in all the activities in which we engage: the securing of work, the way in which we operate within our consultancy practices or with colleagues, the management of our clients and the nature of the assignments and interventions in which we are involved.

☐ *Moral awareness.* A desire to operate ethically requires us to be able to identify the moral issues and to be able to make the appropriate decisions. This should not be seen to happen 'naturally', rather it occurs through an active process of reflection.

☐ *Philosophical platform.* An initial step in the process of reflection is the examination of our philosophical platform. What is the overall guiding theory which will shape our thinking?

☐ *Examining the context.* A second step within the process is the examination of the context. Having considered the platform we also need to consider those various factors that impact both the awareness of the issue and the nature of the judgement.

☐ *Ethical decision-making wheel.* The third step is the path of reflection that allows us to make a judgement and act accordingly. The Wheel, used here, offers a route that raises a variety of questions, regardless of the platform from which you operate, that enable a just decision.

☐ *Why operate ethically?* The idea that it might be 'good for business' needs some exploration of meaning. Is it about bottom line or market advantage? But this might miss the point. Is not operating ethically simply 'good business'?

## FURTHER READING

Barher, R A (2002). *An examination of organizational ethics.* Human Relations, 55: 1097–1116.

# CHAPTER 13

## NEGOTIATION SKILLS

### INTRODUCTION

Conflict, power, and persuasion. These words capture the essence of what an effective negotiator has to come to terms with. Negotiation is the most efficient way to find a solution to a problem, and the best means to manage conflict. For both reasons, it will be, therefore, an essential component of the consultant of the future. To be persuasive, the consultant has to know something about conflict itself, including his or her own reaction in conflict situations.

Most negotiators fall into one of two types: those who measure success by winning, and those who measure success by not losing. Negotiators in the first group do everything they can to break the other side's bottom line, to get the last dollar they can extract from the other party. They believe that the other person must lose, not them. The second type of negotiator is preoccupied with avoiding losing. They try to resist moving too much or making too many concessions. Success for this type of negotiator means not losing; it means getting out with a deal that is, at the very least, just a little better than one's bottom line. This chapter presents an approach to negotiation that improves upon both of these two styles.

### NEGOTIATE FOR SUCCESS

We all want to win. Nevertheless, our society's definition of winning sets us up for disappointment much of the time. We designate winners and losers in the games we play as children and as adults – in sports, in business and in politics. There are the rich and the poor – the winners and the losers.

To be a winner in a 'win or lose world' is very difficult for anyone. So, we have a choice. Either we adjust our thinking and our expectations – 'You win some and you lose some' – or we begin to think differently about winning.

Negotiation is a way of getting what we want by persuading the other side to give it to us. Negotiation is an opportunity to win, but it is winning of a different kind. It is hardly a negotiation if the other side gets everything – unless you wanted them to and giving them everything makes you feel happy, as if you have won. Negotiation is a 'give and take' process. Trade-offs are made. Negotiation can be a very dynamic exchange and the winnings can be great. More than this, negotiation requires an ability to create solutions together to overcome the problems that divide the parties in dispute.

Our survival as a human race shows that we are able to live in a world of give and take and trade-offs. We enrich each other by negotiating, by settling differences in a way that both sides experience some sense of victory. There is room for both participants to come away winners. Is this possible? The answer is 'Yes'. However, it takes self-knowledge, skill, and hard work.

## NEGOTIATION DEFINED

There are many definitions of negotiation. One of the simplest is given by Roger Fisher and Bill Ury:

> ❝It is a back and forth communication designed to reach an agreement when you and the other side have interests that are shared and others that are opposed. ❞ [1]

The key elements of negotiation when defined in this way have been identified by Professor Alan Henrikson.[2] First, negotiation is not just communication, but rather a specific kind of communication:

- ☐ Communication that is explicit.
- ☐ Communication that is reciprocal.
- ☐ Communication that takes place directly between the parties.
- ☐ Communication designed to reach an agreement.

Second, negotiation takes place when:

- ☐ Both sides have interests that are shared.
- ☐ Both sides have interests that are opposed.

Thus, negotiation is a response to conflict and, in turn, has cooperation and competition built into it. Yet it is neither purely one nor the other. Conflict is the perception of incompatible interests and negotiation is a unique means of managing conflict. In negotiation, the tension between the need to assert your own interests and the need to satisfy the interests of your adversary is always present.

## WHAT IS A 'GOOD' OUTCOME?

The only reason to negotiate with another party is to obtain something by negotiating that you could not acceptably obtain in any other way. What is it we seek in negotiation? Obviously, almost 'everything under the sun' as negotiation pertains to goods and services, which are traded and exchanged between people. We can also establish, build and enjoy a relationship with the other people with whom we negotiate.

It should be fairly clear how to determine whether the outcome of our negotiation is good or not. Did we get a good price for our goods or service? Did we pay too much? Did they throw in extras that made the deal a really good one? Did I get the raise in pay I was after?

[1] Roger Fisher and Bill Ury, *Getting to Yes: Reaching Agreement Without Giving In*, Boston, Houghton Mifflin Co, 1981.
[2] Alan Henrikson, *Negotiating World Order*, Wilmington, Del., Scholarly Resources, 1986.

Most negotiations, however, are not as simple as these questions suggest. There are many elements that go into an agreement, even an apparently straightforward deal like buying a car. Moreover, it is unlikely that we can treat any negotiation as a one-time event or as a single meeting between two parties striking a deal. We live in a world that is quite small when it comes to our relationships and our work. We meet the same parties over and over again, and the opportunities to negotiate keep arising. Yesterday it was salary and benefits, today it is the amount of work that needs to be completed, and tomorrow it will be holidays or who will cover the phones at noon, and so on. Even buying a car includes the concerns about warranty, ability of the dealership to service the car, and the feeling of trust and confidence that does or does not develop during the negotiation.

The bottom line is seldom the only issue to think about when we negotiate. Life is more complicated than that. Beyond recognizing that we negotiate many times with the same party because it is a small world, there are other considerations in measuring a good outcome.

Will our agreement 'stand up' outside the room in which it was negotiated? Will it be seen to be well thought out and considerate of those who have a legitimate stake in it?

We rarely negotiate within a closed system. There are usually third parties who must be considered – children, in-laws, colleagues, clients or constituencies such as the membership, the alliance, the sisterhood or brotherhood – with whom we are involved.

Then there is always the question, whether expressed or not: 'Will they keep their end of the bargain?'

Negotiated agreements break down for any number of reasons. Was there really an agreement? Was the agreement that you thought you had the same one the other side thought it had? Did the other side have the authority to commit to an agreement, or was it only an agreement in principle that required ratification? Was the other side able to carry the agreement back to its constituency and mobilize the resources to execute their end of the bargain? Sometimes the players change and old ground has to be covered once again, or the ground itself may shift. Sometimes we have to reopen negotiations to get the other party to honour their previous commitments.

What constitutes a good outcome in negotiation is really a much more complicated question than simply determining whether you got what you wanted, especially if this means a clear bottom line. Bottom line thinking with regards to negotiation is too simple, or shallow. More is at stake in most negotiations and a better measure of success is therefore necessary. Four criteria have been identified by Susskind and Cruikshank[3] to measure a good outcome.

A negotiated agreement is considered good if it is:

1 Fair;

2 Wise;

3 Efficient; and

4 Endures.

A level of success on the first three measures is necessary to achieve an agreement that will endure. If it is not fair, lacks wisdom and is not efficient it will most likely break down during implementation.

[3] Susskind and Cruikshank, *Breaking the Impasse*, New York, Basic Books, 1987.

☐ **Fairness** – A very inefficient, dragged out, and costly negotiation, which finally reaches a fair agreement may not have been worth the effort. You have to think of the cost in human and economic terms. Sometimes we get stuck on noble ground. We are stuck, nevertheless. Furthermore, what constitutes fairness is itself a subjective measure, calculated in a number of ways. We may compare our deal with others that are similar. We might consider the special circumstances of our particular deal, for example, knowing that the other party has given as much as it reasonably can, even though a slightly better deal may be 'more' fair. We may in the end rely on 'instinctive' sense of justice.

☐ **Efficiency** – Efficiency refers to the ease with which a settlement is reached and the degree to which the settlement includes the maximum amount of joint gain possible. Thus, the transaction costs are a consideration, as is the matter of how much the negotiators were able to extract from the potential that both parties brought to the table. The objective is to get as rich an agreement as is feasible within reasonable transaction costs. To insist on fairness as the only measure of a good outcome is to place too much emphasis on one point. In the end, we are aiming for an agreement that meets the whole test, as well as it can, with varying degrees of success for each measure of fairness, efficiency and wisdom.

☐ **Wisdom** – How do we know if an agreement is wise? Who is to say whether it is wise or not, especially when it has not stood the test time, and when the advice of others may not be immediately available when negotiating the specific details of an agreement? Moreover, who cares if it is wise, provided that I get what I want?

When you negotiate and strive for a wise agreement, you are conscious from the outset of things that otherwise you may have totally ignored. You may now think of the implications of this agreement for other negotiations that you will be involved in. Or you may consider the implications of this agreement for other people, such as your children, your colleagues, less powerful third parties whom you care about. You will be guided by these things. This kind of guidance gives you strength in your negotiation and it may slow you down when you would have rushed in.

Nothing short of perfect hindsight at some future time, maybe in weeks, months or even the years ahead, will really answer the question of whether it was a wise agreement. Nevertheless, starting out with that in mind will help make it so.

☐ **Endure** – If you strive for an agreement that is fair and wise and efficient, it will most likely endure. Fair in this case is meant to mean fair to you and to the other side. There will be a stronger commitment to maintaining a fair agreement. That commitment should ensure durability, which means that the negotiation will be honoured and the agreement will hold up over time. Unless, however, it was made with someone who lacked authority, was unable to deliver for some reason beyond his or her control, or who was unscrupulous.

But you want any deal you make to stand up. You want to be able to count on the agreement, on every part that was negotiated and agreed to. Be aware from the beginning that you are interested in getting a durable outcome and it will guide your behaviour. Are you clear about the actual authority you have? Can you commit to this or that? Can you deliver? Ask the same of the other side. Think about taking a little more time if it is necessary to let the other side feel comfortable with the proposal you have placed on the table, or to get more information for yourself. Yield on some points that you can give on and are important 'plusses' to the other side. You know that the other side must feel it is a fair deal and you must feel that too. Make it as fair as possible under the circumstances, knowing that fairness is an investment in the future, in durability and all that it brings with it.

## ACHIEVING A 'GOOD' OUTCOME

Seven elements have been identified as common to each and every negotiation by the Program on Negotiation, at Harvard Law School:

1  *Alternatives* that are available away from the table.

2  The *interests* of the parties.

3  *Options* that are invented in the negotiation to satisfy each party's interests so that agreement may be reached.

4  *Communication* in all its aspects as it plays a role in negotiation.

5  *Standards of legitimacy* that are used to persuade the other side of our case.

6  The *relationship* with the other party and relationship issues generally.

7  *Commitment*, both in terms of commitment expressed during negotiations in respect to a particular proposal or course of action, and commitment to honour the final agreement.

Let us consider each of the seven elements.

### Alternatives

We negotiate because negotiation promises to be the best way to get what we want. However, there are alternatives to negotiating. Our first task is to consider what are the alternatives to a negotiated agreement. List them and select the best of those that you have listed. Identify the best alternative that is available to you without ever having entered negotiation. This best alternative to a negotiated agreement, often called a BATNA, is a deceptively simple concept, yet one of the most critical elements in every negotiation strategy. It tells you whether you should negotiate, if only because you think you can do better than this best alternative. It gives you power when you are negotiating – the better your alternative, the less you need what you are trying to obtain in the negotiation. It tells you whether you should accept the offer, deal, or proposal in front of you or whether you should walk away.

### Interests

> Union: 'We want a 6 per cent raise in pay! That's our bottom line!'
> Management: 'All we're offering is 4 per cent, take it or leave it!'

> Resident: 'I don't know what your position is, but I'm not moving on this. There will be no toxic waste storage in my backyard!'

> Group spokesperson: 'I think we've got to make our position clear and find out theirs. We've got nothing to say to them if they refuse to recognize our position.'

Every day we read and hear statements like these. Individuals and groups about to enter negotiations or already engaged in them, assert their position. We also detect in these statements the basics of an adversarial stance. Declarations are made. Turf is staked out. The pronouncements are presented as both a sword and a shield: 'This is our position, take it or leave it.'

It is true that we do take positions on issues and matters of concern to us. People want to know our position and if we do not have one, we run the risk of being thought of as meek or weak-minded. It is more useful in both the negotiation preparation stage and when engaged in discussion with the other party, to determine what *interests* lie behind the positions presented.

In the first statement given above, for example, we can conclude that the union is very clear in what it wants. Unless it gets a 6 per cent raise, the negotiation is off. And we can imagine where things will go from there. However, is the 6 per cent being demanded because each year the union sets its goal based on the agreements negotiated in other collective bargaining settlements and since 'the others' got 6 per cent, so must they? Or is 6 per cent demanded because the union has calculated a straightforward cost of living increase from last year and this must be gained in negotiation just to keep up with costs? Or is the 6 per cent tied to something behind the scenes that the public will never really know? The 6 per cent figure becomes a symbol of a fair and just agreement given recent company profits, increased production quotas on the plant floor, or personality clashes at senior union and management levels. Is that 6 per cent now part of a power struggle?

We hear the demand for 6 per cent and we assume that it must be tied to some reasonable, defensible argument. Why, otherwise, not ask for 3 per cent or 9 per cent? However, the position is stated and presented with a challenge or threat in it. '6 per cent – that's our bottom line.' What, we must ask ourselves, are the true interests of the union when it states it wants 6 per cent? From the management's side, it may be a financial fact that a 6 per cent raise cannot be given to the union, at least not across the board, when costs have risen for management just as they have for everyone this year.

Behind declared positions are the real interests: the fears, concerns, expectations, beliefs and values. What are those interests? This is the question each negotiator must ask of himself and of the other party. What are my interests? What are their interests? 'They want 6 per cent, but why?', we ask as management.

'They won't give us 6 per cent and are offering 4 per cent, but why?', we ask as the union. Some answers might be that management's costs for material and other overheads, especially energy, have in fact really risen this year and the business is not so profitable. Or they are not pleased with the production output in the moulding shop and do not want to reward that shop along with the rest of us. Or the new vice-president in charge of operations has been trying to establish a name for himself and ran into a real clash with our lawyer over a disciplinary case three months ago. Now he is going to do everything he can to save face with the boss, including driving us down to a lower figure.

If management can determine what interests lie behind the union's position they will be better prepared to meet with them, to keep the communication on a constructive path and perhaps be able to offer a package that will meet the union's interests, and their own.

The challenge is to come up with creative solutions that meet real interests. These interests may be raises that keep up with costs, reassurance that employees are a valued part of the team, or a need to save face. We want to avoid the extreme costs associated with positional bargaining and to get the best agreement with the resources that we have between us.

List their interests and ours. Use a simple chart like the one in Table 13.1.

| | INTERESTS | |
| --- | --- | --- |
| | Ours | Theirs |
| Union's version | To keep up with the cost of living | To make profits |
| Management's version | To remain competitive | To make more money |

TABLE 13.1: Interests

## Options

The options we develop are proposals put forward in the negotiation. They may change or be discarded altogether the moment we learn something critical at the negotiating table. Options are thought about before we enter the face-to-face negotiations, but they really come together at the table. They typically include ideas of what one side will do in exchange for what the other side will commit to. Options follow a clear 'fleshing out' of the interests of both parties during negotiations. In a truly efficient negotiation, options are the creative solutions developed jointly by the negotiating parties. An option must be something that is only achievable through the negotiation, otherwise it is an alternative that can be achieved away from the table.

In our example, a good number of possible options come to mind in response to the interests that lie behind the positions: '6 per cent, that's our bottom line' and '4 per cent. Take it or leave it.' For instance, consider Table 13.2.

| INTERESTS | | OPTIONS |
| --- | --- | --- |
| Union | Management | |
| Getting an agreement that meets real costs of living | Getting an agreement that keeps labour costs down | Spread increase over two years to enable management to meet its legitimate interest, based on: 1. Actual cost of living increases 2. Projected costs/profits in year two |
| Getting an agreement that shows the membership that its leaders do as well as other union leaders | Getting union to stop protecting the moulding shop | Form a joint union-management team charged with developing a bonus plan for performance |
| | Save vice-president's face | Issue a joint statement |

TABLE 13.2: Options

This simple example does not do justice to the real world complexity of collective bargaining, which usually has many issues on the table from overtime pay to disability pensions, not to mention the attention paid to schemes for participatory management and innovative ways of organizing the work. Nevertheless, it does help us realize how much of a difference there is between stated positions and interests, and how it is possible to develop creative options to meet interests.

## Communication

When preparing for negotiation, we want to know ahead of time who 'they' are, what their typical style of negotiating is, whether they will send someone with authority to negotiate an agreement, or whether it will be a person who has to report back to head office. We would also like to determine whether this party is likely to use threats in the negotiation, and if they have the will and ability to execute any threats. Since we have armed ourselves with a very good 'best' alternative to a negotiated agreement, however, we have weakened the power of any threats they might make. We must determine our own information needs and be on top of these throughout the negotiation. We need to ask for information, seek clarification, restate in our own words what we believed we have heard. In addition, we need to communicate our interests clearly and to tell the other party that we are paying attention and are willing to reinforce behaviour that we consider worthy.

What are good communication skills? Consider the following questions: How do you appear when you present your case? Do you make demands, requests, or suggestions? Do you distinguish clearly among these so that the other side knows where you stand? Do you suggest and present some options you have already developed that might help the other side to meet your needs? Do you ridicule or ignore the other side? Do you ask for clarification, when in fact you do not understand? Do you present a fighting image all the time, or stand firm only when that stand is necessary? Do you look weak because of your body language; slumped in the chair, withdrawn? If there are two negotiators on your side do you present your case as though you are in agreement? Do you take time out to get agreement among yourselves and return to present a unified and clear message? Do you communicate in a way that will build confidence and trust?

Negotiation is the art of persuasion. What we communicate and how we communicate must be persuasive. We need to know when to 'go first' and 'how much to disclose' about our interests and needs and our willingness to yield. We need to know 'what would be persuasive' to the other side, either to shore up our case or to weaken their claim. And we need to know when and how to present that argument.

## Standards of legitimacy

What is going to convince the other side of the legitimacy of our case? So often when we fail to persuade them, we go away thinking they are obstructive or just plain stupid. 'Can't they see my point?', we ask ourselves, 'What's wrong with them anyway?' We all seem to think that it is quite natural that good standards, some objective evidence (be it an account of a similar past case), statistics that are available to anyone and therefore 'plain to see', or the opinion of some expert on the topic, should be persuasive.

However, our evidence often fails to persuade. Does this mean that evidence is unimportant? Not at all. It is critically important that some objective standards are presented to make our argument or claim legitimate. These standards help to elevate the negotiation beyond the 'position-taking' approach and all the traps that go with it. We want to minimize personality conflicts. You may have a relatively simple concern about the other person's style or appearance or, more rarely, a personality clash. Standards of legitimacy help us to focus on the problem at hand and not on the personalities. Standards are an honourable tool in the art of persuasion. We recognize that they help to disentangle the opinions and beliefs, the personal 'stuff' from the realities of the problem at hand. That is a useful function for standards. Standards also contribute to our sense of fairness when the standard is seen as legitimate by both parties.

Nevertheless, standards of legitimacy must be relevant to the other party, and they must be introduced at the right time, in the right way.

We have to come to the negotiation with standards that we believe will be persuasive to the other side and we have to examine the ones presented to us. We must be prepared to agree on those that are acceptable. Furthermore, we must move forward in the negotiation even where no prior standard exists, perhaps building on precedents, or developing new standards that should apply in this case. Each negotiated agreement is the creative product of the people at the table. Today's agreement may be tomorrow's standard.

## Relationship

Getting to know the other side's interests, developing options together, communicating to persuade and develop enough trust and confidence to close the deal, agreeing or disagreeing on presented standards are essentials of negotiation. They point out clearly that when we speak about negotiation, we are speaking about relationship.

Even the most straightforward negotiation is full of relationship issues. Probing for interests, dealing back and forth, building some trust, making a commitment and living with the other party after the deal has been struck are all important aspects of negotiation.

When we do not trust the other side, negotiation is most difficult. We are reluctant to accept their standards and we are unsure if they are really telling the truth about their interests and the proposals they put forth are suspect, no matter how sound they may seem. Perhaps they are not at the table in the spirit of seeking an agreement at all, we think to ourselves. Will they cheat? Will they deliver on their commitment? We are talking about a relationship here. A certain level of trust has to be established.

It is no surprise that many of us need to take our time when we are negotiating something that is important to us. We need the 'space' for trust building. If we are negotiating a partnership or any long-term arrangement, we need to feel more than comfortable with the facts. We need to trust the other party. A 'marriage' of kinds is happening.

Time away from the negotiating table may be necessary to gain some understanding of the agreement that is being developed. It might make perfect sense on paper, perfect business sense. But the relationship has not been nourished enough. We need some time to reflect and to feel confident. In a very intense or long negotiation, it may be best to schedule breaks that provide an opportunity to meet informally. The wisdom of eating together or going for a walk is evident.

Many people find that negotiating is a powerful kind of experience that can actually suck them in, like a centripetal force, drawing them into an agreement that they would rather not have made. The excitement and dynamics of making a deal, of problem solving and creating a brilliant agreement, compels them despite themselves. For strong positive reasons, some of us are caught up at the negotiating table to our later regret.

Other people find that they cannot tolerate the tension of negotiating. They are uncomfortable in competitive situations or wish to avoid conflict as much as possible. Some people cannot stand the thought of being offensive. They work very hard to preserve a relationship, sacrificing their personal interests and needs, building a one-sided agreement. For strong negative reasons, some of us are caught up at the negotiating table to our later regret.

In either case, the facts and substance of the negotiation, including the final agreement, whether to make a simple purchase or commit to a long-term partnership or joint venture, were not at issue. Relationships were. We ignore relationship in favour of the ideas and the excitement of the event or we sacrifice ideas and points of principle because we have a great need to avoid conflict at any cost. We may crave relationship to a fault.

While relationship runs through all negotiation, it must be established on individual strength, mutual respect and the honouring of commitments. You may want an agreement because you are excited about what you have just created at the table. But you will regret that you lost sight of your best alternative to a negotiated agreement. Was what you created really better than your BATNA? If so, only then can you enjoy the outcome long after you have taken pleasure in negotiating.

You may be interested in the relationship more than in the substance of this particular agreement. But if you are that dependent on the relationship, and the other party sees you as a tool for meeting its needs, you are weak and vulnerable. It will occur to you one day that you have given away too much, too easily. We do not want to sacrifice fairness, wisdom and durability; we should not compromise our legitimate self-interest.

Trust is critical to negotiating and it is especially important in a world as small as ours where we are likely to do business over and over again with certain parties.

Nevertheless, do not overload trust. This means we should not be naive and trusting fools. You want to be trustworthy. When you say something, you want people to know you mean it. And you want to say what you mean. Yet that does not mean that you automatically and instantly disclose everything to the party you are negotiating with. You do not want to be used. You do not want to create an opportunity for the other side to exploit. You are prepared to share your interests if they do not make you vulnerable, or if they are likely to be interpreted correctly.

You may want a bigger piece of the pie than they are willing to give. You may know that the least your union members will accept in this negotiation is 4.5 per cent, but that is only if management will give you more say in how the work is managed. If you disclose immediately that you are prepared to take 4.5 per cent what have you got left to bargain with? Your reputation? The fact that you are an honest and open person? Unlikely!

We want to make some trade-offs. The package has got to be better than you can get away from the table, i.e. by striking, by working for another company or by setting up your own employee-owned company. You must know what it is you can trade, what is of lesser importance to you and ideally, of more importance to them. We need to share information and both sides need to have a sense of trust. At the very least, this means that they can proceed step by step with a confidence that comes with the ability to predict certain behaviour. Sometimes our rock-bottom notion of trust is predictability: 'I can count on them to do this.'

Our task as negotiator has now reached beyond fact finder, master of argument, or any of the more simple notions we may have begun with. We have gone further than treating negotiation as merely communication. A good negotiator is a builder of relationship. A good relationship is comprised of strong individual players bringing something unique to the table that the other side wants, where the players are capable of making and keeping commitments.

## Commitment

From the very outset, we have touched upon the idea of commitment, although commitment itself is not given much attention in most negotiation discussions. It seems that commitment is recognized implicitly as a central element and the term is used quite casually. Obviously, we are naturally concerned from the first encounter with the other side about the extent to which they are committed to their position, and to what extent they are committed to the negotiation. However, we need to think about commitment in terms of its strategic value in negotiation.

It can be a source of power and a beacon that guides and secures our outcome. It can also be misused, misunderstood, a source of weakness, and of bad relations.

Our approach to negotiation has been to clarify our best alternative to a negotiated agreement and to try to determine what the other side's best alternative is. We do not want to commit ourselves to an agreement that is no better than our best alternative.

We have also said that our approach to negotiation includes a conscious effort to identify the interests that we and the other side have, as distinct from the positions that are stated or raised in the negotiations. This means that we probe behind positions and do not take the lead from positions, no matter how strongly we or they seem committed to them. When a position is stated in hard and clear terms, we may be able to acknowledge the interest that lies behind it, if we believe it is a legitimate one. Furthermore, we may be able to come up with a creative proposal that meets the unstated interests, when we would have become stuck and frustrated by positional stances otherwise. When strong commitments to positions are stated, we are challenged to identify the interests and to create solutions that move the negotiation forward. This is a sign of our commitment to the process and it helps to build the relationship. It assumes that we believe a negotiated outcome can be better than the best we could obtain without dealing with these people.

Because we believe that our interests and needs can be better met in negotiation than by other means, we are tempted to accept proposals that appear to meet those needs as soon as they are presented. The stronger our need or interest, the more likely we are to jump on a 'suitable' proposal. Nonetheless, committing to the first proposal may be far less satisfactory than if we had delayed. And it is very important to understand the relationship between commitment and power. Frequently, we assume there is a direct and obvious relationship between them. We think, 'If I show them my commitment to this they will feel and respect the power of my commitment.'

Consider this example. We are negotiating how to finance a new computer software and desktop publishing shop, which we are planning to start under a partnership arrangement with another party. Assume that one of our positions is to make sure that we own 50 per cent of the business, although the other party clearly has more money to put into the project. They also have less expertise than we do. We have expertise in computers and printing, and knowledge of the publishing industry. The ideal arrangement for us would include an agreement that gave us equal ownership, without investing as much money upfront. We are prepared to contribute our skill and knowledge and have that factored in as a contribution in lieu of cash lay-out to ensure some of our equal ownership.

However, in order to be certain that we do not have to give up the 50 per cent ownership position if pressed, we have determined that we can put the required money in to hold our share. Our expertise would then have to be compensated for in some other way, for instance, by wages or a 'director's fee'.

We would like the other party to put in more money upfront, and we therefore decide that our best strategy is not to mention our willingness to put the money in, but to bargain for equal ownership on the basis of our expertise contribution to the project. We really want the 50 per cent ownership. In preparing for the eventual encounter over our claim to 50 per cent ownership, we are ready to show our degree of commitment by bargaining from a position of strength. We make the assumption that the best position of strength we can demonstrate is to show that we are able to make the financial commitment of equal contribution to the new business.

Early in the negotiation, the other party acknowledges that we are experts in desktop publishing and that an arrangement with us would be great. They make it clear that they have several things to offer the new enterprise, including some accounting support which they have through their work in other businesses, and the influence they will have in referring people to the new shop. They ask, 'How will this new business be capitalized?', knowing our claim to be 50 per cent owners. They propose in the same breath, that a loan be taken and jointly guaranteed by both parties.

Now, we know that we can guarantee the loan. And we were prepared for that question but thought that it would come up later, perhaps if they had begun to haggle over the equal ownership proposal. What do we say?

Remember, we are very interested in maintaining a 50 per cent share of ownership in this business. We have expertise in the field and a personal interest in it. We also want them to know how strongly we are committed to that 50 per cent target.

Do we say: 'Sure, that's a reasonable proposal, which we are prepared to do', not mentioning the 50 per cent ownership interest?

Or 'Sure that's a reasonable proposal, which we are prepared to do, especially because we are committed to owning 50 per cent of the business, even though we are putting expertise in', thereby committing to the specific proposal and declaring our chief interest?

Or 'No, we can't accept that proposal because we are prepared to put our expertise into the venture in exchange for some of the financial costs and we would like to suggest the following . . .', thereby showing that we are committed to reaching an agreement but only under certain conditions?

Or do we say 'That's one approach that may be the best, but we'd like to suggest the following . . .', thereby revealing a willingness to work to an agreement but not revealing any readiness to commit to anything unacceptable to us?

There are a number of obvious reasons why we would find the first couple of answers in our example to be the least helpful to us. In the first case we have jumped right to a commitment, which gives up any negotiating power that may have come from holding back on sharing the financial costs. We have undervalued our expertise card, virtually acknowledging that it cannot be used as credit in exchange for ownership. And we have no assurance whatsoever that the 50 per cent ownership has been secured. The other party might reasonably be thinking at this point, 'If they have committed to that, what else will they commit to?'

In the second case, we commit to the 50–50 financial obligation as a direct means of securing the 50 per cent ownership. However, we have left ourselves open to being pressed for more concessions to keep that.

Furthermore, in both of the first responses we have done ourselves another disservice. We have been unable to determine what their interest is and to what extent our expertise was of value to them. They may have been prepared to contribute more cash upfront, and that was just their opening position. They may have been willing to give considerable value to our expertise. They may have even settled for less than 50 per cent ownership, fearing that the whole thing will not happen without our involvement.

Answers three and four give more room to move. The third case may be more limiting because it flatly rejects the proposal the other party suggests, whereas the last answer should not put them on the defensive. In it, we say: 'Yeah, that's an idea, but let's consider some others.' This one gives us a chance to regroup, to take a lead in offering proposals and it conveys no commitment to anything at this point.

We can now examine some of the other things that were happening in this scenario. This will illustrate the problems that come with confusing our interests with our position, and of equating positional bargaining with commitments. We often say, 'This is our position', meaning that to be seen as a commitment. Since it is a commitment we assume it has power, and it may. However, this kind of formula, or logic can put us at a disadvantage in negotiation.

Recall that we were committed to 50 per cent ownership. But under any circumstance? Surely not. We wanted our expertise to be factored in. And we probably wanted a number of other things as well, all of which would come out as the negotiation proceeded.

We wanted to get 50 per cent ownership so badly that we confused our commitment to it as a position of strength from which we would bargain. Knowing that we were so committed to 50 per cent ownership, we had already begun to figure out ways we could argue for and secure it. If push came to shove we had worked out that we would show how strong we were in our position and that we could defend it. How? By arguing the value of expertise? By developing options to secure 50 per cent over time in exchange for our 'consulting services' to the business? Or by other creative ideas, such as folding our share of the profits into the purchase of a full 50 per cent ownership? No.

We assumed that demonstrating our ability to guarantee one-half of the loan upfront would show the other side that we were ready and able to claim our 50 per cent interest. We did not bargain for 50 per cent, throwing in any number of our assets to secure it. We were committed to 50 per cent and began to develop proposals, meaning concessions, that we were prepared to make to secure it. Not only that, but when we got into the negotiation itself, and gave in right away on the loan issue, had we chosen either the first or second response in our example we would have weakened our other bargaining advantages.

You have a position. You are committed to it. But how far will you go or what will you give to get that position? You believe your commitment to your position makes you strong. You invent a variety of concessions you are prepared to make to secure that position. But what are you asking the other party to give up? And if they know you are committed to your position, do you run the risk that they will put you on the run the moment they see you concede something of value that you had hoped to use as a bargaining strength?

We respect people of commitment. It is clear that commitment can convey power. But do not confuse staking out a position as a sign of commitment which guarantees you automatic bargaining strength. In fact, our strength is often reduced because we commit to a position.

We confuse a position, i.e. 50 per cent ownership, with interest. In this scenario, 50 per cent ownership may have implied that we would have executive authority, the ability to significantly influence the business plan and so forth. These things were our real interests, but they need not be equated with the position of 50 per cent ownership.

Commit very carefully and commit late. And finally, honour any commitments you make.

## SUMMARY

1  Negotiation has both cooperative and competitive dimensions. We have outlined an approach which encourages a climate of negotiation that helps identify the interests of the parties; more can be achieved than sticking to a strictly positional approach. In fact, we have shown how positions mask deeper interests and the challenge is, in part, to determine what those interests are. Then you can offer a good proposal, and even come up with jointly developed options that are richer (more efficient) than you might have expected had you taken a concession/counter-concession approach.

2  Negotiation, as old and as universal a practice as it is, will never conform to a cut and dried formula. Negotiation reaches deep inside our individual personalities and values to engage the other party we are dealing with. This occurs within a broad, and often vaguely sensed, cultural context; although we become very aware of culture when the negotiation takes place in a cross-cultural context. We negotiate all the time, sorting through and expressing what is of value and importance to us. We negotiate on behalf of others, needing to respect, plan for, and attend to their interests, and we also negotiate when others, perhaps our children, or unrepresented third parties have their interests at stake, even though they are not at the table.

3  The approach here does not concentrate on a strategy to win at negotiation, where a win for 'our' side necessarily means a corresponding loss for 'their' side. It does, however, strive to achieve the greatest amount of gain possible in a world made up of individuals, groups, and nations that have self-interest and who must live together in some degree of cooperation for any gains to be achieved.

4  There is no negotiation 'pill' that we can take to make us good negotiators. There is no substitute for informed practice and critical review of what we did 'at the table'.

# CHAPTER 14

## THE SPIRITUAL DIMENSION OF LEADERSHIP

### INTRODUCTION

The days when consultants could be merely advisors – bystanders in the world of work – are all but gone. Today, clients expect their 'consultants' to become involved in delivery and implementation, to be problem solvers. They also expect them not just to follow, but to lead. It is, therefore, reasonable to speak of leadership in the context of consulting, but why spirituality and leadership? It sounds like a contradiction in terms, particularly in the ultra-rational world of consulting. The word 'spiritual' derives from the Latin *spiritus*, which means breath or life. Immediately our exploration leads us to something that gives life, animates or enables. If we put the word 'spirituality' into an internet search engine we would be overwhelmed with definitions. For most people, the concept of spirit or spirituality is very subjective and unique: in fact, we might say that there are almost as many definitions as there are people! Furthermore, not everyone wants to acknowledge that they have a spiritual side to them.

Yet we may talk in the workplace about 'team spirit', or a 'soul-destroying job'. What does this mean to the modern leader? Are they words or phrases that we use without thinking too much about them? The evidence is that more and more people acknowledge the importance of the spiritual in the workplace and in leadership development. This is demonstrated by the increase in the number of books, journals and articles.[1] Words or phrases such as 'attitudes and beliefs which animate people's lives' or 'help them live life to the full' frequently crop up. Other definitions focus on the way we live and do things – in other words, practices and behaviour. How do our beliefs and attitudes impact on the way we behave at work, especially if we operate in a leadership function? Are our beliefs and attitudes very different from the way we behave at home or socially when out with friends? The distinguished management writer, Charles Handy, once asked his radio audience 'Would you take your daughter to work with you?'[2] How much of the behaviour that you display in the workplace, the boardroom or the shop floor would you want to reveal to your children? The quest for meaning in life, truth

[1] For instance both the *Financial Times* and the *Harvard Business Review* have published a series of articles on the spiritual dimension of work.
[2] Charles Handy, BBC Radio 4, 'Thought for the Day'.

and ultimate values is another theme. How aware are we of the aspects of life apart from the physical and material? What sense of awe, wonder and mystery does this awareness give? Does this spiritual dimension help us to develop a sense of our own identity, worth and value in our relationships, especially with the significant people in our lives and society as a whole? Matthew Fox gives this definition about a spirituality of work:

> '. . . spirit means life, and both life and livelihood are about living in depth, living with meaning, purpose, joy and a sense of contributing to the greater community. A spirituality of work is about bringing life and livelihood back together again.'[3]

Even the most cursory examination of business literature will reveal the importance of change and relationships in the spiritual dimension. The spiritual dimension is not static, it is an ongoing process and involves growth, change and conversion so that we can become fully human. The Greek philosophers had a word for change called *metanoia*. This was not superficial change. It meant a radical reorientation of the self, the ego. Furthermore, the realm of the spiritual dimension is all-encompassing. Many ancient philosophies and early writings on spirituality emphasized the submission of the body to the spirit. Simplistically, the fight for the soul was seen as a conflict between good (spirit) and evil (body). The insights of modern psychology have enabled those concerned with the spiritual dimension to understand spiritual growth as a holistic process, which embraces intellect, emotions, the body and the soul. Therefore, if these elements are the four walls of the house, spirituality is the foundation. For some, the spirit can have an existence outside of the body. When we die, the spirit (or soul) will continue to live. In fact it is only then that we will have attained complete fulfilment. Yet, for some, death is the end of everything. For others, there is a possibility of reincarnation into a new body or form.

## SPIRITUALITY AND RELIGIOUS PRACTICE

Many people in the world of business and organizational change have difficulties in accepting the spiritual dimension because of its long association with religion and religious practice. They see the two spheres, spiritual and religion, as inseparable. However, as recent research in North America has shown, it is both possible and desirable that in a secular organizational context they should be kept separate. Ian Mitroff and Elizabeth Denton[4] make the point that whereas individuals and organizations are willing to accept the necessity of the spiritual dimension in the workplace, there is far greater reluctance to accept the religious beliefs that frequently accompany it. Nevertheless, in spite of the reservations that people may have about religion, many have some belief in a higher power or energy that sustains and drives them forward, especially during times of crisis or difficulty. They may even try and communicate or listen to that power. Some may call this process meditation or prayer and there are many techniques. In addition to the more classical approaches, usually evolved from Western religious traditions of prayer and worship, the religions and philosophies of the East now offer a different approach through Yoga, Tai Chi (moving meditation) and similar practices.

One of the most useful ways to understand the spiritual dimension is in terms of relationship. Let us imagine two axes, vertical and horizontal, like the four points of the compass (see Figure 14.1). At the centre is the individual person made up of four elements: body, soul, emotion and intellect. The vertical axis, which passes through the centre, represents the relationship between some higher power or energy and the inner self. This inner being is deep down inside of us, probably not known or recognized, or only superficially. Then there is the

[3] Matthew Fox, *The Reinvention of Work: A New Vision of Livelihood for our Time*, HarperCollins, 1984.
[4] Ian Mitroff and Elizabeth Denton, 'A study of spirituality in the workplace', *Sloan Management Review*, Summer, 1999.

second axis, the horizontal one. Again the individual is at the centre. The relationship is a continuum with the world as perceived by the individual at one end and as perceived by others at the opposite end. If we can imagine, these two axis are intersected by a series of circles of varying circumference. The small one, nearest the centre, represents our relationship with significant people in our lives. The next might be our relationship with close friends. The third circle, larger still, is our relationship with our workplace, especially those we work with or for. Then there are further circles, increasing in circumference representing the myriad of other relationships we have. The options are countless. When we think about it, we have relationships of varying intensity with a wide variety of people (individual and groups), creatures and inanimate objects. They might include other stakeholders in the workplace enterprise (e.g. customers, suppliers, equity holders, local community). Also of importance might be the environment and developing world. How do all these relationships impact on your spirituality, and vice versa, how does your spirituality impact on them? What is the significance of the vertical relationship in your life? If you get that right, are the other relationships more harmonious or right? How are you affected when significant people for instance your spouse, children or other members of family, get pushed out and other concerns, such as your leadership role in the workplace, become more dominant?

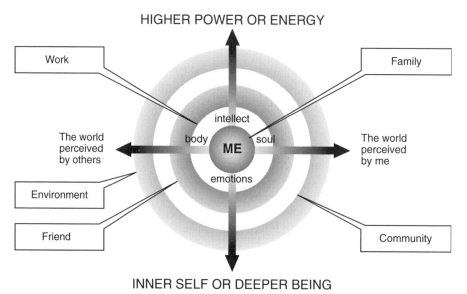

FIGURE 14.1: Spirituality as relationship

## THE WORKING WOUNDED

Relationships have the ability to transform and change us, sometimes quite fundamentally. It may be a chance encounter with a particular person, even a stranger. Perhaps it is something we have read, a piece of poetry or some sacred narrative. Alternatively, it might be a piece of music, a work of art, even a building, landscape or spectacular view. How often have we undergone a 'mountain top experience' without even having to climb the mountain? Our daily work can transform us. Because of our creative ability and talents, we can transform the workplace and others in it. Yet, how easy it is to be crushed rather than transformed by our work and responsibilities. There is evidence that this is happening more and more to people in the workplace, especially to those with leadership roles. The battalions of the 'working wounded' never cease to grow. Diminishing resources and the emphasis on profitability with greater shareholder return and value, sometimes mean that people are forced to take 'short cuts' to get the job done. Expediency and effectiveness tend to outweigh excellence and value. Over the last few years, *Management Today*[5] has conducted a number of surveys on work-life balance. Missing the children growing up, having to put work before home and family and strain on marital relationships, often leading to divorce were some of the areas highlighted. The negative impact of some of these factors results in low morale, skills shortage, and high staff turnover. Moreover, we should not underestimate the debilitating effects of negative stress or distress upon leadership, frequently leading to burn out and physical or mental illness.

How did the managers in the surveys want things to change? Interestingly, money came fairly low on the list. Rather, a desire to work fewer and more flexible hours, change the company culture and reduce or avoid commuting were important. Thus business organizations are starting to realign many of their corporate goals and values, adapting recruitment policies and management training to accommodate these and other shifts.

## LEADER OR MANAGER?

What are the qualities of the leader? Are they the same as for a manager? Traditionally, recruitment and training in the business world and for that matter most other professions, have placed great emphasis on the intellectual and professional qualifications needed to do a job. For the most part, these are function or task-oriented. Intelligence, academic and professional qualifications determine our ability. This has been described as IQ of leadership. Although not completely ignoring other qualities, which we will touch on in a moment, this takes the view that leadership is part and parcel of our intellectual ability. However, we soon realize that good leadership requires more than just a sound knowledge and experience of business functions, such as accounting, financial control and planning, marketing, strategic planning and so on. Perhaps, more than anything, it is other forms of 'intelligence' that differentiates the leader from the manager. In recent literature on management development, these forms are frequently referred to as 'emotional intelligence' and 'spiritual intelligence'. Since the mid-1980s in particular, there has been an increased emphasis on what have been called the 'soft skills' of the modern leader. Emotional intelligence, or EQ as it is called, is the intelligence that gives us awareness of our own and other people's feelings, for example, empathy with others, compassion and motivation. The contribution of the management psychologist Daniel Golemen has been important in this area of development.[6] The latest insight is SQ, or spiritual intelligence. This is the intelligence that we use to address and solve problems of meaning and value. The thesis is that neither IQ or EQ can totally express the complexity of life. SQ gives the ability to discriminate between good and evil. Therefore, it has a moral and transformative quality.[7]

## WHY LEAD?

Why do men and women want to be leaders in business organizations? What motivates them to devote most of their waking day to running an organization? What drives and sustains them? Is it greed, a lust for power, wealth or status? The majority would probably say 'Definitely not'. Perhaps it is simply a need to allow their talents to be fully utilized. The satisfaction of seeing a difficult job well done. The challenge of climbing the mountain because it is there. Modern insights into management motivation can be of great benefit to our understanding. The job of a leader can be lonely and isolated. How are they supported

[5] Ceridian Performance Partners, 'The Great Work Life Debate', *Management Today*, June 1998.

[6] Daniel Goleman, 'Leadership that gets results', *Harvard Business Review*, March/April, 2000. Daniel Goleman, *Emotional Intelligence*, Bloomsbury, 1996.

[7] Danah Zohar and Ian Marshall, *SQ Spiritual Intelligence: the Ultimate Intelligence*, Bloomsbury, 2000.

and affirmed? How can we ensure that they are equipped to deal with the complexity of tasks and the speed of response? What enables them to hold their nerve and keep their cool in times of crisis or failure?

Table 14.1 shows some typical styles, which a leader might adopt. Although one particular style will tend to dominate, he or she may vary the style depending on circumstances.

| | STYLE | ACTION BY LEADER | RESPONSE BY FOLLOWER | RESULT |
|---|---|---|---|---|
| 1 | AUTOCRATIC | Power, coercion, threats, punishment | Alienation, fear | Afraid, oppressed, dependent, distanced |
| 2 | BENEVOLENT | Paternalistic, rewards and teaches | Preserved, feels safe | Dependent, serves, obeys, loyalty |
| 3 | BUREAUCRATIC | Institutionalizes and dictates | Laws, handbooks, regulations, procedures | Dedicated, committed, institutionalized |
| 4 | LAISSEZ-FAIRE | Listens, supports and clarifies | Listens, supports, clarifies | Cooperation |
| 5 | DEMOCRATIC | Participatory and gifted | Become more independent | Productive, goal-oriented, collaborative |
| 6 | PARTICIPATORY | Team work, serves others | Creative and empowered | Interdependent and takes responsibility |
| 7 | PROPHETIC | Visionary, spiritual and truthful | Liberated and synergized | Bonded, fulfilled and trusted |

TABLE 14.1: Leadership styles

Most people in leadership are familiar with Abraham Maslow's hierarchy of human needs: security, relationship, self-esteem and self-actualization. Using these and other psychological insights, Richard Barrett in *Liberating the Corporate Soul*[8] develops seven levels of human (employee) consciousness: survival, relationship, self-esteem, transformation, organization, community and society. The last three are spiritual levels of consciousness provoked by our need to be of service to society, to make a difference to our community and to gain meaning in our life from the organization we work for. In contrast to the first three, which are primarily motivated by self-interest, the spiritual levels of consciousness are motivated by the 'common good' or the needs of others. The two groups are linked by transformation or as we have described it earlier conversion or *metanoia*. This is the key, the bridge focused on self-knowledge and renewal. Richard Barrett says:

> During transformation, the culture of the organisation shifts from control to trust, from punishment to incentives, from exploitation to ownership, and from fear to truth.

## THE SPIRITUAL TOOLS OF LEADERSHIP

What are the spiritual tools of leadership and can they be acquired or developed? Is it a question of connecting with the inner qualities and character traits that are already there, or can they be learned through some regular practice and discipline? What differentiates a spiritually motivated leader from an ordinary one? Is a gifted leader one who can take the appropriate skill from his or her spiritual tool-kit at the right time and the right place? The management guru, Steven Covey, laments the fact that in the last 50 years or so, the focus of much North American management development literature has been on a personality rather than a character ethic. Up until 1955, this literature emphasized the importance of:

[8] Richard Barrett, *Liberating the Corporate Soul: Building a Visionary Organization*, Butterworth-Heinemann, 1998.

‘ humility integrity, fidelity, temperance, courage, justice, patience, and the *Golden Rule*[9] . . . Now it is focused on personality, public image, attitudes, behaviours and techniques which lubricate the process of human interaction. ’ [10]

This is an interesting and important observation because it brings those responsible for leadership development, including leaders themselves, face to face with a more recent philosophical trend, which concentrates on 'virtue ethics'. To put it simply, it is not so much the activity of the leader or the different leadership tasks that have to be addressed. Rather, it is the qualities (or virtues) of the leader that we must examine. Although management literature is more familiar with the concept of values and mission statements, it does not often speak in terms of 'virtue'. Yet anyone who recognizes the importance of the spiritual dimension of leadership, has to accept that this also implies recognition of the importance of the virtues (as we shall continue to call them from now on), and in this context, particularly those that are most applicable to the leadership of business organizations. Why is virtue important in the context of the spiritual dimension of leadership? Because, more than anything else, it is what differentiates a manager from a leader and a good leader from an excellent leader. The virtues are key to good leadership, especially in the context of relationships. They indicate an ability to engage, trust and respect and to inspire and motivate others. They give us the ability to transform ourselves, and by our deeds and example, transform others.

Two people can be used to illustrate the importance of virtue in leadership. These are the Greek philosopher Aristotle (384–323 BC) and founder of Western Monasticism, Benedict of Norcia (c. AD 480–526). Surprisingly, neither were businesspeople, in fact they were both very suspicious of business activities. However, they knew a great deal about the qualities of spiritual leadership, which are as relevant today as they were many centuries ago. Aristotle, in his *Nicomachean Ethics*, written some 23 centuries ago defines the types of virtue and their importance for living a fulfilled life or 'achieving happiness', as he called it. For Aristotle, the purpose of studying ethics (and learning about virtue) was not to learn what good people are like, but rather to learn how to act as good people in order to be good citizens of the community in which we live. Or we can paraphrase this by saying 'be good leaders in the place in which we work'. Virtues could not be learned in a day, it was the task of a lifetime!

‘ Happiness is not so much the end but the way. Happiness comes as we acquire and live the virtues necessary to transverse the dangers and opportunities of our existence . . . it decidedly is not something that can be accomplished all at once. ’ [11]

For Aristotle, a virtue was a 'moral excellence', a settled or consistent attitude conducive to achieving a good outcome in some aspect of our behaviour. The virtues were concerned with character traits such as courage, fortitude, temperance, patience and truthfulness. However, above all, the good leader needs to possess 'practical wisdom', that is to be good at thinking about what he or she should do. Consequently, one of the most important qualities of a leader is knowing how to think about how to act. President Lyndon B Johnson, in relation to US foreign policy, was once asked by a journalist if he was sure that America was doing the right thing. The President replied, 'Hell, boy, doing the right thing is easy. It's knowing what the right thing is that's the difficult part.'[12]

Aristotle did not underestimate the difficulty of teaching virtue. He realized that it was something that could be done only with people who had gained a certain level of intellectual and emotional maturity and above all 'judgement'. We all recognize that one of the essential qualities of good leadership is sound judgement or practical wisdom. Assuming that we have

153

---

[9] The Golden Rule exists in many cultures and sacred texts. Invariably it can be paraphrased in the words 'do not do to another what you would not want done to yourself'.

[10] Steven Covey, *The Seven Habits of Highly Effective People*, Simon & Schuster, 2002.

[11] Aristotle, *The Nicomachean Ethics*, translation by J A K Thompson, Penguin, 1976.

[12] Cited by R C Smith in *Wall Street Ethics Today*, New York University, Salomon Centre, Work Paper Series, 1990.

learned to think about how to act in the right way, we grow in practical wisdom through experience, learning from different situations (either firsthand or indirectly), from various narratives (newspapers, media, TV, journals, books) and other people. Practical wisdom is learned rather than taught. Making mistakes is an integral part of the learning process. Sometimes making a mistake can lead to great failure. In our results-oriented business environment, failure is seldom tolerated, or is viewed at least in very negative terms. Failure is seen as crisis rather than a stepping stone to ultimate success. Nevertheless, does not our personal experience confirm that we grow most in character and virtue at times of crisis, isolation and failure? The good leader is continually tested and transformed by the many difficult situations and by the complex and seemingly insurmountable decisions that have to be made.

Over the centuries, the list and types of virtues has developed. For instance, humility, faith, hope and love feature prominently as Christian virtues. Most religions and philosophies have their 'sacred texts' where types of virtue and traits of character are used to define the good person, someone who is successful or fulfilled. In the sixth century, Benedict of Norcia compiled a rule for monks. It was not intended as a manual for leadership development. Instead, it was 'a little rule for beginners' who wanted a life in this world that would eventually lead to happiness in eternal life. At the heart of the rule was the role of the leader of the community or, as he or she was called (respectively), the 'abbot' or 'abbess'. The abbot or abbess was the spiritual and temporal father or mother, of the community. In referring to the choice and qualities of the community leader, Benedict makes no mention of academic ability, professional qualifications or success at recruitment. The focus is entirely on the virtues. This is what he writes:

> ' Goodness of life and wisdom in teaching must be the criteria for choosing the one to be made leader, even if he or she is last in community rank. Once in office the leader must keep constantly in mind the nature of the burden that has been received and remember to whom he or she will have to give an account. Let leaders recognise that their goal must be profit for the community not pre-eminence for themselves. The leader must be chaste, temperate and merciful . . . hate faults but love each member of the community using prudence and avoiding extremes. Let the leader strive to be loved rather than feared. A leader should never be excitable, anxious, extreme, obstinate, jealous or over suspicious because they are never at rest. Instead, being discerning and moderate, they must show foresight and consideration in all they do . . . therefore drawing on this and other examples of discretion, the mother of virtues, they must so arrange everything that the strong have something to yearn for and the weak nothing to run from. ' [13]

Above all, says Benedict, let the leader be humble. How appropriate is the virtue of humility for a leader? Does it indicate some degree of weakness or subservience? What does humility in a contemporary business leader look like? Here is a list of attributes that came out of a recent workshop.[14] Humility in the workplace means being grounded, authentic, listening, being the same to all irrespective of who people are, affirming, accepting mistakes and learning from others.

For both Aristotle and Benedict, being virtuous meant achieving excellence rather than being effective. It was about changing oneself rather than changing the organization. We can change others, but only by being a model or mirror of what we should be striving to be, rather than do. When the people in a business look at their leader, they are more likely to be influenced by what the leader is rather that what the leader is doing.

[13] Timothy Fry (Ed.), *The Rule of St Benedict*, The Liturgical Press, 1982.

[14] Dermot Tredget, Spirituality in the workplace, 'Coping with success and failure' at Douai Abbey, Reading, England, May 2002.

# SUMMARY

The central theme of this chapter has been that the spiritual qualities of leadership are indispensable, in particular to the business organization. The importance of this can be evidenced by growth in business literature on the spiritual dimension of the workplace, soft skills, business ethics and emotional intelligence. The core concept used to describe spirituality is 'relationship' or 'connectedness' with a focus on the vertical relationship of the individual with some higher power or energy. At the same time, working on a horizontal plane, is the leaders' relationship with other individuals, the wider community, nature and the environment. This can be made up of many categories or stakeholders such as customers, suppliers, employees, local households or developing countries. The categories are limitless. This relationship also has an impact on the environment. In short, whatever the leader does has an effect on somebody or something somewhere. Conversely, much of what happens in the business environment, often beyond the control of the business organization, for instance market forces or political intervention, has an effect on the business leader. Hence the importance of the ethical activity which is an integral part of the spiritual dimension of leadership. In this chapter, drawing on examples given by Aristotle and Benedict of Norcia, it has been suggested that the focus should be on the spiritual qualities of leadership, in particular the virtues such as integrity, prudence, temperance, courage, humility, faith and love. In other words the qualities of the decision-maker are more important than the decision-making process itself. What the leader *is* rather than what the leader *does* characterizes the spiritual dimension.

# CHAPTER 15

## KNOWLEDGE SHARING IN THE CONSULTING CONTEXT

Francis Bacon (1561–1626) the famous philosopher and politician, said 'Knowledge itself is Power'. Until recently, if people thought about knowledge at all, they did so with the equation that knowledge equals power. People, therefore, tended to hoard knowledge. People were promoted because of it; many consultants made a good living from building, packaging, protecting and selling it; business schools have researched and disseminated it. However, with the accelerating rate of change, the life-span of knowledge is decreasing. Whereas you used to be able to consult textbooks or the library for methods and solutions to business problems, increasingly problems have no clear answer or appropriate problem-solving method.

People and companies are looking again at the equation of 'knowledge equals power', and coming to the conclusion that knowledge is best shared in order to help individuals and companies to fulfil their true potential. At the strategic level, an organization needs to sense the environment in which it operates, challenge basic assumptions and evaluate options. At a tactical level, countless decisions are made every day by employees and stakeholders. It would be more advantageous if people talk openly, share their experiences, have access to expert input when needed and are better equipped to understand the impact of their decisions. As successes are seen and shared, they can be replicated quickly and effectively to everyone's benefit. This chapter explores the implications of this shift for consultants.

## CONSULTING ON THE GROUND AND IN THE AIR

Since the early 1990s, the major means of communication between consultant and client have changed dramatically due to technological development. In many ways, these technological developments have forced an increase in the rate of change in consulting and client behaviour. If we reflect on the changes on consulting activity and possibilities, we will see a significant shift from consulting on the ground to consulting in the air. By consulting, we refer to that activity, which is conducted either by an expert external to and contracted by the organization or a specialist (internal consultant) employed by an organization. For the purposes of this chapter, we have separated these into two sections. In practice, many of the observations refer to both.

## Implications for external consultants

We believe that the future role of the consultant will have more to do with knowledge management. That is, the effective consultant will be one who has the capability to search for and capture knowledge and apply it appropriately. Actually 'having knowledge' will become less important. The advances in internet technologies and the effectiveness of search engines mean that it is all too easy to access knowledge in terms of content. The added value contribution from the consultant will be the ability to access relevant knowledge and to select it, assess its value, integrate it with other knowledge, to apply it in practice and to communicate effectively with the client. Real edge will come from being able to do this more accurately and more articulately than the next consultant, as well as responding quickly.

The worldwide web is having an amazing effect on the work of consultants. While face-to-face dialogue is still important, increasingly the collection and the distribution of information is carried out electronically. There are dangers in this, but the result is that clients expect quicker, more efficient service and at lower cost.

These changes will impact the way consultants work together and the type of business they may be asked to deliver. This is because there are many factors involved, both in the selection of the company to be sent an 'Invitation to tender' and in the final choice of supplier. Costs can carry a positive image – 'They can afford to charge these fees because they employ the best and get results', but perhaps these days they start to carry a different implication – 'They have elegant offices which are much of the overhead that we (the client) have to pay for.'

We now see networks of consultancies springing up, which are harnessing the power of the new technologies. Smaller consultancies, including the single operator, are now able to find like-minded consultants with complementary skills and can link up globally in order to take on the bigger projects, which hitherto might have been the preserve of the big consultancy firms. Small consultancies are able to make themselves appear big and can assemble teams without the overhead of employing consultants who are unassigned to a project. Many consultants are re-framing how they view other consultants. Rather than seeing them as competitors, they look at them as collaborators or even potential customers. Thus, there are now important roles for the consultants to the consultants, for instance providing sales and marketing, public relations and technical services.

In such a fragmented market, there are even valuable roles for intermediaries, who connect various consultancies and consultants to clients. The ability to do this is increased by the power of the internet.

There are a number of valuable guidelines to follow when consultants use the internet.

## Talk before you write

The essence of any consulting activity is to develop confidence and understanding. This still requires some face-to-face meetings, because that is where we assess and convey emotion, passion and interest. For all of its user-friendly features, the web is still an impersonal vehicle. Messages are received and dispatched, as if by magic. Nevertheless, when they are received, they may not be understood in the spirit in which you wrote them. There is a tendency, once you have the facility of internet communication, to move into arms-length communication where messages are sent into cyberspace and returned, without any direct human contact. Meeting a person will tell you far more than what they write – although some consultants say quite the opposite. It is possible that they have developed their own personal and intuitive skills to operate, without meeting their clients. However, the arrival of the web camera enables even meetings to be held electronically. In the future, many meetings will be held at a distance. However, we still advise: talk before you write.

## Do not confuse reports with action

The internet is a great vehicle for sharing and comparing information. It is also a great deceiver. It encourages the report mentality. It is often assumed that if you write a good report, that is sufficient. The report may provide an excellent diagnosis and a first-class solution, but it will not necessarily lead to any action. This, of course, has always been the case in consulting. How many times have you seen consultants' reports gathering dust on the shelves, with no action taken on the issues? The same occurs with reports written via the internet, only now they do not gather dust. They are out of sight, out of mind. The value of any consulting is not in the report, but in the action taken to effect meaningful and useful change. It is essential, therefore, that consultants influence others to get action. This means working with those involved to gain direction and energy for action. This is a political, with a small 'p', activity. You need to arrange meetings, and ensure those people who can influence change are there. At the meetings, you need to help people to talk through problems and difficulties, which otherwise might not be resolved. Do not let virtual communication be a substitute for action. You may have everyone sending e-mails and writing reports, but no one acting on them.

## Involve the client

Wherever possible, ensure that the clients contribute in a substantial way to problem solving. In that way, they will be more interested in following through the proposals to improve things. Special efforts have to be made to include the views of clients. They may not, for example, be at ease with the web as a means of communication. If so, their views should be elicited in traditional ways, written up and circulated, so that they are part of the debate.

## Research on the web

The great advantage of the internet is that it is an excellent way to do research, without leaving your office or home. In the past, any consultant had to go to the library to get books and articles. Now, at the touch of a finger, you can access the latest information through systems like Anbar and PALS. Moreover, many sources are free to use. Note, however, that your clients can do likewise. It is often the consultant's role to bring forward relevant material and thinking, which the client has not found or has not had the time to find. However, research on the internet is more than passive access to existing literature. There is an amazing opportunity for doing real-time research. You can send out questions to a selected audience, at a fraction of the cost of traditional market research. The success of research on the internet depends on the thought that goes into it. It requires well thought out questions. That is easy to say and hard to do. The answers you get are only as good as the questions you pose. It is wise to trial these questions in advance and refine them, before going live.

## Tips on developing your website

Most external consultants direct you to their website early in the conversation. This may put you off because it can give the impression that they do not wish to spend any further time with you. Therefore, be selective about when you advertise your web presence. Before you advertise your website, make sure that you have it fully tested and constructed. No one wants to see a half finished site, or to look and get little reward. It will be a long time before they go back. Make your site lively and use colour. People are used to seeing good sites that stand out. You have to compete at all levels, but beware of gimmicks that can appear superficial and lead to frustration in terms of download times. Make your site easy to navigate. Have the main buttons that will lead people to the key areas on your homepage. Cut out the tours. One of the design objectives when developing the PALS websites (www.pals.co.uk and www.palszenith.com) was to help a visitor find what they want with 'three clicks'. Tough to do, but it does lead to rigorous design. If you want to gain business through your site, it is best to offer some business. What can you give away that is free and that indicates the focus and quality of your service? This is increasingly an important aspect of consulting on the web. The internet is a veritable Aladdin's Cave for discovery, providing you know what you want to find out. It is useful to join professional groups who discuss topics in your area, or set up your own group. The web is a very exciting medium for consulting. It adds to what is already a fast and furious level of activity for most consultants. Keeping a balance between 'on the ground', and 'in the air' consulting will be hard to do, but essential for success.

## Implications for internal organizational development consultants

The internal consultant can support organizational development and knowledge initiatives in very important ways. There are new paradigms operating which open up a range of opportunities:

☐ **Knowledge strategy** – Get involved in your organization's knowledge management strategy.[1] Do not be put off if you do not think that you know enough about the subject. It is critical to link specific networks, knowledge domains and communities of practice to business success and strategic goals. One of the first tasks, therefore, is to identify in your workplace the communities and networks already in place – and make them visible. Study them to understand how knowledge sharing is already taking place. Be aware that the people involved in them will be constantly moving and changing. The skills obtained through working with teams cannot be directly translated into working with communities.

☐ **Working with communities** – Etienne Wenger's *Communities of Practice*[2] lays out a solid theoretical foundation to understand the dynamics of practice communities. Facilitating community development is a natural role for internal organizational development (OD) consultants. There are new roles to be defined in the organization and these will lead to new reward systems. Skills need to be developed so that people create new knowledge by collaboration – not just cooperation.

☐ **Use of technology** – The use of new technologies can greatly assist in the knowledge revolution. However, the supporting infrastructure can only be effective if it more easily facilitates the natural processes that exist in an organization.

---

[1] Recent surveys by The Conference Board and the American Management Association show that at least 50 per cent of US companies, and up to 72 per cent of overseas firms, have some kind of knowledge management initiative underway. Other studies put the figure closer to 80 per cent for global corporations.

[2] Etienne Wenger, *Communities of Practice*, Cambridge University Press, 1998.

☐ **Ethics** – This topic is covered in Chapter 12. Trust is important in e-networks. From experience, this trust exists in the beginning, but it can be quickly eroded. Internal consultants have a unique opportunity to champion understanding of the new business paradigms and the ethical underpinnings for success.

## COMMUNICATION AND INFORMATION SHARING IN E-NETWORKS

Common sense would indicate that there are different dynamics for communicating with people who are in the same time/same place, those who have occasional face-to-face interaction, and those with no face-to-face interaction.

From observations of working with e-networks, we believe that the members' experience of working online is important. It is through experience that they learn to articulate their thoughts, questions and insights. Their own personality starts to shine through. In addition, they become more familiar with the technology. In time they learn to concentrate on the content rather than the technology itself.

For many people, the professional reputation and integrity of the network members seems to generate trust and openness from the outset. This is a swift trust but is temporary and must be reinforced.

One other important point, regarding virtual communications, is response times. The more immediate response to a virtual communication (usually an e-mail), the more trust is built. Generally speaking if you are going to get answers to an e-mail question, they will arrive in a couple of days. However, this does not necessarily mean that only those members replying have something to contribute. Therefore, in order to glean the maximum amount of useful information, you may want to send out the same (or similar) question in a few days' or weeks' time. A more sophisticated way is to identify the sources from where you would expect to get a reply; match up the replies and then send out a personalized message to those people not responding.

In fact there are a whole series of variables that need to be taken into account for the e-network to work at an optimum level:

☐ Time demands on the individual network member. If a network has a particularly heavy workload and the question requires some thought and a well-crafted response, the e-mail may be left until a later time.

☐ Lack of an effective system for filing e-mails and creating a to do list. If e-mails are left in the inbox, it is likely that after a couple of days it will be forgotten about. To improve efficiency, encourage your network members to have a 'To do' e-mail folder. Also keep track of questions that need further work.

☐ Perception by the individual member that their input cannot add anything. Know your network member! Help to facilitate replies. Think about how you manage meetings in order to tease out information from the quiet ones.

☐ Incorrect understanding of the network request. Some people are better at expressing themselves than others when writing e-mails. If the recipient does not understand what the e-mail is about, they may not ask for clarification but just ignore it. To a certain extent this can be avoided if you operate the network using a moderated list. That is, all the questions and responses are sent into a central point where they are checked and validated before being sent to the network.

☐ Work habits of dealing with e-mail, for example, once a week. This comes back to knowing the preferences of the member. For instance, some people do not like receiving network messages throughout the day, which disrupt their work patterns. They may prefer them batched and sent out once a day or once a week. They may then allocate time in their diary to review and answer them.

☐ Availability of network member – travel, holiday. We often know when a member is away because they provide an automated e-mail response, but of course this is not always the case. This point overlaps with overload. Holiday periods and big sporting events also affect the number of people replying.

☐ Perceived urgency of the request. Interestingly, network members do tend to take notice if the message clearly indicates that it is urgent and they will respond. However, this technique should be used sparingly. The downside is that people reading the message late – for example, returning from holiday – may not bother to contribute and valuable knowledge may not be shared.

☐ Needs for confidentiality and anonymity. This mainly applies to people asking questions, although it can be a contributing factor to not responding. When a number of different organizations are involved in a network, clearly people need to be careful about the type of questions they ask. However, this is also important when operating an e-network within the same company. People do not want to show their lack of knowledge or perhaps give away changes that may be in the pipeline. Operating a moderated list helps to maintain confidentiality and anonymity, because the e-mail address of the originator cannot be detected by the network members and any references can be edited out by the moderator.

☐ Familiarity with technology. The more comfortable people are with technology and writing e-mails, the more they use the network facilities. This means knowing about the capabilities of the network member. Sometimes a telephone call is required to find out some useful information, which can then be written up and shared with the other members.

☐ Ease of sharing information and knowledge. The more difficult a process is to use, the less it will be used.

☐ Relevance to the network of the information and knowledge. Clearly members will not be interested in every single topic that is raised through the network at the time it is raised. Therefore, at any one time, only a small percentage will be able to respond. It is important to keep the content quality as high and as relevant as possible. You may stop reading some output from networks simply because they are not controlled and much of the content is trivia. This can be a pity, and some good quality input may be missed.

It may be desirable for some members to form their own focus groups in order to discuss some topics in greater detail.

☐ Complexity of input required. This relates to a point made earlier. Sometimes a question simply cannot be answered in a few lines and requires a much more detailed and considered response. On these occasions, perhaps an 'expert' from outside the network could be asked for their input. There may be other occasions when anonymity is required.

☐ Understanding and appreciation of the 'rules' of the network. People new to the network will at first be unsure of the culture, process and procedures. Over time they will become familiar with other members, the type of questions being asked and the quality of replies being given. They will watch at first and gradually contribute.

☐ Previous experience of using the network. This is very similar to the previous point, except that people new to one network may have previous experience of using similar ones. Therefore, they may be willing to make contributions much earlier.

☐ Culture of the organization in terms of sharing knowledge and information. Clearly if an organization operates a culture of employees keeping information to themselves, it will be more difficult to get members to share knowledge through a network.

The proliferation of the internet and other technologies is contributing to a sharing of information, but does this translate into knowledge? The concern is that the information is presumed to be 'knowledge' without a critical review.

True collaboration is about sharing information and a willingness to help interpret that information's relevance and meaning with other people. There is a direct link here to communications and trust. By taking the time to share information and summarizing its relevance, you are demonstrating that you have commitment to the network. These are all actions that build trust.

The very process of using e-mail also gives the organization a real opportunity to turn the knowledge stored in a person's head (and rarely gets documented) into more widely available knowledge. By sending e-mails, the knowledge is written down and its relevance pointed out – it can then be put into more detailed documents in a shared library.

The organization needs to ensure that the culture of information sharing is prevalent. The best way to do this may be through the performance management system. For example, part of an employee's remuneration could relate to their contribution to the company's electronic network and knowledge management system. By contribution, we mean quality and relevance, rather than quantity. Once a culture of information sharing has taken hold, the organization needs to implement other technology solutions to facilitate the acquisition, storage, and retrieval of information. This, in turn, requires an understanding of the e-networks within and associated with the company, as well as the support environment necessary to nurture and develop the e-networks to their full potential.

## CASE STUDIES – ACTION LEARNING MEETS E-LEARNING AT GUINNESS UDV

An interesting example of projects combining in the air and on the ground consulting have been set up in the Guinness UDV – the spirits business of the global drinks giant. A series of Value Improvement Projects™ were established across the organization in order to address such issues as:

☐ Developing the leadership capability of senior managers.

☐ Improving the shared service centre's approach to knowledge management.

☐ Creating a strategy for global projects working to develop best supply chain practices.

The client organization did not want to use traditional approaches, for example, training courses or business school programs in order to tackle these issues. A key objective was action and a desire to avoid consultancy dependency.

The approach taken entailed use of the Value Improvement Projects™ and the Online Management Development System™ (OMDS) which combine action learning approaches with e-learning technologies.

Action learning was developed by Professor Reg Revans[3] following his work with leading world scientists and, subsequently, with many industries where he revolutionized management education. Revans emphasizes the importance in the management development process of leading with action and allowing theory to follow. Revans stresses the importance of asking penetrating questions and says, 'judge the man not by his knowledge but by the quality of his questions'. This approach is similar to that developed as far back as 430 BC with the work of Socrates. Revans is very critical of the concept of an expert (and presumably the 'consultant as expert'). In action learning 'sets', managers question and challenge each other as 'comrades in adversity' and learn by doing and action.

In the Guinness UDV case, the projects were based around the specific business issues, and individuals were asked to define their personal learning objectives. They worked in action learning sets to address real business issues and were required to capture and define their learning as they proceeded. Throughout these projects, individuals accessed the OMDS, which provided an 'in the air' forum for discussion, communication with each other and with key stakeholders, access to materials and online diagnostic surveys, web links, and facilitation.

The role of the consultants was to establish the infrastructure educationally, technically and politically and then to participate on projects as facilitators. Facilitators were drawn from the external consultancy commissioned to lead the process and from internal personnel who were inducted into the role. This supported the objective of reducing consultant dependency and a key role of the consultant was as coach to the internal consultants.

Internal politics were crucial considerations and the consultants had to be sensitive to understanding the politics of relationships within projects and between project members and other stakeholders, such as their managers and directors. A pivotal skill was knowing when and how to intervene in such relationships in order to oil the wheels of communication. Additionally, the project members needed to understand the dynamics of their own relationships and this is where the consultants as facilitators were able to provide support and

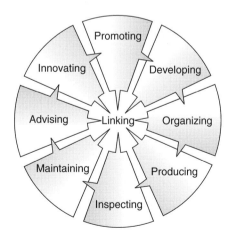

FIGURE 15.1: Representation of the Margerison-McCann Types of Work Model

© TMS Development International Ltd, 2001. Reproduced by kind permission of TMS Development International Ltd, 128 Holgate Road, York, YO24 4FL Tel. +44 (0)1904 641640. www.tmsdi.com

163

[3] Reg Revans, *ABC of Action Learning* (new edition), Lemos & Crane, 1998.

feedback. A critical process tool used here was the Types of Work Model and Team Management Systems approach developed by Margerison-McCann.[4]

Projects were rolled out over a defined period of 90–100 days and participants were required to present the results of their actions, their learning and the 'value added' to the business at the end of this period. Some results showed year on year returns of ten times the investment. For the consultants, while there was a commitment to avoiding consultancy dependency, the relationship evolved from initially taking a lead in driving projects, to training internal staff to run projects, to licensing and then through referral to doing the same in other parts of the global organization.

[4] C J Margerison, *Team Leadership*, Thomson Learning, 2002.